In *American Originals* the prizewinning biographer and historian Geoffrey C. Ward probes the distinctive personalities of more than forty fascinating Americans whose diverse talents, accomplishments, virtues, or vices have affected the course of our history—for better or for worse.

Seeking always to discover the private person behind the public figure and drawing upon a decade of his published articles and reviews, Ward writes about men and women as various as Abraham Lincoln and Alger Hiss, Roy Cohn and Robert E. Lee, Clara Barton and Josephine Baker, Ernest Hemingway and Shirley Temple.

Among the other statesmen and showmen, reformers and reactionaries, heroes and heroines, villains and villainesses who undergo Ward's informed scrutiny are Frederick Douglass, Fiorello La Guardia, Thomas E. Dewey, the Barrymores, Jack Dempsey, Paul Robeson, Charlie Parker, John Wilkes Booth, Henry Morton Stanley, Lillian Hellman, Mark Twain, H. L. Mencken, Dorothy Thompson, Thomas Hart Benton, Margaret Bourke-White, Edward R. Murrow, U. S. Grant, John L. Sullivan, George Armstrong Custer, George C. Marshall, Harry Truman—and the Roosevelts, Theodore, Franklin, and Eleanor.

AMERICAN ORIGINALS

AMERICAN ORIGINALS

★

The Private Worlds of
Some Singular Men and Women

GEOFFREY C. WARD

*Harper*Collins*Publishers*

For Diane

FIRST EDITION

Designed by Helene Berinsky

LIBRARY OF CONGRESS CATALOGING-IN-PUBLICATION DATA

Ward, Geoffrey C.
  American originals : men and women who made a difference / Geoffrey C. Ward.—1st ed.
    p. cm.
  Includes bibliographical references and index.
  ISBN 0-06-016694-0 (cloth)
  1. Celebrities—United States—Biography.   2. Biography—19th century.
3. Biography—20th century.   I. Title.
CT215.W37   1991
920.073—dc20
[B]   90-56401

91 92 93 94 95 CC/RRD 10 9 8 7 6 5 4 3 2 1

CONTENTS

COMBATANTS

DELANOS AND ROOSEVELTS

PREFACE

When my family lived in Hyde Park on the South Side of Chicago in the late forties, there were two neighborhood movie theatres to which my best friend and I were allowed to go on Saturday afternoons. The Frolic was closest. Small, crowded, and redolent, with sticky floors, it specialized in B-pictures during the week and cartoon marathons on weekends. But when my mother heard that some of the back-row seats had been slashed by what were then called "hoods" or "rowdies," it was thought best that my friend and I move on to the more distant, more refined Piccadilly, where even kids' seats cost thirty-five cents.

The Piccadilly was everything the Frolic was not: enormous, hushed, thickly carpeted. Lightly draped statuary lined the lobby and real butter inundated the fresh popcorn sold there for a dime; polished brass railings led down marble steps to a tiled, echoing men's room as big as the Baths of Caracalla; inside the theatre itself, carved and gilded boxes rose on either side of the heavy gold curtains that hid the huge screen between showings. The balconies were roped off; no one ever actually sat in the boxes, either; and there were always acres of empty seats in the mezzanine, all of which we then thought was wonderful but which was actually evidence that television had already doomed the Piccadilly.

It was from the splendid isolation of seats like these that a good many members of my generation first encountered the American past, or rather, Hollywood's version of it. War movies were okay with us then—lots of shooting, precious little mush—but it was the big westerns for which we most eagerly saved our allowances, the big western stars like Jimmy Stewart and John Wayne with whom we most wanted to identify.

There is no pedantry more relentless than a ten-year-old's: one contemporary of mine used to dazzle my baseball-loving father by rattling off the batting averages of old-time players of whom I'd never even heard: "I was *just* like that at his age," my father would chuckle appreciatively, while I looked for a way to change the subject. My field of obsessive expertise was the history of the Wild West, which did me absolutely no good at home, but won a certain amount of grudging respect at the Piccadilly. At least my friends were nice about it and never told me how little fun it must have been to sit next to someone who relentlessly muttered scornful corrections: "Apaches lived in wickiups, not teepees," "Cochise didn't have blue eyes," "That's thir- teen shots Wild Bill's fired without reloading."

But, for all my elaborate disdain, I could never get enough of films like *Fort Apache, Shane, High Noon, Red River, The Searchers, Winchester '73, She Wore a Yellow Ribbon.* Neither my own solemn, boyish version of western scholarship nor the real thing, encountered many years later, ever seriously dulled the impact on me of those epics.

There may really be no record of Indians ever having attacked a circle of covered wagons; Bat Masterson may never actually have killed *anybody;* the supposedly untamed cattle towns of Abilene, Caldwell, Dodge City, Ellsworth, and Wichita, together, may have had fewer than fifty homicides between 1870 and 1885, fewer than my own section of Manhattan now experiences in any given year.

Tell it to John Ford. The movie western was history as all my friends and I wanted it to have been.

It is that tension—between the history that really happened and those versions of it which appear in print or on screen—that sparked most of the essays in this book.

These pieces appeared in a number of places, but most were written as columns for *American Heritage* magazine, where my friends and successors as editor, Byron Dobell and Richard F. Snow, have kindly let me have my say about new books—and films, and television pro- grams—for nearly a decade now.

I lit on most of the men and women I've profiled here because someone else had done so first, and my debt to their biographers is therefore as great as it is obvious.

The subjects range from Roy Cohn to Robert E. Lee, Ernest Hemingway to Shirley Temple, Clara Barton to Josephine Baker— plus a full complement of Roosevelts and Delanos (about whom one might think I'd already said more than enough elsewhere). They may not have had much in common other than their fame or notoriety, but the authors of the best of the books that occasioned most of these pieces about them do:

all understand that a writer's first task is to tell a story, to give a vivid sense of a real life lived;

all treat their subjects as human beings, not quaint artifacts of a supposedly simpler time;

all take pains to place their subjects within a historical context that helps explain how they lived their lives, even when it cannot excuse it;

and the best and boldest among them, to my way of thinking, are those willing to take still another step and venture into the realm of psychology.

Psychobiography is in bad odor these days, partly because of the grandiose claims made for it by its least supple practitioners, partly because of the evident terror the merest whiff of psychological speculation strikes in the hearts of some traditional historians.

At its worst, psychobiography is everything its enemies charge—reductive, jargon-ridden, ahistorical, pseudoscientific. But no life can really be understood, it seems to me, unless its chronicler is willing to think hard about how his or her subject got that way, and to accept that challenge is inevitably to explore the world of family—the power of parents and siblings and surroundings to shape a personality and influence the actions that personality eventually takes.

There really shouldn't be anything startling about this. We do the same thing in our everyday lives, without a second thought: who does not remember the sudden gleam of understanding experienced at high school graduation or college commencement, when the parents of some until-then inexplicable contemporary turned up to make everything about their offspring seem suddenly self-evident?

It is one of the good biographer's greatest pleasures to come to that kind of understanding of his or her subject—and then to share it with the rest of us.

There are a few people I'd like especially to thank for helping in one way or another to put this book together: Carl Brandt; Buz Wyeth, Pamela LaBarbiera, and Florence Goldstein at HarperCollins; Ann Adelman, (again) for her sensitive copyediting; Byron Dobell and Richard F. Snow, Barbara Klaw, the late Carter Cooper, Sam Sifton, Bruce Fretts, and Mary Elizabeth Wise at *American Heritage;* Les Line and Gary Soucie at *Audubon;* Byron Hollinshead, Rob Cowley, and Barbara Benton of *MHQ;* Barbara Epstein of the *New York Review of Books;* D. J. R. B. Bruckner, James Chase, and Eden Lipson at the *New*

York Times Book Review; Don Moser and Tim Foote at *Smithsonian;* my oldest friend, Robert M. Strozier, then of *Success!;* and Dick Friedman, then of *TV Guide.*

The Rathore Mahal
Sariska Tiger Reserve   Geoffrey C. Ward
Rajasthan
October 25, 1990

POLITICIANS

★

THE HOUSE AT EIGHTH AND JACKSON: ABRAHAM LINCOLN

O NE GOOD MEASURE OF OUR APPARENTLY INEXHAUSTIBLE IN-
terest in Abraham Lincoln is that every year half a million of
us are led through his house at the corner of Eighth and Jackson
Streets in Springfield, Illinois, so many people edging past the
horsehair furniture and stomping up and down the narrow stairs that
the National Park Service had to close the place down in 1987, take
much of it apart, and put it back together again, newly decorated and
sturdily reinforced with steel, to withstand the next generation of
pilgrims.

I use the word "pilgrims" advisedly, for the refurbished house, its
windows freshly sealed against dust and weather, its air climate-
controlled for the sake of the artifacts, the sanctioned path past its relics
marked out by a narrow gray carpet and bound by wooden railings,
seems more shrine than home. It is hard to believe that a prairie lawyer
and politician, his wife, four sons, and a perpetually shifting cast of
cooks and hired girls, cats and dogs, all ever really lived in these chaste
rooms. No small boy ever tracked black Illinois mud across these
bright Belgian carpets; no dirt ever sullied the broom that leans against
the kitchen wall; no visiting pol ever missed the brown-and-white
ceramic spittoon in the corner of the sitting room.

The site's curious sterility is not really the fault of the Park Service,
which has labored hard to make this old house a home again. The
structure's modest size and the long lines of people who wait out front
of it each day to take the twenty-minute tour demand that severe
limitations be placed on visitors, much of the period furniture that fills
the rooms has no genuine link with the Lincolns, and a good deal of
educated guesswork has inevitably gone into the restoration; no one
is even entirely certain any more just where everyone slept.

And it should not surprise us that Lincoln's home remains a shrine.
He himself sympathized with the impulse to revere heroes: "Let us

believe as in the days of our youth," he once said, "that Washington was spotless. It makes human nature better to believe that one human being was perfect—that human perfection is possible." From the moment of his assassination—and despite the hard work of a host of scrupulous biographers—Lincoln has remained a martyred saint to most of us: unfailingly modest and loving, candid and forbearing, selfless and self-depreciating.

But even as the Lincoln home has grown more immaculate, more monument-like, discoveries made as the work went forward offer further clues to the real human being who lived here for seventeen years, adding fresh details to a Lincoln portrait that will always be tantalizingly incomplete.

Reconstructing the daily lives of the Lincolns is a tricky business. Precisely one letter from Mary Todd Lincoln to her husband written during the Springfield years has survived and, while a handful of Lincoln's letters home do still exist, he was always reticent about his private life—"the most shut-mouthed man that ever lived," a close friend said—and routinely left the details of daily living to his wife; most of his letters mirror little more than his genuine affection for Mary and for the boys he called "the codgers." The result is that much of what we think we know about the Lincolns' domestic lives is distinctly second- and third-hand, drawn from the memories of friends and neighbors and family members, some unwilling to be anything but worshipful, a few with old scores to settle. Opinions differ even as to the quality of the meals prepared in the Lincolns' small kitchen: one frequent Springfield visitor remembered that they were "famed for the excellence of many rare Kentucky dishes and, in season . . . venison, wild turkey, prairie chickens, quail and other game. . . ."; another guest at the Lincolns' gate-leg table enjoyed Lincoln's wit but remembered the food as "an old-fashioned mess of indigestion, composed mainly of cake, pies and chickens. . . ."

Most of the finds made during the recent renovation were important primarily to specialists: a staircase once led from one garret to the other; a cistern was uncovered behind the house and a pump relocated to conform to it; the Lincolns' flowered wallpaper was a good deal gaudier than had once been thought.

But two discoveries were of wider interest. The first of them has permanently altered one of the oldest legends about the Lincolns. The dwelling to which the Lincolns brought their year-old son, Robert, in 1844 was a story-and-a-half Greek Revival cottage, built by the Reverend Charles Dresser, the Episcopal minister who had married the couple two years earlier. Tradition has always held that although the family eventually grew to five—Edward Baker Lincoln was born here in 1846, William Wallace in 1850, Thomas, known as "Tad," in 1853—Lincoln earned too little money to make any improvements on their increasingly crowded cottage until 1856, when Mary sold off 80 acres of land inherited from her father and took it upon herself to order up a second story. Lincoln was said to have been away circuit-riding while the work went on, and to have claimed not to recognize his old house when he got back, asking a neighbor, "Stranger, do you know where Lincoln lives?"

If he did ask such a question, he meant it purely as a joke, for it is now clear from structural evidence and the town tax records that the Lincolns together improved and expanded their home not once but six times while they lived in it—in 1846, 1849, 1853, 1855, 1856, and 1860—and apparently approved a seventh renovation from the White House in 1863.

This record of constantly growing affluence and comfort is further proof that Abraham Lincoln's celebrated penury was always relative. Illinois was traditionally a Democratic state and the Whigs, with whom he identified from boyhood until their party went out of existence, were widely denounced as "aristocratical"; it was not merely good politics, it was probably *essential* politics, that Lincoln appear always a little more threadbare than he really was.

In fact, as the relative spaciousness and affluent furnishings of his home attest, he had come a very long way from the dark, crowded one-room cabins of his boyhood in Kentucky and Indiana, and a considerable distance from the log houses of New Salem. He understood better than anyone else that his rail-splitting youth was a prime political asset, but he did not much like to dwell upon it: his whole boyhood, he once told a campaign biographer, could be "condensed into a single sentence and that sentence you will find in Gray's Elegy, 'the short and simple annals of the poor.'"

His marriage to the daughter of a wealthy Kentucky merchant banker had helped make the "flourishing about in carriages" of Springfield's most fashionable citizens seem less intimidating than it had been when he first arrived in 1837, and the home he and his wife occupied and steadily improved together nicely symbolizes the great and growing distance his will to succeed had put between the circumstances of his own life and those of his father, a gulf so wide he finally did not try to bridge it. No member of Lincoln's family was asked to attend his marriage; neither his father nor his stepmother ever met his wife or saw their grandchildren. Lincoln revered the memory of his mother, Nancy Hanks Lincoln, dead when he was nine, but was frankly scorn-

ful of his father, Thomas, who, he said, "never did more in the way
of writing than to bunglingly sign his own name." He visited Thomas
Lincoln from time to time but never invited him to his home in
Springfield, did not go to see him on his deathbed in 1851, never even
ordered a headstone for his grave. In fact, only one member of Lincoln's family is known to have stayed with the Lincolns, a cousin
named Harriet Hanks, who lived at Eighth and Jackson for a time
while attending a local seminary for young ladies, and later said she
had been treated as a servant by Mary Lincoln.

He may have sometimes been irritated by the pretensions of his
in-laws—he is supposed to have wondered why, if God was content
with one "d," the Todds demanded two—and they evidently never
quite thought him worthy of Mary; but it was the kind of life that
Todds, not Lincolns, led that he wanted for himself and for his children.

The aggregate of Lincoln's own schooling, he once said, was less
than a year—asked in 1860 to summarize his education, he answered
simply "defective"—but when it came time to educate his eldest son,
he sent him to Phillips Exeter and Harvard, evidently intending to
make of him an Eastern gentleman. He may have succeeded too well:
on the centennial of his father's birth in 1909, Robert would refuse to
attend the dedication of the big Greek temple which now harbors the
small Kentucky cabin in which Lincoln is alleged to have been born.
Archie Butt, military aide to the main speaker, President Theodore
Roosevelt, thought he knew why: ". . . if it be true, as I hear, that Bob
Lincoln . . . does not relish the perpetuation of this cabin," he wrote,
"I cannot blame him. The very thought of it . . . would make any
member of his family shudder with horror. It does not bear the stamp
of poverty alone, but degradation and uncleanliness."

If we are made a little nervous by the notion of a resolutely aspiring
Abraham Lincoln, apparently willing to put behind him the people
from whom he sprang in the course of bettering himself, we are still
more wary when asked to consider him as a vote-seeking politician.
Yet "Politics were his life, newspapers his food, and his great ambition
his motive force," as his last law partner, William Herndon, remembered: "He delighted [in politics], he revelled in it, as a fish does in
water, as a bird disports itself on the sustaining air."

His party's declining fortunes in Democratic Illinois led some of
Lincoln's early biographers to portray Lincoln as a political failure; in
fact, he was a considerable success, a state legislator at twenty-five, a
promising Whig leader well before he married.

But a second discovery made during the renovation of his home reminds us that there was nothing inevitable about his rise to power, that in order to become the Emancipator we remember best, Lincoln first had to master the small, sometimes seamy world of state and county politics, and to learn to take seriously the importuning of ordinary citizens.

In 1849, Park Service experts now speculate, someone—probably five-year-old Robert, or one of his playmates—fed some of his father's old papers into a crack above the baseboard in the kitchen's north wall. They were soon obliterated by a shower of plaster shaken down upon them by further alterations to the house. A field mouse then constructed its nest atop the plaster. (When what was left of the papers was uncovered in 1987, the infinitely delicate skeleton of the nest's builder still lay folded up inside it.)

There was nothing momentous in this cache; nothing in Lincoln's own hand, in fact, except part of a franked but empty envelope addressed to the Washington landlady in whose boardinghouse he lived while in Congress. The papers include two more or less intact letters from Illinois political allies, termite-chewed fragments of two additional letters from constituents seeking favors, and a copy of an 1849 speech by a fellow Whig congressman, James Wilson of New Hampshire, opposing slavery's spread into lands newly acquired from Mexico, its pages still uncut.

One letter, from David Dickinson, a political backer from Lacon, Illinois, was written in early 1846, while Lincoln was maneuvering to assure his own nomination for the state's single safe Whig congressional seat. Lincoln believed that he had an agreement with the two other leading party hopefuls—Edward D. Baker (for whom his second son was named) and John J. Hardin—that they would rotate the nomination among themselves, and that 1846 was his turn. But Hardin, a former incumbent (and Mary's distant cousin), had other ideas, and schemed to seize the nomination for himself. Lincoln finally forced him to withdraw by insisting to party leaders that "Turnabout is fair play," but he was evidently still wary of a last-minute betrayal, for Dickinson wrote to reassure him that he had been scouting Putnam County, on the lookout for Hardin's "moccasin tracks," and that all was well: Lincoln need have no fear about Putnam's vote at the coming convention.

During his single term in Congress, Lincoln was besieged by letters from constituents demanding services. Two of these survived beneath the mouse nest: one voter asked him to register a patent for a "compound vegetable" elixir that cured "Dyspepsia . . . weakness . . . or a

bad cold. . . ."; the other hoped the congressman could arrange for him
a commission in the army, then fighting the Mexican War. "I hope to
obtain your *interference* in my behalf," the aspiring officer wrote,
"and if I succeed rest assured sir that it will never be forgotten by
me. . . ." It is unlikely that the young congressman's interference did
his eager constituent much good with the Democratic administration;
Lincoln was a freshman and a Whig who believed the current struggle
in the Southwest "a war of conquest brought into existence to catch
votes." But it is likely that he did his best; he could not afford to be
forgotten by any voter.

Lincoln's first love may have been politics, but he made his money as
a lawyer, at least $5,000 annually by the 1850s, and the result was that
he wasn't home much; for almost six months of every year—roughly
three months in spring, three in the fall—he was away trying cases on
the Eighth Circuit, a vast shifting area that once encompassed fourteen
counties, one fifth of the state. "During my childhood and early
youth," Robert Lincoln once recalled, trying to explain why his father
had never found the time to tell him much about his own boyhood,
"[my father] was almost constantly away . . . attending court or making
political speeches."

During all that time, year after year, Mary was left to run her
household and raise her children largely on her own, and it is understandably her impress rather than her husband's that is most evident
in their house. It was Mary who studied *Miss Leslie's House Book or
Manual of Domestic Economy for Town and Country;* who saw to it that
the ceilings were freshly whitewashed and the oil lamps were filled and
their wicks trimmed; who arranged the seashells on the what-not
shelves in the parlor. (Lincoln's own mussed, intensely masculine
world was epitomized by the law office, eight blocks away, where he
spent most daylight hours when he was in Springfield; it was so
disheveled, a clerk recalled, that government seeds brought back with
him from Washington actually sprouted in one unswept corner.)

A reporter from upstate New York, ushered through the house
shortly after Lincoln was nominated for the presidency, reassured his
Republican readers that they need not fear that they were being asked
to vote for an untamed frontiersman. The candidate's "house was
neatly without being extravagantly furnished," he wrote. "An air of
quiet refinement pervaded the place. You would have known instantly
that she who presided over the modest household was a true type of
the American lady. There were flowers upon the tables . . . pictures
upon the walls. . . . The thought that involuntarily blossomed into

speech was—'What a pleasant home Abe Lincoln has.' "

Making that home pleasant was a demanding task, especially for a woman who came to her marriage speaking fluent French but unable to prepare the simplest dish. But the newly restored house barely hints at the difficulties she faced every morning. The Lincolns' backyard today is as well groomed as a putting green; the freshly painted back porch is kept bare of everything but an empty woodbox whose purpose has to be explained to visitors, most of whom have never seen one. But a photograph of the same scene, made while the Lincolns' wartime tenants still occupied the house, suggests something of the shabbier reality of daily life in their time: the grass is ragged; the paint is peeling; logs overflow the woodbox and bark litters the porch, which is crowded with fire-blackened pots and battered washtubs. And even the old photograph cannot convey the perpetual buzz of flies in summer or the pervasive reek produced collectively by the milk cow kept tethered behind the house, the two horses in the barn, the privy at the back of the garden, the hogs rooting along the unplanked streets just beyond the fence.

Mary had a string of hired girls to help her, but her relations with them were frequently turbulent and she complained because "the wild Irish" whom she often had to employ were not as admirably submissive as the slaves who had served her family in Kentucky.

Her problems may have rested less with her servants' temperaments than with her own. Mary Todd's wit and coquettish vivacity had made her a great prize when Lincoln began to court her: "Mary could make a bishop forget his prayers," her brother-in-law once said. But beneath that surface she was insecure, quick-tempered, sharp-tongued, seeing slights where none were intended, suffering from migraine headaches that frequently drove her to bed in her darkened room, living in daily dread that those she loved most would be taken from her—as her mother had been by death at six, as her beloved father had been by his remarriage to a stranger who bore him nine children and had little time for a stepdaughter.

In 1849 and 1850 her worst fears seemed confirmed as first her father died, then the grandmother who had done all she could to fill in for her dead mother, then her own Eddie, not yet four, who succumbed to diphtheria despite fifteen days of his parents' desperate nursing. She was inconsolable for months and increasingly fearful thereafter, especially when her husband was away, certain one of the other boys would fall ill and die, that the house would catch fire or be hit by lightning. When a bearded umbrella mender knocked unexpectedly at the front door one day, she screamed "Murder! Murder!" so loudly that a neighbor ran over and escorted the astonished man away. At night, afraid of burglary or worse, Mary often had her boys sleep alongside her, but even that was sometimes not enough to allay her fears. One of her maids was "a bad girl," a neighbor remembered; "the boys and men used to come to [Mary's] house in L.'s absence and scare her; she was crying and wailing one night, called me, and said: 'Mr. [Gourley], come, do come and stay with me all night, you can sleep in the bed with Bob and I.' "

Mary herself once called Lincoln "My Sainted Idol. . . . A sainted man who had a holy smile." Her own tumultuous personality had a good deal to do with the myth of his saintliness, for if, as some of her husband's closest associates said, she was a "she-devil" and "Hell-Catical," the old argument ran, was Lincoln not all the more wonderful for having put up with her for so long?

In fact, his home was not a "hell on earth," as William Herndon claimed, and many of the stories that seem to suggest it was and that Lincoln was "woman-whipped and woman-carved" were amassed by his junior partner, whose loathing for Mary Lincoln was surpassed only by hers for him. Although a photograph of the two partners hung on her parlor wall, she would not have Herndon in her home: "Mr. Herndon had always been an utter stranger to me," Mary wrote many years later, "he was not considered an *habitué* at our house. The office was more in his line."

There is no reason to suppose that Lincoln ever regretted having had "Love Is Eternal" engraved on Mary's engagement ring. The Lincolns called one another "Molly" and "Mr. Lincoln" at first, and "Mother" and "Father" after the boys were born. Their letters are full of bantering affection for one another.

Mary Todd Lincoln may not have been easy to live with, but neither was her husband, and some of his wife's eccentricities were certainly exacerbated by his. Mary Owen, to whom Lincoln had once been engaged, gently recalled that he had been "deficient in those little links which make up the chains of a woman's happiness," and even Herndon believed he "ought never to have married anyone. He had no quality of a husband."

Despite Mary's best efforts, an early writer said, Lincoln was inherently "unparlorable." His company manners had improved a good deal since he moved to Springfield, still capable of stalking into a fashionable ball with friends wearing muddy boots and shouting, "Oh, boys— how *clean* those girls look!" But despite her exhortations to "dress up and look like somebody," he continued to appear in rumpled clothes, his hair unbrushed; the stove-pipe hat he hung on the arched hat tree in the front hall every evening usually looked "as if a calf had licked it." He was perpetually—and unapologetically—late for meals, used the wrong knife to spread his butter, and persisted in answering the door himself instead of allowing the serving girl to do it, sometimes in his shirtsleeves and without his boots; once, to Mary's acute embarrassment, he told some visiting ladies his wife would be down "as soon as she gets her trotting harness on."

Lincoln could be solicitous, insisting that Mary not try to do everything herself, and genuinely concerned when she fell victim to one of her headaches: " . . . *he* was never himself—when I was not perfectly well," Mary remembered. But he was also laconic and undemonstrative—no one who knew him well ever slapped his back or called him "Abe." At the best of times he spoke and thought and moved so slowly, a friend remembered, it seemed as if he needed oiling, and he dealt with her tantrums by stalking from the house until she calmed down, his forbearing silence only adding further to her frustration.

At his worst, he was given to spells of severe and morbid depression which must have frightened his wife and from which even she could sometimes not rouse him. The closing stanza of "Mortality," his favorite poem, hints at the sort of lugubriousness that sometimes gripped him:

Tis the wink of an eye, 'tis the draught of a breath,
From the blossoms of health, to the paleness of death.
From the gilded saloon, to the bier and the shroud.
Oh, why should the spirit of mortal be proud!

The last letter fragments found in the kitchen wall came from a Whig editor to whom Lincoln had sent the poem in 1846; the newspaperman wanted to know whether Lincoln himself had written it. "Beyond all question I am not the author," he replied (the Scottish poet William Knox was). "I would give all I am worth and go in debt, to be able to write so fine a piece as I think that is."

Her husband's frequent absences were difficult enough for Mary to bear, but even when at home, he often seemed to disappear within himself. She dealt with his strange, brooding withdrawals as lightly as she could when guests were present. Her half sister Emilie Helm remembered an evening in the sitting room when Lincoln and Robert were playing checkers and someone asked her brother-in-law a question. There was no answer. "Your silence is remarkably soothing, Mr.

Lincoln," Mary finally said, "but we are not quite ready for sleep just yet." Everyone including Lincoln laughed.

But when the Lincolns were alone together, Mary was evidently less forgiving: after suggesting three times that he poke up the dying fire without spurring him to the slightest action, she once went at him with a stick of wood. Another time, a neighbor woman had just reached the back door when Lincoln burst through it with his wife close behind, hurling potatoes.

The Park Service has done its best to evoke the lively presence of the Lincoln sons throughout the restored house: their original stereopticon rests on a table in the sitting room; wooden hoops, alphabet blocks, and a little book called *The Passionate Child* lie scattered about the room the curators believe the two younger boys occupied just across the hall from their mother's bedroom, where a child's table and chairs are clustered at the end of the bed in which they often slept.

Inevitably, these period artifacts convey nothing of their individual personalities. Robert was high-spirited as a small boy but increasingly reserved as he got older, evidence perhaps of the impact of his younger brother's death when he was only six and of the responsibility he felt for keeping his anxious mother calm while his father was away. Willie and Tad were uniformly boisterous—even their mother called them her "noisy boys." Willie was his father's favorite, perhaps the brightest of his sons and fond of poetry as well as mischief. Tad suffered from an impediment so severe that outsiders found it hard to understand him, and may also have been what we now call hyperactive, unable to sit still for long, unable to read until he was twelve.

The Lincoln literature is filled with stories of his sons' wildness. One kicked over the chess board while his father was trying to concentrate on his next move; Tad smeared black ink all over the white marble counter at the telegraph office and raced through a reception swinging a side of bacon to scatter the formally dressed guests.

No one found the boys more tiresome than Herndon, who often had to clean up after them. "Sometimes," he recalled, "Lincoln would, when his wife had gone to church, *to show off her new bonnet*, or when she had kicked him out of the house, bring to the office Willie and Tad—*these* little devils . . . would take down the books, empty ash buckets, coal ashes, inkstands, papers, gold pens, letters, etc., etc, in a pile and then dance on the pile. Lincoln would say nothing, so abstracted was he, and so blinded to his children's faults. Had they s--t in Lincoln's hat and rubbed it on his boots, he would have laughed and thought it smart."

"Mr. Lincoln . . . was very exceedingly indulgent to his children," Mary later wrote, trying to explain the boys' behavior. "He always said: 'It is my pleasure that my children are free, happy, and unrestrained by parental tyranny. Love is the chain whereby to bind a child to its parents.' " Some have taken this at face value, seeing in it further evidence of Lincoln's patient wisdom, his foresightedness in understanding the advantages of the more permissive style of child raising familiar in our own day. It seems at least as likely that Lincoln was a fond but preoccupied and often absent father who, when he did make it home, wished to enjoy his children, not to discipline them. Child raising, he believed, was woman's work: "Since I began this letter," he wrote to a friend when Robert was small, "a messenger came to tell me, Bob was lost and by the time I reached the house, his mother had found him, and had him whip[p]ed—and, by now, very likely he is run away again."

The boys' chronic obstreperousness may simply have been the only way they knew to attract their oblivious father's sustained attention. According to Herndon, they rarely held it long: "On a winter's morning," he remembered, "[Lincoln] might be seen stalking and stilting it toward the market house, basket on his arm, his old gray shawl wrapped around his neck, his little Willie and Tad running along at his heels, asking a thousand little questions which his father heard not, not even then knowing that little Willie or Tad was there, fast running after him, so abstracted was he. When he thus met a friend on the road, he said that something that he had just seen, heard, or left put him in mind of a story which he heard in Indiana or Egypt [southern Illinois] or elsewhere, and tell it he would and there was no alternative . . . but to patiently stand and hear it."

The stories his friends stood to hear were often strong stuff. After Lincoln's death, an old woman who had known him as a youth began to recite for an interviewer a piece of doggerel she believed he had written, then stopped, blushing furiously, and explained that since the "poem is smutty . . . I can't tell it to you, will tell it to my daughter-in-law; she will tell her husband; and he will tell it to you." When a friend asked Lincoln why he didn't publish his stories, he wrinkled his nose: "Such a book," he said, "would stink like a thousand privies."

Such redolent tales would not have been spun out in Mary Lincoln's parlor, but they were surely told in the upstairs bedroom, where her husband often retreated with his political friends, and that room remains, it seems to me, the place in the restored house most successfully evocative of its owner: oval portraits of his Whig heroes, Henry

Clay and Daniel Webster, hang above the black "Paris Parlor 19" stove; on a baize-covered table rests the battered mahogany lap desk he carried in his saddlebags while riding the circuit; his original shaving mirror is nailed to the west wall, startlingly high. Bargains were struck in this room; campaigns were planned; political news was received and tactics altered to fit new circumstances.

Mary may not have been immediately privy to the salty intriguing that went on next door to her own bedroom—few women in her time wished to be considered "political females"—but she was always intensely interested in his career, amiable to his allies, unforgiving of his enemies, and unwilling to allow setbacks to impede his progress. The Lincolns "understood each other thoroughly," Mary's half sister recalled, "and Mr. Lincoln looked beyond the impulsive word and manner, and knew that his wife was devoted to him and to his interests."

Lincoln wondered at the skill with which she served as his hostess, sometimes presiding over *levées* attended by three hundred guests—and once, if the local newspaper is to be believed, "thronged by thousands" inching their way through the downstairs rooms. But he also reserved the right to be a little bemused by it all. At one reception, the guests were expected to serve themselves from pyramidal shelves piled high with sandwiches, fruit, and frosted cakes: "Do they give you anything to *eat* here?" Lincoln murmured to the man ahead of him in line.

Mary's ambition was every bit as consuming as Herndon said her husband's was, and while the evidence offered by some of her most admiring biographers that she greatly influenced his political thinking seems thin, at least to me, she was certainly his most effective and persistent booster: "Mr. [Stephen A.] Douglas is a very little, *little* giant by the side of my tall Kentuckian," she told a relative before there was much objective evidence to back her up, "and intellectually my husband towers above Douglas, just as he does physically." When the Whigs won the White House in 1848, it was she who wrote more than forty letters to Washington applying for a federal post and signed his name to each—and she who helped talk him out of taking the dead-end ones offered in response. He was destined for greater things, and so, she thought, was she.

During the 1858 Senate race against Douglas, a sudden downpour forced Lincoln and a reporter to take shelter together in an empty flatcar. "My friends got me into *this* business," he told his companion as the rain splattered through the open door. "I did not consider myself qualified for the United States Senate, and it took me a long time to persuade myself that I was. . . . Mary insists, however, that I am going to be Senator and President of the United States, too." He clasped his long arms around his knees and laughed: "Just think of such a sucker as me as President!"

Lincoln's legendary humility was the public product of private self-assurance; we can be certain that he had himself often thought about the presidency. Mary shared her husband's aspirations and helped to focus his energies upon realizing them, but she did not create them.

Lincoln's subsequent loss to Douglas was disappointing but not devastating. "I believe . . . you are 'feeling like h-ll yet,' " Lincoln told one supporter a few days after the votes were counted. "Quit that— you will soon feel better. Another 'blow-up' is coming; we shall have fun again." A national figure at last, he was flooded with invitations to speak from as far away as New Hampshire. He turned down the most distant ones, but in early September, he packed his bag, said good-bye to the boys as he had so many times before, and set forth on a political swing through Ohio. This time, his wife went with him.

In Cincinnati, on the 7th, a large crowd turned out at Market Square to hear him. Mary sat proudly near the platform. "There is no permanent class of hired laborers among us," she heard him tell his audience. "Twenty-five years ago, I was a hired laborer. The hired laborer of yesterday, labors on his own account today, and will hire others to labor for him tomorrow. Advancement—improvement of condition—is the order of things in a society of equals."

For Lincoln, the comfortable house in which he and Mary and their children lived provided vivid, reassuring proof of how far a man might rise in the society of equals which he would one day give his life to preserve.

American Heritage April 1989

"SIMPLY A MAN":
FREDERICK DOUGLASS

IN AUGUST OF 1863, FREDERICK DOUGLASS CALLED UPON THE Secretary of War, Edwin M. Stanton, to explain why the recruiting of black troops for the Union had been slower than some had expected. Blacks wanted equal pay, he said, and a chance for promotion. And they wanted some assurance that the Union really would retaliate if the Confederate Congress made good on its pledge to treat captive black soldiers as rebellious slaves rather than prisoners of war.

Stanton was "cold and businesslike . . . but earnest," Douglass remembered. His visitor was earnest, too: "I told him," Douglass recalled, "that the negro was the victim of two extreme opinions. One claimed for him too much and the other too little[;] that it was a mistake to regard him either as an angel or a devil. He is simply a man, and should be dealt with purely as such."

That fact, so apparently self-evident, so rarely acknowledged either in Douglass's time or in our own, was the tirelessly reiterated lesson of his extraordinary life, and it provides the key to William S. McFeely's distinguished biography, *Frederick Douglass*. McFeely's Douglass is undeniably great—and undeniably human, as well.

Abraham Lincoln has traditionally been our model self-made statesman, but his rise to prominence seems almost effortless compared to the climb Frederick Douglass had to make. He was born Frederick Bailey in 1818 on a Maryland plantation (even the name by which he later became famous was his own creation, adapted from a poem by Sir Walter Scott to confuse slave-catchers after he fled north), the son of a white man whose identity he could never quite pin down, and of a slave woman who, perhaps because she harbored bitter memories of his fathering, seems to have showed little interest in him. His grandmother raised him until the age of six, somehow managing to instill in him a sense that he was destined for great things, then handed him on to the big house to be trained as a servant.

Douglass experienced both slavery's brutality and its paternalism during his first twenty years, and it is hard to tell from the three vivid but increasingly romanticized accounts of his youth he published during his lifetime which angered him the most. But he taught himself to read and write and at twelve secretly bought a book, Caleb Bingham's *Columbian Orator.* Words could be weapons, Douglass learned; oratory was power.

His oratory helped make Douglass black America's best-known champion, but he was far more than a magnificent voice and a majestic presence. He was his own man, cunning about tactics but uncompromising in his convictions, and unwilling ever to follow anyone else's script, including that drafted by the white sympathizers who thought him their creation. No man did more to undermine slavery before the Civil War, and none was more prescient about the subtler, more stubborn evil of racism that survived intact to permeate the postwar world.

These were great achievements but, like the achievements of other great men of every color, they were purchased at fearful cost to those around him.

His family suffered most. He had married at twenty, long before he had been introduced to the wider world. His wife was Anna Murray, about whom very little is known except that she was the daughter of former slaves, and unable either to read or write. During the forty-four years of their marriage, she bore five children and ran the house, McFeely writes, while staying mostly in the kitchen and "emerging only to serve her husband as if he, like his friends, were a guest in her house."

It is impossible to reconstruct Douglass's feelings for his wife once he had become a public figure—it remains one of the enduring mysteries of his life that he never taught her to read or write—but his response to one of his daughters, who had surprised him with news of her own wedding plans, may echo his own unhappiness. "I should rejoice to see you married tomorrow, if I felt you were marrying someone worthy of you," he wrote. "It would spread a dark cloud over my soul to see you marry some ignorant and unlearned person. You might as well tie yourself to a log of wood as to do so. You are altogether too refined and intelligent a person for any such marriage."

In any case, Douglass turned for the companionship he craved to a succession of educated white women, whose constant presence in his life embittered his wife, bewildered his children, and threatened to destroy his career.

The first was Julia Griffiths, an Englishwoman who traveled with her sister all the way to Rochester, New York, in 1849 to help Douglass raise funds and run his newspaper. She stayed for six years, living much of that time in his home. When an old friend warned him that rumors about his relationship with an unmarried white woman were threatening to undermine his effectiveness, Douglass professed not to care: "Individuals have rights not less than society," he wrote. He was "a husband and a father—and withal a citizen"; only he would be the judge of his own domestic arrangements. But the whispers continued, his wife's resentment intensified, and Griffiths finally felt obliged first to move to lodgings of her own and then to sail for home, where she eventually married a clergyman but never stopped corresponding with the man she continued to love.

Her successor, Ottilia Assing, arrived in 1856. A high-strung German intellectual, initially drawn to Douglass by his autobiography (which she translated into German) and to his cause by her liberal upbringing, she, too, was soon in love with him. McFeely concludes that their partnership was probably physical as well as emotional, but prudence now dictated that they live apart; she took rooms in a Hoboken, New Jersey, boardinghouse and lived for his infrequent visits, and for the long, lazy summer afternoons when she was allowed to come to his garden in Rochester and read aloud to him from Dickens and Goethe.

After a quarter of a century, the strain of continuing this passionate but doomed relationship evidently began to tell, and in 1881, suffering from what a physician had warned Douglass were dangerous "self-slaughterous" tendencies, she returned to Europe—from where she soon wrote to an American friend to ask that he send her a box of Douglass's favorite cigars so that their aroma could remind her of him.

The following year, Anna Douglass suffered a fatal stroke.

In the spring of 1884, Douglass quietly got married again, to his secretary, Helen Pitts, an Ohio abolitionist's daughter, twenty-one years younger than he—and white. Her father announced he would not have his new son-in-law in his home. Douglass's children, who refused to attend the wedding, never called their stepmother anything other than "Mrs. Douglass." Even the black *Weekly News* was appalled: "Fred Douglass has married a red-head white girl. . . . Goodbye, black blood in that family. We have no further use for him. His picture hangs in our parlor. We will hang it in the stables."

Again, Douglass was unmoved: "What business has the world with the color of my wife?" he asked a friend. "Helen and I are making life go very happily. . . ."

Julia Griffiths wrote to congratulate him on his remarriage. There seems to be no record of how Ottilia Assing took the news, but a few

weeks later, she left her Paris hotel, wandered into the Bois de Bou-
logne, and swallowed poison. In her will, she asked that all her letters
be destroyed and left a $13,000 trust fund, its annual income earmarked
for Douglass and the cause for which they had labored together so
long.

His reaction to her death is unknown, but his new marriage did
brighten his last years, which were otherwise mostly dark. He never
stopped agitating, first successfully for black voting rights and then in
vain against the betrayal of Reconstruction and the steady growth of
Jim Crow, but he did so always from within the Republican Party for
which he worked, as he himself once admitted, as a "fieldhand." In
return for his dogged fealty, he received a succession of largely empty
honors—the presidency of the already moribund Freedman's Bank,
marshal of Washington, recorder of deeds, minister to Haiti (where his
enthusiasm at living in a black republic evidently helped blind him to
the bloody-mindedness of its president, Florvil Hyppolite). The favored treatment he received at white Republican hands served to point
up the hardships endured by other blacks: he once found himself
playing croquet at the home of the Washington hostess Kate Chase
Sprague, who was then employing in her stable one of his own sons.

But from time to time even during his sad, final years, Douglass
displayed something of his old fire. He was asked to speak at "Colored
People's Day" at the Columbian Exposition at Chicago in 1893. The
white press treated the occasion as a joke, and as Douglass, now a
weary, stooped old man, began to read his speech, he was drowned out
by jeering whites. He seemed genuinely shaken at first. His voice
faltered, he removed his glasses, set down his manuscript. Then, the
poet Paul Laurence Dunbar remembered, he ran his fingers once
through his white hair, straightened his back, and began to speak once
again in the huge, echoing voice of his youth, "compelling attention,
drowning out the catcalls as an organ would a penny whistle."

"Men talk of the Negro problem. There is no Negro problem," he
said. "The problem is whether the American people have loyalty
enough, honor enough, patriotism enough, to live up to their own
Constitution. . . . We Negroes love our country. We fought for it. We
ask only that we be treated as well as those who fought against it."

American Heritage February 1991

A FRESH LOOK AT THE LITTLE FLOWER:
FIORELLO LA GUARDIA

SOME TWENTY YEARS AGO, A FRIEND LET ME LEAF THROUGH several photograph albums compiled by his grandfather, an army surgeon who had spent the 1880s and 90s stationed at dusty Western outposts helping to keep a wary eye on the Indians, only recently subdued. There, among the tea-colored pictures of leathery one-time warriors, clusters of bored-looking officers and their still-more-bored-looking wives, and distant snapshots of the low-slung forts themselves, barely distinguishable from the sagebrush that surrounded them, was a striking portrait of a regimental bandmaster with bright black eyes, waxed mustache, and crisply barbered beard. Beneath it was the man's grandiloquent signature: "Professor Achille La Guardia."

I wondered idly as I turned the big page whether this showy westerner could somehow have been distantly related to Fiorello La Guardia, the quintessential New Yorker who served three terms as mayor of his city. Not only were the two related, I later learned from Thomas Kessner's biography, *Fiorello H. La Guardia and the Making of Modern New York,* but Fiorello was the bandmaster's eldest son; born in New York in 1882 but raised from the age of three on army installations elsewhere, he did not move back permanently to the metropolis whose brassy symbol he became until he was twenty-three.

I suppose I shouldn't have been surprised. The overwhelming majority of La Guardia's constituents were brought up somewhere else, after all, and La Guardia's variegated heritage could hardly have been tailored for broader voter appeal. His father was Italian—*Fiorello* means "Little Flower," and his middle name was Enrico until he had it changed to Henry. But his mother was Jewish, and he was raised at least nominally as an Episcopalian.

La Guardia's Western boyhood was central to his development. Early exposure to crooked Indian agents helped inspire in him an aversion to politics-as-usual so strong that in 1941 he insisted that the *International Who's Who* describe him as a "municipal officer" rather than a mere politician. His adolescent admiration for swift, frontier-style justice never left him, either—it was no accident that he wore an outsize Stetson when he set out to tame New York's streets. But it was his demanding father—who beat him regularly in a doomed effort to make him "the second John Philip Sousa" and who urged his teachers to beat him, too—who really shaped his character, inculcating in him an instinctive sympathy with the victimized, an unslakable desire to excel, and a deep suspicion of authority, along with a crippling inability to trust or confide in anyone that would make this famously outgoing man virtually friendless.

La Guardia became a Republican in part because Tammany corruption genuinely appalled him, but also because there was little room for an ambitious Italian in an organization run by Irishmen primarily for Irishmen. The GOP was not hospitable, at first: it was run by establishment WASPs made frankly uneasy by an obstreperous recruit who was happy giving better than he got in the savage ethnic political wars that still mystified old-school New Yorkers. "I can out-demagogue the best of demagogues," La Guardia liked to boast, but he endured as many setbacks as successes before winning a seat in Congress in 1916 by just 357 votes out of 18,670 cast—his winning margin in part due to his having lured flophouse voters to the polls with coffee and doughnuts before the fatally complacent Tammany men could get to them.

He had barely been sworn in when the United States entered World War I. La Guardia volunteered for the Air Service Bombing Squadron and ended up a major, though he had too little patience for smooth landings: "I can't take the buzzard off and I can't land him," he told a member of his squad, "but I can fly the son of a gun." He returned from one combat mission with two hundred bullet holes in his plane, and when King Victor Emmanuel III personally awarded him the Flying Cross, he called him "Manny," to the delight of the newspapers back home.

Back in Congress, La Guardia found the gentlemanly traditions of the House a strain: "Are you quoted correctly . . . ," an enraged general asked, "in calling me nothing but a beribboned dog-robber?" "No sir," La Guardia replied. "I was not aware that you had any ribbons." He was a master of dramatics, "the Belasco of politics," according to an envious ally. Once, to point up the hypocrisy of Prohibition, he invited the press to room 150 of the House Office Building to watch him make illegal beer, and when opponents dared him to do it again out from under congressional immunity, he cheerfully restaged the whole thing in a Manhattan drugstore and was irate when no Prohibition agents turned up to arrest him.

La Guardia spent a dozen years in Congress, offering forthright progressive views on every conceivable topic in his loud, shrill voice: "It was like he owned the U.S.," his widow remembered. "Nobody should do anything to it." "The function of a progressive . . . ," he told an interviewer, was "to keep on protesting until things get so bad that a reactionary demands reforms."

But he was not really content to wait that long. He wanted to run New York, and he got his chance at last in 1933, when, in the depths of the Depression, enough city voters wearied of Tammany scandals to sweep him into office on a Fusion ticket.

For those too young to have first-hand memories of La Guardia's gaudy days at City Hall, he remains the lovable but eccentric figure of the old newsreels, racing to fires, smashing slot machines, exuberantly reading Dick Tracy over the radio to children deprived of their Sunday funnies by a newspaper strike.

But there was far more substance than style to Fiorello La Guardia. He literally transformed his city: clearing slums; building airports, parks, and public housing with funds tirelessly lobbied from Albany and Washington; ramming through a revised city charter; creating a non-political civil service; and so drying up opportunities for graft that the bank holding the mortgage on the Tammany wigwam felt compelled to sell it out from under the organization.

Kessner is properly admiring of his subject, but not blind to his faults. La Guardia was a little man—just over five feet tall and wide enough to seem still shorter—and acutely sensitive about it. Once, when a remarkably heedless aide suggested that a candidate for a city job was "too small" to work in a dangerous neighborhood, the mayor came around his desk, jumping up and down and screaming, "WHAT'S THE MATTER WITH A LITTLE GUY? WHAT'S THE MATTER WITH A LITTLE GUY?" He was something of a bully, too, and relished dressing down subordinates in front of others: "If you were any dumber," he once shrieked at a stenographer in the presence of a department head, "I would make you a commissioner." But he was also relentlessly hardworking and scrupulously honest: "Beware of the nickel cigar," he told motor vehicle inspectors. "Accept no favors. . . . Oh, they will want to know if you're interested in fights or ball games. Look out, that's the preliminary necking. If you succumb to the preliminary necking, you're done."

La Guardia himself never succumbed to any necking. When he

died in 1947, his modest home was still mortgaged and he had just $8,000 in savings bonds in the bank. It was power, not money, that drove him, and in the end it drove him too hard.

Congress had never satisfied him. Neither did being America's most celebrated mayor, and he had taken it into his head that he would succeed his sometime patron Franklin D. Roosevelt in the White House in 1940, although his ethnic background, his irrepressible brashness, and his noisy disdain for party loyalty all militated against any party ever rewarding him with its presidential nomination. Then the war in Europe began, FDR won a third term, and La Guardia was left at City Hall to nurse his disappointment. Everything seemed to sour: day-to-day duties bored him and the cockiness that had once been winning lurched toward megalomania; he set investigators upon his critics, and frantically lobbied Roosevelt for a big federal job that would keep him in the headlines.

FDR obliged by naming him director of the Office of Civilian Defense. He got the publicity he craved—"positively swollen with importance," Rexford Tugwell wrote after hearing him deliver one of the fifty "preparedness" speeches he gave a month—but he was quickly forced out after quarreling with his staff and foolishly patronizing his deputy director, the President's wife.

He continued to beg for federal favors: "Dear Chief," he wrote FDR in 1943, asking to be made a brigadier general. "Soldier La Guardia reports to the C in C that he awaits orders. He believes General Eisenhower needs him now more than ever."

The orders never came. La Guardia left City Hall in 1946 rather than run for the fourth term that no longer interested him, and then was given the sort of position with which he might under other circumstances have rebuilt his reputation—rescuing millions of displaced persons from misery and starvation as director general of the United Nations Relief and Rehabilitation Administration. But the task now just seemed overwhelming to La Guardia, weary and already suffering from the cancer that would kill him ten months later, and he resigned when he proved unable to persuade policy makers preoccupied with offsetting Soviet power that their policy of offering assistance only to those hungry people who happened to live under friendly regimes was as wrong overseas as it had been in New York, when he was young and Tammany had bought its votes with bread.

American Heritage February 1990

THE PROSECUTOR: THOMAS E. DEWEY

WINNERS WRITE HISTORY, OF COURSE, OR THEIR ADMIRERS do. All that most losers can hope for is to be treated with magnanimity. Thomas E. Dewey was many times a winner: as America's most celebrated racket buster during the 1930s, three times as governor of New York, and as a leader of the moderate wing of the Republican Party that put Dwight D. Eisenhower in the White House and ended twenty years of Democratic rule. Yet he is remembered, if at all, as a loser because he was twice defeated for the presidency, first by Franklin D. Roosevelt (to the surprise of almost no one), then by Harry S Truman (to the utter astonishment of almost everybody).

As *Thomas E. Dewey and His Times,* the richly detailed, full-scale biography by Richard Norton Smith, makes clear, to recall Dewey only as a beaten candidate is to miss a lot, both about him and about the political history of the middle years of this century.

"Everything came too early for me," Dewey admitted toward the end of his life. And it showed. Like Richard M. Nixon (whom he championed early), Dewey always displayed the overly sober mien of a young man to whom success has come too soon. Even his delivery resembled Nixon's: resonant, studied, unctuous, like a young divinity student's. He seemed to many voters literally too good to be true.

Dewey was in fact very good at what he did.

He was born in the tiny Michigan town of Owosso in 1902. His father, a fervently Republican country editor, drummed into him early the ancient doctrine that far-off Tammany Hall embodied "all that is evil in government," and it became an article of faith. Dewey was a national celebrity before he was thirty-four, relentlessly pursuing gangsters and grabbing headlines as New York's special prosecutor for organized crime. His methods sometimes alarmed civil libertarians, but the results were statistically impressive: seventy-two convictions out of seventy-three prosecutions in just two years. No one ever questioned Dewey's courage: when a caller threatened to kill him on his way home at night, he refused to alter his route, even turning on the light in his car to make himself a better target. Two 1938 movies, *Racket Busters* and *Smashing the Rackets,* were based on Dewey's exploits. By 1940, the thirty-seven-year-old crime fighter had become a leading contender for the GOP presidential nomination, even though he had held just one elective office, as Manhattan's district attorney. (It was the year for amateurs: Wendell Willkie, who nosed Dewey out, had never been elected to anything.)

Dewey became governor in 1942 and built a solid, prudent, but progressive record during his dozen years in Albany. He constructed highways, launched the state university system, won enactment of pioneering civil rights legislation—and managed to cut taxes in the bargain. (He viewed Nelson Rockefeller, his free-wheeling, free-spending Republican successor, with bemusement: "I like you, Nelson," he once confided, "but I don't think I can afford you.")

But he was never able to put himself across to the nation as a whole. Few men as talented and successful as Dewey have inspired so many hostile cracks. He was the little man on the wedding cake; the man you really had to get to know to really dislike; the only man on earth who could strut sitting down.

His appearance had something to do with it. He stood just 5 feet 8 inches tall; both his vice presidential running mates towered over him. His dark smear of a mustache didn't help, either: "Remember fellows," he told a Boy Scout delegation, "any boy can become President—unless he's got a mustache." His toothy, irregular smile was more grimace than grin. He was stiff, formal, uncomfortable with strangers, impatient even with admirers.

"I don't think he was ever happy," recalled his campaign manager, Herbert Brownell. "He got joy out of attainment. . . . But as for happiness in the usual sense of the word. . . . He wasn't really geared to our political system." Even with his closest aides, one of them remembered, he was "cold—cold as a February icicle." When he was district attorney, his desktop held a blotter, a letter opener, a brown leather folder, and a carafe of water. When the carafe needed filling, his biographer writes, "A buzzer brought a secretary, and a finger was pointed at the offending pitcher." (This happened often: Dewey drank three quarts of water a day, sipping religiously even while cross-examining witnesses.) He had a phobia about germs. In building his case against Lucky Luciano as a procurer, he had to meet a large number of prostitutes; after each handshake he retired to the washroom to scrub his hand. Later, touring prisons as governor, he would not touch a doorknob without first surreptitiously wiping it off with a folded handkerchief concealed in his palm.

The attributes that made him an effective prosecutor—rectitude, efficiency, precision, a nearly limitless capacity for hard work—are admirable but bloodless. "His greatest fun was finding out someone else had made a mistake," said an employee, and that attitude communicated itself directly to the voters. Roosevelt saw what was wrong. "You ought to hear him," he marveled to a friend. "He talks to the people as if they were the jury and I were the villain on trial for his life."

Everyone knows that Dewey failed to convict either of his Democratic opponents, but Robert Smith's recounting of those campaigns manages to be both fresh and provocative. Roosevelt's uproarious defense of "my little dog, Fala," against Republican slander is often cited as a masterstroke that demolished Dewey in 1944; thereafter, the old joke runs, it become a contest between Roosevelt's dog and Dewey's goat. In fact, Smith writes, Roosevelt's speech almost backfired, for it goaded Dewey into delivering the most effective address of his campaign, an all-out partisan assault on Democratic pretensions to indispensability that galvanized Republicans and nearly doubled the crowds that came out to see him. More of the same might have made the difference, but Dewey believed he had been undignified, out of control—it had been "the worst damned speech I ever made in my life"— and he drew back to his fatally cool prosecutorial style. In 1948, Dewey's worst enemy was not himself, his biographer argues, so much as the Republican-controlled Congress, whose overeagerness to repeal the New Deal (especially for agriculture) cost him precious farm votes during the last two weeks of the campaign.

Democrats did not like Dewey. Even Roosevelt, who was normally tolerant of political foes (once he had trounced them), never warmed to him. "I still think he is a son of a bitch," he said to an aide as he wheeled himself to bed on election night.

A good many Republicans agreed, especially the conservative followers of Dewey's perennial rival, Senator Robert Taft, whose reserved, unyielding personality was a match for Dewey's own. For fifteen years these two unlikely politicians jousted for their party's favor. Dewey's crisp aggressive style worked best behind the scenes. He was instrumental in edging the GOP back from isolationism. He did his best to block the most zealous red-hunters: a proposed bill to outlaw the Communist Party amounted to unconstitutional "Thought control," he said. On the domestic front, he preached what he had practiced in Albany. "It is our solemn duty," he declared, "to show that the Government can have both a head and a heart, that it can be both progressive and solvent, that it can serve the people without being their master." Unable finally to win the White House for himself, he hoped by drafting Eisenhower to thwart those who wanted to take the party "back to McKinley."

Smith is at his sensitive best when seeking to discover how Dewey's sadly crippled personality came into being. The adult Dewey could not bring himself to speak well of his dead father. His strong-willed mother (whom he called "Mater" and to whom he was devoted) was ambitious for him: it was she who made sure that he alone of all fifty-eight of his Owosso classmates was never late or absent in twelve years of schooling. But she was also oddly scornful of his accomplishments, and since neither she nor his wife, Frances, ever really approved of politics, his victories could never fully be savored and his defeats were all the more nakedly humiliating. When he announced in 1950 (prematurely, as it turned out) that he would not run for a third term as governor, his mother told friends how pleased she was that her son was "finally going to make an honest living."

Frances Dewey appears to have been simultaneously devoted to her husband and resentful at having abandoned a promising operatic career to marry him. Perhaps to compensate, she became the vigilant guardian of his dignity: she would make sure he was not seen to act more like a sweaty, glad-handing politician than was absolutely necessary. Vacationing in Arizona after the 1948 debacle, Dewey went out behind his hotel to pitch pennies with his two sons. As he rolled up his sleeves and squatted in the dust, his wife rushed to stop him, afraid that a photographer might snap an unseemly picture. "Maybe if I had done this during the campaign," he said quietly, "I might have won."

His wife's bitterness was deepened toward the end by her long struggle against cancer, relieved only by heavy drinking. After her death in 1969, he turned for companionship to the actress Kitty Carlisle Hart, who provided him with a warm but belated introduction to the lighter side of things. Watching *Catch-22*—the first movie he'd seen in twenty years—Dewey began to rumble that the army was nothing like that. "Relax," Mrs. Hart said. "It's supposed to be funny."

During his last years, politicians and presidents of both parties sought his counsel. In 1964, Dewey persuaded Lyndon Johnson to move a filmed tribute to John Kennedy from the first night of the Democratic Convention to the last in order to prevent emotional delegates from forcing Robert Kennedy (whom Dewey detested) onto the ticket. And only death may have prevented him from performing one final service to his party. In early 1971, five members of the Nixon cabinet grew so alarmed at their chief's isolation behind the Haldeman-Ehrlichman wall that they planned to dispatch Dewey to the Oval Office to urge that the President's top aides be supplanted by a new chief of staff, Melvin Laird.

Dewey died instantly of a massive heart attack in Florida on March 16, 1971. His body was found lying fully clothed on his hotel bed. His bags were piled neatly next to him. On top of the suitcases sat his hat.

New York Times Book Review August 22, 1982

DEAR BESS: HARRY S TRUMAN

BESS TRUMAN MAY BE REMEMBERED BEST TODAY FOR A FEW seconds of newsreel film that show her in a rare moment of public embarrassment. Surrounded by dignitaries at the christening of a new bomber, she beats an inexplicably resilient champagne bottle time after helpless time against its fuselage. Her expression is unreadable beneath a big, sheltering hat.

Elizabeth Virginia Wallace Truman was perhaps the most private and least known of all the modern First Ladies. She granted few interviews, disliked speechmaking, did not comment on politics. Cherishing her privacy, she stayed away from Washington as much as possible, preferring to live at home in Independence, Missouri, in the house her grandfather had built at 219 North Delaware Street shortly after the Civil War. Until she died in 1982 at the age of ninety-seven it was assumed that none of her husband's early personal papers had survived; even his daughter, Margaret, believed her mother had burned all his letters. But after Bess Truman's death hundreds of hoarded family letters were found scattered through some of the seventeen rooms of her old home, among them some 1,200 written to her by her husband. Without her, it now seems clear, Harry S Truman might have stayed a dirt farmer all his life.

They met in Independence, at the Presbyterian Sunday School in 1890. He was six. She was five, and, as he never seems to have tired of telling her, the prettiest girl in town. They lived around the corner from one another as children and he claimed later to have set his heart then on someday having her; but the social barrier that separated them was nearly as broad as the Missouri River that flowed just north of town. Her grandfather was co-owner of the local mill, producer of "the finest biscuit and cake flower in the world," called Queen of the Pantry. Her father was David Wallace, a town official and sometime Democratic politician who liked to lead parades. The Trumans stood on the sidelines. They were country people—"clodhoppers," Harry called them—upright and respected but often in debt.

He did not dare try to win Bess until he was twenty-six, in 1910. The return of a borrowed cake plate to the Wallace kitchen provided the pretext he needed to make his first nervous call. His prospects had not improved since childhood: he was working from dawn to dark on his father's farm near Grandview, twenty miles from Independence, forced to abandon his plans for college to help provide for his younger brother and sister. But he always had aspirations for something better, dreams encouraged by his devoted, college-educated mother. Still, Bess Wallace might have remained forever beyond his reach had it not been for a family tragedy: one evening in 1903, for reasons never fully understood, her father went into the bathroom, sat down in the tub, and shot himself. Bess shouldered the burden of caring for her embittered mother, and other, more likely suitors shied off.

Harry worked hard to win her, riding the train to Independence after a full day's work in the fields for an evening of vaudeville, and even taking time out from sowing clover to mark out and mow a tennis court to her specifications so that she might come out to the farm "Saturday afternoons and play in the shade all the time." But he was unable to see her as often as he liked and so pressed his suit by mail, scribbling long letters in bed before returning to the fields at 5:00 A.M. He would continue to write to her whenever they were apart—sometimes twice a day—for the rest of his life. *Dear Bess: The Letters from Harry to Bess Truman, 1910–1959*, the collection edited by Robert H. Ferrell, is at once a love story, an astonishing record of what one industrious man managed to accomplish, and an intimate look into the heart and mind of the thirty-third President of the United States.

Missourians are not normally demonstrative, and he was no exception: "A weeping man is an abomination unto the Lord," he once wrote to Bess. And he took particular pride in his toughness, perhaps to compensate for the fact that his mother often told him he had been "intended for a girl." He gave up serious study of the piano at fifteen, in part because he had been made to think it sissified, and he once described himself to Bess as "a guy with spectacles and a girl mouth." But when he wrote to her, all the barriers came down. "I know your last letter word for word," he told her in 1913, not long after she had agreed eventually to marry him. "I read it some 40 times a day. Oh, please send me another like it. . . . You really didn't know I had so much softness and sentimentality in me, did you? I'm full of it. But I'd die if I had to talk it. I can tell you on paper how much I love you. . . . But to tell it to you, I can't. . . . When a person's airing his most sacred thoughts he's very easily distressed."

Like most farm boys who grew up to be President, Truman loathed working the land. "Riding a plow," he wrote to Bess, "gives one a chance to think of all the meanness he ever did and all he intends to do." He tried everything he could think of to free himself from it— working in a bank, running a zinc mine, drilling for oil, haberdashery. Nothing worked. "They say debts give a man energy," he wrote. "I ought to be a shining example of that quality if they do." He was, and he kept at it, convinced that "when the motive's strong enough, a man can do almost anything if he's got the stuff in him."

Bess became the motive; he had the stuff. She was "the superlative of excellence," he said, and she filled his dreams: "I dreamed of you last night. Thought we were going down a grand street in some very big city . . . trying to find somewhere to eat when I discovered that I had no hat on and then I woke up. I hope to see that place in that manner some day with you." With her support, anything was possible. "My mother is for me, first, last and all the time," he told her, "and I know you are. Why shouldn't I win? Such backing should overturn the worst of hoodooes."

Mother Wallace was another matter. He worried that even if he managed someday to prosper, she might never "care for me well enough to have me in the family," and he may have been right. Though she would live with the Trumans until her death in 1952, she is said never fully to have approved of her son-in-law and, if the neighbors interviewed for Merle Miller's *Plain Speaking* are to be believed, she may have favored the more genteel Thomas Dewey for President in 1948. That there is no word of complaint about her in *Dear Bess* is a tribute to Harry's forbearance and sturdy sense of family obligation.

"I am crazy to marry you," he told Bess in 1917. "I see myself in an ideal country home with everything in it as it should be and you to run it and me." World War I further delayed the wedding, but his letters from "Somewhere in Parlez-Vous" reflect his first real triumph, as an artillery officer. "I'm plumb crazy about my Battery," he wrote home. "They sure do step when I ask them to." He and Bess were finally married when he came home in 1919; their courtship had stretched nine years. Because the Trumans now lived together (in his mother-in-law's house), the flow of letters slowed but it never stopped. They trace his life in politics, first in Jackson County, where he managed to flourish as the creation of Tom Pendergast's noisome Kansas City machine without ever becoming its creature, then in

Washington, as senator, Vice President, and President.

Dear Bess contains no startling revelations. Harry Truman's letters confirm what his friends and enemies alike always said about him: he was precisely what he seemed, no less, no more. What is startling is how little he seems to have changed over nearly fifty years. The voice of the young farmer of 1910 is almost identical with that of the President he became. President Truman's distrust of military brass seems foreshadowed in Captain Truman's unromantic view of the trench warfare he saw in France. "It is a great thing to swell your chest and fight for a principle," he wrote, "but it gets almighty tiresome sometimes." And there are echoes of Sunday School in his brisk explanation of his cold war obligations: since the Soviets could not be trusted, he told Bess, "We've got to organize the people who believe in honor and the Golden Rule to win the world back to peace and Christianity." The presidency itself was just another job at which to work hard; there was no more to it "than running Jackson County, and not any more worry."

Harry Truman was a man of many prejudices. His letters are peppered with the standard-issue epithets of the world in which he grew up—"dago," "nigger," "bohunk." Nor did they soften much with the years: New York was a "kike town" when he first saw it on his way to war in 1917, and it was still "the U.S. Capital of Israel" when he visited it again as an ex-President forty years later. It is not surprising that he retained the petty bigotry bred into his bones; his grandmother, after all, had thought the only thing wrong with John Wilkes Booth had been that he made his move too late. But when it came to a question of what he considered elemental fairness—integration of the armed forces, for example, or the creation of Israel—he was able to overcome his heritage and act on principle.

Bess Truman herself remains as elusive as ever. While some of her replies to her husband's letters have survived, they are not yet open to researchers. We see her only through her husband's adoring eyes, and if photographs do not quite bear out his belief that she was "the prettiest girl in the world," he thought she was and lived accordingly. "Most of my associates think there's something wrong with me because I believe in that oath I took in a certain little Episcopal Church," he wrote her from a West Coast hotel room in 1944, "but I don't care what they think."

There were inevitably tensions between the Trumans. She didn't spend enough time in Washington to suit him, and she didn't write often enough; he sometimes came home too late to suit her, and she was never afraid to tell him so. "I guess I'm a damn fool," he told her after one White House scolding, "but I'm happier when I can see you—even when you give me hell I'd rather have you around than not."

"I miss you terribly," he told her again in 1946, "no one here to see whether my tie's on straight, or whether my hair needs cutting, whether the dinner's good, bad or indifferent." But he needed far more than that from her. He had never wanted to be "a No. 1 man in the world," and it was up to Bess and Margaret, "to those I have on a pedestal at home," to help him keep things in perspective and cool the temper he himself called "hotter than a depot stove."

Back in 1913, Harry described himself to Bess as "just a common everyday man whose instincts are to be ornery, who's anxious to be right." For nearly sixty years, Bess Truman did her best to keep him right, and these letters suggest that for him no achievement in his remarkable life ever quite matched the winning of her. On June 29, 1949, he wrote from Blair House. It was their anniversary, and he was now President in his own right. "Thirty years ago," he said, "I hoped to make you a happy wife and a happy mother. Did I? I don't know. All I can say [is] I've tried. There is no one in the world who can look down on you or your daughter. That means much to me."

New York Times Book Review August 7, 1983

ENTERTAINERS

★

THE BOSTON STRONG BOY:
JOHN L. SULLIVAN

AMERICANS HAVE ALWAYS ADMIRED SIZE. WE LIKE BIG STAT-ues, big buildings, big burgers. And when it comes to boxing, it is the heavyweights we follow most avidly, fascinated by their sheer volume and by the terrible damage they can do: according to one study, a top heavyweight's knockout blow hits its objective with the equivalent force of 10,000 pounds. The swift, spidery smaller men so popular in other countries usually appear here on the undercard.

John L. Sullivan was both the last of the bare-knuckle heavyweight champions and the first prizefighter ever to make his living in the ring; it was he, more than any other man, who transformed the American fight game from an illicit pastime into a (more or less) legitimate big business and blazed the trail out of big-city slums followed first by other Irishmen with the requisite speed and skill and hunger, and then by Jews, Italians, blacks, and Hispanics equipped with the same fierce talents.

Sullivan himself is irresistible, but the most recent book about him, Michael T. Isenberg's *John L. Sullivan and His America,* is oddly disappointing. Like a good many academic biographers, the author seems uneasy simply chronicling his hero's colorful career. He too rarely allows his subject to remain onstage, nudging him into the wings to make room for detailed descriptions of two Manhattan bars Sullivan may never even have visited, to list the name of every tank town at which his barnstorming train stopped, and to offer numbing disquisitions on everything from cowtown violence and Social Darwinism to Irish attitudes toward women.

"Write any damn thing yuh please, young fella," Sullivan told the youthful Theodore Dreiser when he came to interview the ex-champion in retirement, "and say John L. Sullivan said so." But even Sullivan might have been flummoxed by Isenberg's grave search for greater meaning in every corner of his life and career. The relatively humane Marquis of Queensberry rules under which Sullivan preferred to fight, for example, required among other things that a felled man be back on his feet by the count of ten: this, his latest biographer assures us, elevated the "timekeeper . . . to a position of prime importance, consonant with the growing significance of time in the industrial age."

(To be fair, Isenberg is not alone in his earnest quest: Writers from Homer to Norman Mailer have labored altogether too hard to find high-minded reasons for the visceral pleasure they take in watching two total strangers try to batter one another senseless. Even A. J. Liebling, the undefeated champion among boxing essayists, could be uncharacteristically portentous about it: ". . . [a] boxer, like a writer," he once intoned, "must stand alone.")

John L. Sullivan saw boxing in simpler terms as the best way he could think of to make money and get famous fast. He was born in 1858 at Roxbury, Massachusetts, now part of Boston, the son of Mike Sullivan, a stumpy laborer from Tralee, and his immense wife, Catherine Kelly. He inherited his heavy drinking and his combativeness from his father, whose hard life laying brick and digging ditches also inspired him to seek a new and more lucrative way to exploit the size and strength that were the legacies of his mother.

Sullivan's boxing career began in Boston on the stage of the Dudley Opera House in 1878 when he shed his coat, rolled up his sleeves, and put on gloves for what, to placate the police, was billed as a mere "exhibition." When his equally green adversary thumped him on the back of the head, Sullivan knocked him into the piano. "I done him up in about two minutes," he remembered. That was how he liked things to go. "I go in to win from the very first second," he explained. "Win I must and win I shall." Win he did—at least forty-seven times, against every blacksmith, tugboat captain, iron puddler, and gandydancer who accepted the challenge he issued to "all fighters—first come, first served. . . ."

Sometimes he liked to pontificate about the supposed scientific skill with which he went about his work: "My objective point in hitting is the corner of a man's shoulder," he gravely explained to one reporter, "and if he ducks his head he is bound to get it in the neck. A man will break his dukes if he goes hitting at his antagonist's skull." In fact, his mode of attack was brutally straightforward: He rushed at his man from the opening bell, swinging his cudgel of a right fist until the opponent fell down. His defensive skills were limited largely to a ferrous chin and the psychological impact of the relentless cheer with which he complimented any man who managed to reach it. "That's a good one, Charlie!" he would say, continuing to move inexorably forward. There can be few more disheartening moments in sports than to land your best punch and see its beefy target smile.

Sullivan may not actually have been able to take bites out of horseshoes, as one widely believed story had it, but his power really was prodigious. "I thought a telegraph pole had been shoved against me endways," said Paddy Ryan, from whom he took the title in 1882; another victim, awakened after being drenched with several buckets of water, wondered dreamily if he might have fallen off a barn. For those who refused to close with him, Sullivan had nothing but scorn: "I want fighting, not foot racing," he liked to say, and he dismissed Charlie Mitchell, the British champion whose footwork helped hold him to a thirty-round draw in 1887, as "the bombastic sprinter."

Isenberg assures us that Sullivan was "the first significant mass cultural hero in American life." A good many other historical figures, starting perhaps with Davy Crockett, have as much right to have this gassy claim made for them, but the champion's mustached portrait did soon hang everywhere; small boys followed him from saloon to saloon; their fathers followed his feats in and out of the ring in the burgeoning penny press or in the pink pages of the *National Police Gazette;* and people seemed willing to pay to see him do almost anything, including declaim poetry and pose motionless in tights as "The Dying Gladiator" and "Hercules at Rest." For three of his ten years as champion he abandoned the ring entirely in favor of a cross-country tour playing a virtuous blacksmith in *Honest Hearts and Willing Hands,* a melodrama especially written for him—"Mr. Sullivan," wrote one careful critic, "was quite as good as the play"—and he later starred briefly as Simon Legree in a drastically rewritten version of *Uncle Tom's Cabin* in which, according to the author, Mrs. Stowe's harsh overseer had been transformed into a hero so that Sullivan could hold on to the audience's sympathy while pummeling Uncle Tom.

The champion once claimed in court that he had "never been angry in any of the engagements I have been in." Between engagements, however, things were different: Sullivan was "a son-of-a-bitch of the first water," one contemporary said, "if he ever drank any." A mean drunk, sensitive to any slight, real or fancied, his favored brawling technique was to butt his enemies into oblivion. His drinking caused him to balloon to more than 300 pounds; it lost him his first wife, drove off at least one mistress, and almost cost him his life when, staggering out onto the platform between two railroad cars to urinate, he tumbled off the speeding train.

In 1889, he nonetheless announced his qualifications to run for Congress: he was a loyal Democrat, he explained; he kept his promises; and as for people who criticized his occupation, "They don't know what they are talking about. My business is, and always has been . . . to encourage physical culture. . . . Many a young man is bigger and stronger because my example has set him to work." (Gingerly, party bosses politely overlooked his offer.)

One of the young men Sullivan had set to work was James John Corbett, who left his bank teller's cage in San Francisco that same year to pursue Sullivan's title—and the big cash prizes that now went with it. The two men finally met at New Orleans three years later. The champion, badly overweight at thirty-three and breathing hard from the eighth round on, never caught up with his agile challenger, who banged him with counterpunches every time he lunged until he collapsed in the twenty-first round and was unable to rise again.

Nothing in Sullivan's ring career became him so much as his leaving of it: Shrugging off the restraining hands of his seconds who thought he wanted to continue his hopeless battle, he managed to get to his feet and lean heavily on the ropes long enough to deliver a graceful curtain speech: "Gentlemen. . . . All I have to say is that I came into the ring once too often—and if I had to get licked, I'm glad I was licked by an American. I remain your warm and personal friend, John L. Sullivan."

Sullivan lived on for another twenty-six years, sadly little better suited to retirement than most of the champions who came after him. By one estimate he had made and lost more than a million dollars; he failed three times at saloon keeping; was forced to pawn his gaudy championship belt; tried refereeing, hurling lighter men across the ring whenever they dared clinch; and flirted with a comeback: at forty-three and weighing a wobbly 273 pounds, he had enough left to knock out an opponent half his age for five full minutes in 1905.

Instead of resuming boxing, however, he gave up alcohol—"If I ever take another drink as long as I live," he told astonished fellow patrons in a hotel bar in Terre Haute, Indiana, "I hope to God I choke"—and later launched a new career as a temperance lecturer.

Having opened a new way to wealth for poor whites, Sullivan sought to obstruct it for all blacks. He was an implacable believer in the color line. "I will not fight a negro," he used to boast. "I never have, and I never will," and when in 1908, the heavyweight champion, Tommy Burns of Australia, signed to fight Jack Johnson, he piously denounced the foreigner's greed: "Shame on the money-mad champion!" he said. "Shame on the man who upsets good American precedents because there are Dollars, Dollars, Dollars in it." To Sullivan's credit, once Burns was knocked out, he wrote that despite his own "well-known antipathy to [Johnson's] race," the black man had won fair and square.

In 1910, he married a woman he had known since childhood, almost as tall as he and nearly as wide. She moved with him to a Massachusetts farm and kept a careful eye on what little money her husband had managed to retain.

John L. Sullivan died of a heart attack at fifty-nine in February 1918. For the wake, held in his sister's parlor, the undertakers laid him out in a tuxedo, his massive right fist clenched over his heart.

American Heritage September 1988

THE ST. LOUIS WOMAN OF PARIS: JOSEPHINE BAKER

THE PAST KEEPS NO SECRETS MORE SECURELY THAN THOSE OF the stage. Little that happens behind the footlights survives for long in front of them, and the theatrical enthusiasms of one era invariably puzzle the next: Sarah Bernhardt, universally admired on-stage for more than half a century, looked ludicrous sawing the air on the silent screen; recordings of Paul Robeson's rumbling *Othello* are filled with sound and fury that now seem to us to signify mostly overacting.

Josephine Baker is a particularly puzzling case in point. *Chasing a Rainbow: The Life of Josephine Baker*, a British-made television documentary shown recently on PBS, includes film clips of the kind of dancing that made this girl from a black St. Louis slum the queen of the Paris music hall. Slim and long-legged at nineteen, she races, bare-breasted, onto the stage of the Folies Bergère in 1926 and tears into the Charleston, knees bent, elbows flapping, feet stomping; she bumps and grinds and writhes and shimmies and, from time to time, puffs out her cheeks and crosses her eyes and grins into the camera.

e. e. cummings thought her "an incomparably fluid night-mare...." But the French, who have never been wholly reliable judges of American culture—they revere Jerry Lewis, after all—were genuinely undone by this frantically eager-to-please young performer whom they first called simply "Joséphine." Critics called her "the black Venus that haunted Baudelaire" and compared her to a snake, a giraffe, a kangaroo; when she began to parade along the boulevards with a live cheetah, admirers speculated as to which "animal" was more wonderfully savage, the one at the end of the leash or the one holding it.

The fact that Baker and the other members of the cast of the *Revue Nègre* in which she first triumphed in Paris grew up on gritty American city streets and had never even seen Africa was cheerfully over-looked: "Their lips must have the taste of pickled watermelon coconut, sweet pepper and guava," one critic assured his readers. "One sips in through the eyes the sweet saltiness of their perspiration, the sweat of a hamadryad bounding across jungles filled with poisonous flowers."

"The white imagination," Josephine once said, "sure is something when it comes to blacks," and she was derisive when asked by a French reporter if she preferred black lovers to white ones: *"La peau!* Pfftt! Nothing." But the color of Baker's own skin—and what it then symbolized for whites on both sides of the Atlantic—was very nearly everything at the start of her career, for better and for worse, and the most compelling parts of Phyllis Rose's biographical essay, *Jazz Cleopatra: Josephine Baker in Her Time,* examine the strange workings of color that forced Josephine to serve "as a focus for decades of theorizing about race."

To many Frenchmen, Rose writes, Baker's tawny, writhing body was the old colonial dream made flesh—primitive, sensuous, abandoned, above all *exotic.*

> Compared with racism, exoticism is merely decorative and superficial. It doesn't build death camps. It doesn't exterminate. Exoticism cares mostly for its own amusement and tends to find differences of color amusing where racism finds them threatening. Exoticism is frivolous, hangs out at nightclubs, will pay anything to have the black singer or pianist sit at its table. Racism is like a poor kid who grew up needing someone to hurt. Exoticism grew up rich, and a little bored. The racist is hedged around by dangers, the exoticist by used up toys. If one is to be treated as a thing, one would rather be treated as a rare and pretty thing than as a disgusting or dangerous one. But that is still to be treated as a thing.

There was nothing remotely exotic about the girlhood Josephine fled for France; being treated as a thing was nothing new to her. She was born at St. Louis in 1906, the daughter of a vaudeville drummer who did not stick around long, and a would-be dancer who blamed the baby's arrival for having driven him away and largely ignored her firstborn in favor of three younger children, fathered by a second husband. Josephine wore shoes snipped from sacking, scavenged bits of coal from the railroad yards, and at the age of eight was farmed out to a white woman who forced her to sleep in the cellar with the dog and deliberately scalded the little girl's hands when she used too much soap for the laundry. Even this did not keep her home for long: Josephine's mother got her a new job right away, working for a woman whose husband tried to molest her.

It was clear to her early on that she could rely on no one, that if she were to survive at all she would have to seize control of her own life. "There is no Santa Claus," she resolved on her tenth Christmas, "I'm Santa Claus." The following year she was a horrified witness to a race riot, watching as hundreds of black refugees fled their burned-out homes, a searing memory that never left her. To preempt ridicule and mask her fear she began making the goofy faces that would one day delight Paris.

"That such a childhood produced an expatriate," her biographer writes, "is not surprising. 'They' might drive you out of your home any minute, whether 'they' were your parents or rampaging white bigots. What better response to the fear of exile than voluntary expatriation?" Josephine left St. Louis at thirteen and rarely looked back; she worked in a bar, got married and divorced, danced for pennies in the street, and was married again—all by the time she was fourteen.

At fifteen, she graduated from a threadbare troupe called the Dixie Steppers into the cast of *Shuffle Along*, the first all-black musical to reach Broadway during the twenties. (The racial progress it represented was relative: one sketch revolved around a black mayor of "Jimtown" incapable of spelling "cat.") Dancing with more abandon than skill while mugging furiously, she stole scene after scene. "She was not beautiful," the singer Adelaide Hall remembered, "but she was fascinating."

Her Paris triumph was followed by two and a half years of mostly successful touring that took her to twenty-four countries but also reinforced the lesson that race would always impose risks upon her that other performers never needed to run: in Vienna, her dancing was denounced as "decadent"; in Zagreb, students interrupted her performance to shout, "Long live Croatian culture! Down with vulgarity!" The Munich authorities banned her from performing at all.

"I don't want to live without Paris," she said upon her return to the city that would always remain her sanctuary. "It's my country . . . I have to be worthy of Paris. I want to become an artist." With the encouragement of her lover and manager—a former plasterer and sometime gigolo named Pepito who wore a monocle and claimed to be a count—she did just that, mastering French (and becoming a French citizen), tempering the raw energy that first propelled her to stardom, adopting dancing and singing styles better suited to the traditional music hall reviews that now eagerly formed around her. e. e. cummings, who saw her perform again in 1930, could hardly believe she was the same person.

She wasn't, exactly. She had become "La Baker," a fixture of French nightlife and an international star for three decades. Thereafter, her tentative visits to America served mostly to remind her that while French exoticism could be trying, homegrown racism was a good deal worse.

Phyllis Rose is admirably fair-minded, understanding of the special obstacles race placed in her subject's path but unblinking in the face of her follies—her infidelities and profligacy and egotism, the maddening inconsistency that made her admire equally Dr. Martin Luther King, Jr., and Juan Perón. Rose is undaunted even by Baker's chronic desire to reconstruct her own legend, which led her to collaborate in writing four mutually contradictory "memoirs," so muddling the facts, as Rose admits, as to render her life finally "unreproducible in its details." The reasons for this relentless reordering of her past, her biographer believes, lay in Baker's inbred need for total control of every aspect of her life, even in retrospect. For all her onstage self-confidence, offstage she was never sure who she was, let alone who she once had been.

Still, the broad outlines of Josephine's career are remarkable enough to hold any reader's interest. After earning the Medal of the Resistance during World War II for smuggling to Allied agents in Lisbon and North Africa information pinned inside her underwear, she announced she would leave the stage in order to create an international tourist attraction around her château, complete with nightclub, miniature golf, and the "Jorama," a wax museum devoted entirely to gussied-up scenes from its builder's life. It was not a success.

Nor was her next project—amassing a "rainbow tribe" that grew to include a dozen children of nearly every creed and color, adopted one by one during her travels overseas and meant to serve as living proof that color didn't count. (Her third husband finally left her when the tally reached six with no sign of stopping.) Her new role as "wholesale mother" required her to spend most of her time away from her brood, appearing wherever she could get a booking just to pay the bills. It didn't work: in 1968, she and her variegated children were evicted, forced to seek shelter in a villa proffered by another glamorous American expatriate, Princess Grace of Monaco.

She married for a fourth time, continued to tour despite a heart attack, and in 1975, at the age of sixty-eight, returned to the Paris music hall stage in *Joséphine,* a series of gaudy tableaux illustrating the latest revised standard version of her life. She had not been asked to play the city she still considered "my country" for seven years, but the opening was a triumph and she bathed in the applause, tears streaming from beneath her sequined eyelids.

Two days later, she died in her sleep. A cerebral hemorrhage was the official cause, but a friend suggested she had died of joy.

American Heritage November 1989

SURVIVING ANYTHING THAT PAYS:
THE BARRYMORES

A CCORDING TO RECENT STUDIES, ALCOHOLICS "HAVE STRONGER expectations about how alcohol will affect them than other drinkers do. Alcoholics believe that alcohol transforms their personalities," making them more relaxed, entertaining, sexually alluring. This is also more or less the sort of transformation actors hope for when they take the stage: "An actor is much better off than a human being," John Barrymore once said. "He isn't stuck with the paltry fellow he is. He can always act his better and non-existent self." And so it is really not surprising that acting and alcoholism often seem to go together, though rarely have they been so sadly intertwined as in the lives of the Barrymores—Lionel, Ethel, and John—chronicled in *The House of Barrymore* by Margot Peters.

Theatrical biography is never easy: live performances die on paper; the titles of plays and movies and the names of critics and cast members quickly pall; and triple biography is triply difficult. The story of the Barrymore clan remains irresistible, but this latest retelling of it is badly undercut by arch asides that suggest that the author's familiarity with her subjects has bred something like contempt.

Surely, compassion is called for. Given the unsteadiness of the world in which the Barrymores struggled to grow up, it's hard to see how they managed to accomplish anything at all.

Their self-obsessed, quarrelsome parents evidently did little more for them than bring them into the world. Georgie Drew was a gifted comedienne, heir to a great theatrical tradition and celebrated for her wit and beauty, but so distant and so rarely home that even though John, the youngest of her children, was eleven when she died of tuberculosis in 1893, he could truthfully say he had never known her.

The children knew their father all too well. Maurice Barrymore was a British drawing-room comedian—his real name was Blythe; he had lifted "Barrymore" from an old playbill—remarkably handsome, utterly irresponsible, and so self-dramatizing, his daughter recalled, that when he heard that his favorite New York Giants had lost a crucial game, he got off the train on which he was riding and strode up and down the platform, waving his arms and shouting, "God! how could they do this to me!" until she fled in embarrassment. He was a noisy and flamboyant drunk—"Staggering is a sign of strength," he taught his admiring sons; "weak men are carried home"—and a chronic philanderer. Returning home one Sunday morning after a night in a brothel, he found his wife and children on their way out and asked where they were going: "To church," his wife is supposed to have said, "and *you* can go to hell." He did, more or less, ending his days as a victim of syphilitic paresis in the Long Island Home for the Insane, convinced he was still on tour, shouting lines from forgotten plays.

The children's grandmother, Mrs. John Drew, in whose Philadelphia home they were brought up until financial reverses forced them to be farmed out among relatives and friends, was the lonely rock to which they clung. She stood less than 5 feet tall and had a sour temper and none of the family's good looks, but she was capable simultaneously of performing on stage, managing her own theater, and overseeing her household, while somehow persuading Philadelphia society that although hers was a theatrical family, it was still worth knowing. She impressed upon all three of the grandchildren, who called her "Mum Mum," her conviction that "one never disclosed one's deepest feelings."

Lionel, born in 1878, was the eldest of the three, the least enthusiastic about acting and the most determinedly reticent about himself: despite diligent research, Peters has been unable authoritatively to answer such basic questions as whether his first child survived infancy or precisely what it was that confined him to a wheelchair for the last seventeen years of his life. But he suffered from the same insecurities that plagued his siblings, and bad reviews of his *Macbeth* in 1921 so wounded him that he abandoned the stage altogether, supporting his simultaneous addictions to alcohol, morphine, and cocaine instead with undemanding character parts on radio and in the movies—he played crusty old Dr. Gillespie in the *Dr. Kildare* films fifteen times. When a friend suggested that his reputation would not survive such wholesale squandering of his talent, he was unmoved: "You don't know Barrymores. We survive anything that pays."

Ethel, a year younger than Lionel and less haunted than either of her brothers by the memory of their drunken father, was the most stable of the three. Beautiful and stately, with huge, expressive eyes and a voice that one of her many spurned suitors, Winston Churchill, remembered as "soft, alluring, persuasive, magnetic . . . like liquid gold," she was less a great actress than a magnificent presence. She was uniformly protective of her personal life, telling one intrusive reporter that if he wanted to know what she had done he could look it up in the index of the *New York Times*. But she, too, was an alcoholic, her marriage to a brutal, unfaithful stockbroker proved disastrous, and she was only slightly more competent as a mother to her own three children than her own mother had been to hers. Still, she stayed faithful to the stage for fifty years despite shifts in theatrical fashion that made suitable parts harder and harder to come by, then made a second, successful career playing dauntless old ladies on film, a medium for which she never entirely lost her scorn: "You work about two minutes," she said, "then go to your dressing room and read a detective novel."

Adopting a pattern common among the offspring of alcoholics, Lionel and Ethel had sought approval as children by being dutiful solid little citizens who tried to bring order to a world in which their parents were more childlike than they. Their brother John took the opposite tack, vying for his grandmother's attention through relentless misbehavior—pilfering stage jewelry from her dresser drawer, draining her dinner guests' half-empty wineglasses until he was insensible, drawing pictures of the devils and demons that haunted his dreams, secretly blaming himself for all the troubles of his chaotic family.

At fifteen, events conspired to reinforce his worst feelings of unworthiness. First, his father's young and beautiful second wife seduced him, an event that both intensified his guilt and infused him with the chronic distrust of attractive women that would wreck all four of his marriages. Then, his beloved grandmother suddenly died. "He never felt safe after that," his brother wrote many years later. "I am inclined . . . to the theory that he was in revolt against the whole insecure pattern of life, and that the insecurity sprang from the collapse of his frame of reference when Mum Mum died when he was fifteen."

From roughly that time on, he would confess, he was "more or less a chronic drunkard."

At first, his acting outshone his alcoholism. Few performers have ever received the adulation John Barrymore won on stage. He began in light comedy, where the easy charm and celebrated profile he had inherited from his father were all he needed, but he soon eclipsed the memory of Maurice Barrymore, playing an unjustly imprisoned man in John Galsworthy's tragedy *Justice* in 1916, then scoring still greater triumphs in Shakespeare, first as Richard III and then, most memorably, as Hamlet.

Eva Le Gallienne, who saw his Hamlet four times, thought him "the greatest actor we ever had," and she may have been right. We have only a handful of late film performances from which to judge him, but in the best of these—*Grand Hotel, A Bill of Divorcement,* or *Twentieth Century,* for example—he remains mesmerizing. Despite his thinning hair and puffy eyes, and the continuing tension that comes from watching him teeter on the edge of self-parody, it is virtually impossible to look at anyone else when he's on screen; neither Garbo nor Katherine Hepburn nor Carole Lombard—not even his own shamelessly hammy brother—can distract us for long.

But Barrymore's great success only served to deepen his inbred sense of failure. Convinced of his own worthlessness, he had little but contempt for those who praised him. He disdained his art as he disdained himself, and by 1925 he had joined Lionel in Hollywood to begin what turned out to be seventeen years of appallingly public disintegration. Alcohol ravaged his body and destroyed his memory— his lines had to be scrawled on off-camera blackboards. He battled with wives and ex-wives, fell hopelessly into debt, drank perfume when desperate friends denied him liquor, compulsively pursued teen-aged starlets, and, if Barrymore's boozy friend and first biographer Gene Fowler is to be believed, may even have tried to bed his own tormented daughter, Diana.

In *Playmates,* his fifty-seventh film, he was reduced to cruel burlesquing of the great actor he had been. Called upon to intone Hamlet's soliloquy to a comic called Ish Kabibble, he drew himself up and delivered the speech with as much of his old power as he could muster, tears slipping down his face. The set fell silent. "That's the funniest gin I ever drank," he said, and turned away.

He finally died at sixty on May 29, 1942, from an accumulation of ills, most of which were caused by alcohol. Even on his deathbed, Barrymore continued to perform as best he could—pretending to proposition nurses, motioning Gene Fowler to lean down for a final word, then whispering, "Tell me, is it true that you are the illegitimate son of Buffalo Bill?"

But as he drifted in and out of consciousness, Lionel heard him call again and again for "Mum Mum," the exacting little woman who had provided the only stability he had ever known.

American Heritage December 1990

THE MAN WHO RECOGNIZED
NO DEADLINES: JACK DEMPSEY

JACK DEMPSEY LIVED QUIETLY IN NEW YORK UNTIL HIS DEATH
at eighty-seven in 1983. If during his last years he still followed the
sport that made him the best-known athlete on earth during the
1920s, he must sometimes have been puzzled by the lengths to which
boxers of the television age feel they must go to persuade the public
that they are swell fellows, however severe their profession may require them to be with their opponents.

Muhammad Ali composed verse, delivered sermons, and endured
Howard Cosell. The likable Sugar Ray Leonard peddled soft drinks
on TV with his even more likable son, Ray Jr. Ray "Boom-Boom"
Mancini, whose all-out style was faintly reminiscent of Dempsey's,
said he did it all for his dad.

When Dempsey was in his prime, it never crossed his mind that
he needed to be *nice* to be champion. He wanted only to win, not be
winsome, and he was never overly concerned about how he went
about it. Dempsey came snarling out of the mining camps and hobo
jungles of the Far West: he started hungry and stayed that way. Born
in a log cabin near Manassa, Colorado, in 1895, the ninth of thirteen
children, he had just one toy as a child—a wooden top whittled by his
father. His mother hoped he'd be a boxer, like her hero, John L.
Sullivan, and his oldest brother, Bernie—also a fighter but cursed with
a glass jaw—was his trainer. He made the youngster chew pine pitch
to strengthen his jaw and, to toughen his fists and face, had him soak
them in buckets of reeking beef brine, hauled home from the butcher
shop.

Dempsey began fighting professionally at sixteen as "Kid Blackie,"
flattening bullies and barflies in saloons for a hatful of change. His real
first name was William, but in 1915 he graduated to smalltown smokers and renamed himself Jack Dempsey after a legendary Irish middle-
weight nicknamed "the Nonpareil." He rode the rods from fight to

fight for purses of $2.50, and worked as a miner and lumberjack to feed and clothe himself while he learned his craft.

Boxing was much gamier then. It was the age of such celebrated brawlers as Mysterious Billy Smith, who "was always doing something mysterious," Dempsey's manager Doc Kearns recalled. "Like he would step on your foot, and when you looked down, he would bite you in the ear." Niceties such as going to a neutral corner after knocking your opponent down were still years away, and Dempsey was especially effective standing over his adversaries and hitting them on the rise.

It was Kearns who guided Dempsey to his title fight with Jess Willard at Toledo, Ohio, on July 4, 1919. Dempsey was a formidable man: He stood 6 feet 1¼ inches and weighed 187 pounds, but he seemed almost puny standing in front of the hulking champion, who was 5 inches taller and outweighed him by nearly 60 pounds. ("God he was big," Dempsey remembered half a century later.) Size didn't matter: the challenger tore Willard's title from him. The ex-champion had to be helped from the ring after three rounds. He had been knocked down seven times; four ribs were cracked; he left six teeth on the canvas; and his jaw was broken in seven places.

Dempsey's father had once advised him to think of obstacles as stepping stones: if he couldn't get around them, "goddamit, go through them." That was how he fought. Most boxers hope to demolish their opponents; Dempsey seemed bent on obliterating his. He fought from a crouch in furious rushes, teeth bared, and he could hit hard with either hand and from any angle (including from behind, whenever he could get away with it).

It wasn't that he consciously flaunted the rules. It was wrong to call him a dirty fighter, the sportswriter Paul Gallico once explained, "because in his simple way he recognized no deadlines on the body of his opponent and certainly asked for none to be enforced upon his." In against Jack Sharkey (himself a future champion), Dempsey was told he really had to stop hitting his opponent in the *leg*. He reluctantly shifted his sights upwards, and moments later, Sharkey complained of four consecutive blows to his groin, turning his head toward the referee as he did so. Dempsey took that opportunity to knock him out. ("What'd he want me to do," Dempsey asked later, after a reporter suggested he'd bent the rules some, "write him a letter?")

Dempsey's 1923 battle with Luis Firpo, an Argentinian whose ferocity nearly matched his own, was the wildest in heavyweight history. After being knocked down seven times in the first round, the enraged "Wild Bull of the Pampas" stormed back and sent Dempsey sprawling through the ropes. He landed on the typewriters in the front rows and friendly hands pushed him back into the ring before the bell rang. There, refreshed by a bucket of water poured over his head between rounds, he knocked Firpo unconscious in Round Two.

Dempsey ruled as champion for seven years, taking on all comers—except blacks. Dempsey was willing enough (he'd fought and beaten black fighters on his way up), but the memory of the flamboyant Jack Johnson and the sordid search for a "white hope" to unseat him was still fresh, and Kearns saw in it an excuse to draw the color line. (Unable to advance further, the two top black contenders, Harry Wills and Sam Langford, had to be content to fight one another—twenty-three times.)

Dempsey's mastery seemed to desert him whenever he left the arena. There were four marriages, three of them disastrous: his first wife was a prostitute who insisted on remaining at her trade after they were married; the second and third were actresses, beautiful but second-rate, who came to blame him for their failed careers. (His fourth wife, with whom he lived happily until his death, was the owner of a jewelry store and had never heard of him before they were introduced.)

Dempsey soon broke with Kearns, whom he believed had bilked him of a large percentage of his earnings; later, he lost a sizable fortune all on his own in the crash of 1929.

Like many other prominent athletes of the World War I era, Dempsey had been exempted from the draft on the grounds that he was the sole support of his family. After he won the title, some sportswriters (joined by his vindictive first wife) loudly charged that he had dodged the draft. A trial exonerated him, but the taint remained, and the first of the five "Million Dollar Gates" he drew was drummed up largely because so many fans wanted to see him beaten by a handsome French war hero, Georges Carpentier. There were chants of "slacker" as Dempsey shouldered his way to the ring, but Carpentier's medals could not help him once the bell rang: Dempsey knocked him out in four. (Although he was forty-five years old and technically over-age when World War II began, Dempsey rushed to enlist in the Coast Guard and saw action at Okinawa; it was his way of wiping out the humiliation he had suffered in 1920.)

His stubborn loyalty to the old rough-and-tumble ways eventually did him in. In 1926 he lost his title by decision to Gene Tunney, a new sort of darting, defensive fighter whose frank admission that he found "no joy in knocking people unconscious" must have baffled a man who found comparable joy in nothing else. The aging Dempsey was behind on points going into the seventh round of their rematch in Chicago the following year, when he caught Tunney coming off the ropes with a perfect left hook. Tunney went down, and Dempsey crouched over him, fists cocked, just as he always had stood over his victims. But both camps had agreed in advance to observe the new neutral corner rule, and when the referee ordered Dempsey to retreat, he stayed put. "I couldn't move," he said later. "I wanted him to get up. I wanted to kill the sonofabitch." It took some fourteen seconds to straighten things out, time enough for Tunney's head to clear. For the final three rounds, he shrewdly stayed out of harm's way as Dempsey stalked him. Finally, the weary ex-champion stopped in mid-ring and motioned for Tunney to stop his dancing and stand with him, toe-to-toe. When Tunney just spun away again, Paul Gallico remembered, there appeared on Dempsey's "swarthy, blue-jawed fighter's face . . . such a glance of bitter, biting contempt for his opponent [that] I felt ashamed for the man who was running away."

When it was over, Dempsey made no excuses. "It was just one of the breaks," he said. "Tunney fought a smart fight."

After his boxing career ended, Dempsey toured the country fighting exhibitions in which he felled local heroes with nicknames more impressive than their skills—K. O. Christner, Bearcat Wright, Bad News Johnson. He also shambled through several Hollywood movies, including *Mr. Broadway* and *The Prizefighter and the Lady,* his plausibility as a romantic lead undercut by the curious piping voice that emanated from his powerful body. In 1937, he opened his own restaurant, Jack Dempsey's, on Broadway.

In 1964, Doc Kearns's autobiography was published posthumously; in it, Dempsey's embittered ex-manager charged—falsely—that his gloves had been hardened with plaster the day he took the title from Jess Willard. When Dempsey threatened to sue for libel, the publisher settled out of court, but the old champion had been embarrassed again. Ten years later, another blow: Dempsey was forced to close his restaurant when the landlord abruptly canceled his lease.

Still, there was to be at least one more victory. Several years before Dempsey's death, two young muggers spotted a likely victim in the back seat of a taxi stopped for a red light—an old man wearing an expensive suit. They came at him from two sides, tearing open both back doors and demanding his wallet. The driver froze. Jack Dempsey, then in his late seventies, knocked them both senseless.

An abbreviated version of this piece,
occasioned by an upcoming mini-series on Dempsey,
appeared in *TV Guide*, September 4, 1983

LITTLE MISS MARKER,
MOSTLY GROWN UP:
SHIRLEY TEMPLE

URING THE LATE DEPRESSION YEARS, THE BIGGEST MOVIE star was also the littlest, Shirley Temple. "It is a splendid thing," FDR said, "that for just fifteen cents an American can go to a movie and look at the smiling face of a baby and forget his troubles." For anyone born too late to see her films the first time around, it is hard to understand her appeal; it's clear from the five she made with Bill Robinson that she was a talented dancer (so talented that cynics charged she was a midget), but the sturdy, bright-eyed, relentlessly cheerful character she invariably played when standing still is hard for modern eyes to take. "Why they bother with titles, or with plots, either, for that matter is beyond me," the critic Frank Nugent wrote at the height of her fame. "The sensible thing would be to announce Shirley Temple in 'Shirley Temple' and let it go at that." Whether playing *Little Miss Marker* or *The Little Colonel, Curly Top* or *Dimples, Poor Little Rich Girl* or *Wee Willie Winkie*, she was the same—doggedly sweet, determinedly innocent, more dependable than any of the surrounding grown-ups upon whom a child might be expected to depend—in short, too good to be true.

Guess again. As Shirley Temple Black's vivid memoir *Child Star* makes clear without a hint of special pleading, she was in fact far more dependable than the adults closest to her, did try hard to maintain her innocence and hold on to her good humor in circumstances that would have caused a less resilient person to implode. Her book also demonstrates again what a very good thing it is that there's no business like show business.

She was born in 1928, the third child and first girl born to a breezy California bank manager and his starstruck wife, Gertrude. "The owners of a child star are like lease-holders," Graham Greene once wrote, "their property diminishes in value every year." Temple's owners got an extra year out of her by altering her birth certificate to make her seem a year younger than she really was, an act which upped the profits but nearly cost their daughter her life: at a public appearance in 1939, a deranged woman stood up in the front row and aimed a pistol at her. FBI agents, previously alerted to a possible kidnapping, seized the woman before she could squeeze off a shot. Her own daughter and Shirley had been born the same day, the would-be assassin explained later, but her baby had died; clearly, the movie star had stolen her child's soul.

Shirley was barely three in 1931, when her mother led her onto the set of the first of the eight one-reel shorts called *Baby Burlesks* which began her career. These were pedophiliac parodies of grown-up films in which the cast members were dressed as adults from the waist up and wore droopy diapers below. In one, Shirley mimicked Dolores Del Rio in an off-the-shoulder blouse and lace garter; in another, she was "Morelegs Sweet Trick" (Marlene Dietrich) in a black lace bra, feather boa, and spangled diaper run up the night before by her mother.

When discipline became a problem (no performer was over six), mothers were barred and the child welfare supervisor lured away to a dressing room fitted out with a sofa, magazines, and refreshments so that the director could lay down the law. Any child who acted up was banished to "the black box," an airless, windowless chamber on wheels originally built for sound technicians, where the only thing on which to sit was a block of ice. Anyone who told about the box would be put back in it.

Shirley was imprisoned there several times, but when she finally dared tell her mother she was not believed. And when hours spent shivering in the box exacerbated an ear infection that finally had to be lanced, her mother saw that her daughter was back early the next morning for another eleven-and-a-half-hour, ten dollar day. "This business of being mother to a budding star is no joke," Gertrude wrote Shirley's grandmother that evening. "I think I look ten years older and have lost quite a little weight."

Shirley's time in the box did her no lasting psychological damage, she believes, but the "lesson of life" it taught her was "profound and unforgettable. Time is money. Wasted time means wasted money means trouble. Working is more fun than standing in any icy box and getting an earache."

It is the eerie power of her book that without affectation or self-pity she manages to tell most of her story from the viewpoint of the little girl she once was, missing few details of what went on around her but leaving adult judgments to her readers. The result is often harrowing. Here, she remembers a day at work on the last *Baby Burlesk* comedy,

Kid 'n' Africa, in which she played "Madame Cradlebait," a missionary rescued from tiny tribesmen by a jungle boy called "Diaperzan":

> Rehearsal for a jungle skirmish between two groups of barefoot black children painted with white stripes like a mob of tiny zebras called for the bad guys, fleeing down a twisting jungle path, to be suddenly felled by a barrage of arrows from pursuing good guys. The action during rehearsal must not have been convincing enough . . . [and so] a thin piano wire was secretly rigged shin-high across the trail. Down the path bolted the bad guys. Racing into the disguised trip wire, the whole bunch cartwheeled heads over heels into one squirming heap, with yowls rising from the pileup of small bodies. Some shins were bleeding. Out of pure sympathy I burst into tears, my first cry on a movie set.

The mother who put her through her paces is both the most important and the most elusive character in the book. To outsiders, Gertrude Temple may have been the quintessential stage mother, a hard-eyed negotiator, jealous of her daughter's status and her own, ruthless in her wish to push forward her "Presh" (for "Precious"). But to her daughter, she was simply Mother, whose control of every aspect of her life she thought the natural order of things. Gertrude picked her playmates, scheduled her day, dressed her hair (putting in precisely fifty-six pin-curls every single Sunday), and coached her acting, urging her to "sparkle" whenever the cameras rolled: "Arching eyebrows and rounding the mouth in an expression of surprise was 'sparkling' by her definition. So was frowning with an outthrust lower lip, or a knowing half-smile with head cocked to one side." (Tears came a little harder, and once, when Shirley heard that another child had just been killed in an automobile accident and began genuinely to weep, her director gratefully focused in to get the real thing on film.)

It worked. Shirley Temple was the most popular movie star on earth at seven, received 167,000 presents for her eighth birthday (which was actually her ninth, of course), could not cross the street without bodyguards, and was eagerly sought after by everyone from Edwina Mountbatten to Vittorio Mussolini, the Italian dictator's son. Of the two-hundred-odd celebrity laps onto which she was pulled for the photographers, she remembers J. Edgar Hoover's as "outstanding": "Thighs just fleshy enough, knees held calmly together, and no bouncing or wiggling."

She gave in to childhood impulses only rarely: once, picnicking at Val-Kill, Eleanor Roosevelt's Hyde Park retreat, she waited until the

First Lady was bending over the barbecue, then let her have it with a slingshot. Mrs. Roosevelt straightened up sharply, but said nothing, and in her next day's column pronounced her little visitor "A well brought-up, charming child . . . a joy to all who meet her."

Unpleasant things were not to be dwelt upon. At eleven, with adolescence looming over the horizon at last, she left Twentieth Century-Fox for Metro-Goldwyn-Mayer. "First we get rid of the baby fat," Arthur Freed, producer of the children's classic *The Wizard of Oz*, told her at their first meeting. "Then new hair. Teach you to belt a song and some decent dancing. . . . You'll be my new star!" With that, he stood up and exposed himself. Temple burst into laughter, not tears, and was ordered angrily from his office. (She can still be funny about it: she had always thought of Freed, she writes, "as a producer rather than an exhibitor.")

Shirley's producers may have wanted her to grow up, but her fans did not, and sparkling did not work when playing adults. She gave up the screen at twenty-two.

Then she found that while she had made fifty-seven films in eighteen years she had very nearly nothing to show for it. Her father, who had quit his job early on to oversee his daughter's finances, turned out to have spent all but $44,000 of the $3,207,666 she had earned, and had failed even to make required payments into a court-ordered trust fund meant for her. "Baby bountiful," she writes with uncharacteristic but entirely justified bitterness, had paid for everything all those years "parents, brothers, twelve household staff . . . a . . . grandmother, two paternal uncles whom I vaguely remembered collecting handouts at our gate." Friends urged her to sue, but "My attitude has always been get it over with and get on with it. The best and only solution was obvious. Do nothing. Avoid piggish action . . . until death removes any chance of embarassment to the living. Neither word nor gesture."

She did just that: surviving a short, bad marriage to the actor John Agar, continuing to enjoy a long, successful one with a businessman, Charles Black, raising three children, serving as Ambassador to Ghana, representative to the United Nations, and Chief of Protocol.

She seems genuinely to have no regrets and hold no grudges, even against her late parents. Despite her father's betrayal, she dutifully nursed him through his final illness, and the last words of her book, offered without apparent irony, are "Thanks, Mom."

American Heritage March 1989

THE ARROGANT INNOCENT:
PAUL ROBESON

IN THE DENSELY PRINTED, FIFTY-ONE-PAGE INDEX TO TAYLOR Branch's splendid chronicle of the civil rights movement, *Parting the Waters: America in the King Years 1954–63*, there are just three references to Paul Robeson, all of them inconsequential. To blacks and their allies of an earlier generation, Robeson's relative insignificance in that struggle would have seemed inconceivable: as athlete and actor, singer and spokesman, Robeson had been perhaps the best-known black American on earth during the twenties and thirties. He was only fifty-six when Rosa Parks refused to leave her bus seat, and was still just sixty-five when Dr. Martin Luther King, Jr., proclaimed his Dream at the Lincoln Memorial; yet he no longer had any role to play.

Martin Duberman's good biography, *Paul Robeson*, traces the long, sad arc of Robeson's career.

He was born in Princeton, New Jersey, in 1898, the sixth and best-loved child of a Presbyterian minister and former slave who had been driven from his pulpit and forced to haul ashes for a living because of his outspokenness about racial injustice in that Jim Crow university town. The elder Robeson passed on to his son his huge baritone voice and unshakable dignity, his conviction that blacks were at least the equal of whites and that application and goodwill would ultimately prevail over prejudice. "[Paul Robeson] had never learned as a youngster, as had almost all black Americans," Duberman writes, "to deal in limited expectations; treated in his own family like a god, he had met in the outside world far fewer institutional humiliations than afflict most blacks. . . . Ingrained optimism had become a characteristic attitude; he expected *every* set of hurdles, with the requisite hard work and determination, to be cleared as handily as those of his youth had been."

He cleared those early hurdles with astonishing ease, seemed able, in fact, to do anything. Tall, powerful, and magnetic, he earned fifteen varsity letters in four sports at Rutgers, was twice named to Walter Camp's All-American football team, graduated fourth in his class and delivered the commencement oration in 1919 to tumultuous cheers. The class prophecy suggested that by 1940 he would have "dimmed the fame of Booker T. Washington" and become "the leader of the colored race in America."

After college he played professional football, considered a boxing career, earned a law degree from Columbia, sang, acted, and seemed undecided just what field to conquer next when he married Eslanda Cardozo Goode, a pretty, light-skinned woman, as ambitious as she was conventional, who devoted the rest of her life to making what she called the "best and most" of her husband. Known always as "Essie," she steered him toward the stage.

"The general public's idea of a Negro is an Uncle Tom, an Aunt Jemima, Ol' Mammy and Jack Johnson," she told one playwright. "These subjects have always been sold to the public deliberately. Well, now they don't exist anymore except in the sentimental minds of credulous people, and we feel that we certainly must not do anything in any way to prolong their nonexistent lives!!! We feel Mr. Robeson must play a Negro who does exist, who has something to do with reality. That's all he asks. . . ."

He asked too much. He was hugely successful in *Othello* and *The Emperor Jones*, but there were precious few such parts, and in the end he would largely abandon acting for the concert stage. Heard today on records, his voice still astonishes—Brooks Atkinson called it a "cavernous roar," a British critic exulted in its "sheer, carpeted magnificence"—although the self-conscious gravity with which he approached everything he sang now often seems stiff and dated. (In October 1940, with Count Basie, he recorded "King Joe," a blues tribute to Joe Louis, who had just annihilated Max Schmeling: "It certainly is an honor to be working with Mr. Robeson," Basie confided to the record producer, "but the man certainly can't sing the blues.")

"The only thing wrong with Robeson," W. E. B. DuBois once said, "is in having too great faith in human beings." That was not all that was wrong. The size of his voice was matched by that of his ego: he was, he assured one reporter, "one of the great artists of the contemporary period." And his devotion to art and politics was alloyed always with the sins that theatrical flesh seems especially heir to. He routinely ignored his son, Paul Jr., toward whom, he once told Essie, he had "no fatherly instincts . . . at all," and in his pursuit of other women he time and again wounded the loyal wife for whose lifelong willingness to take him back between affairs Duberman seems to me to give insufficient credit. (Essie, a friend remembered, was willing always to "be 'a dragon' so [Paul] could be his beautiful self.")

"That Mr. Robeson should be stripped to the waist is my first demand of any play in which he appears," wrote the drama critic for the London *Graphic,* in what the biographer calls "a fine display of homoeroticism," and women felt the same way about him. Robeson had "many, many, *many* women," the actress Uta Hagen (who was one of them) recalled—including Peggy Ashcroft, his first Desdemona, but not, according to his biographer, the two Englishwomen most prominently rumored to have been his lovers, Nancy Cunard and Edwina Mountbatten.

In 1932, another Englishwoman, whom he had courted for three years and for whom he actually planned to divorce Essie in order to marry, abruptly turned him down, apparently because her father would not hear of her marrying a black man.

Shortly thereafter, Robeson began to manifest a new interest in his own African heritage and in the Soviet Union, which he persuaded himself was entirely free of the racism evident everywhere else on earth. "Here," he said in Moscow in 1934, "for the first time in my life, I walk in full human dignity." Thereafter, he would rarely stray from the Soviet path, and his devotion to the struggle for equality in America was always tangled up with the fate of international socialism everywhere else. "Despising American racism and viewing the Soviets as the only promising counterbalancing force to racism," Duberman writes, "Robeson was inclined to look away when the U.S.S.R. acted against its own stated principles, to look away fixedly as the perversions multiplied over the years, discounting them as temporary aberrations or stupidities ultimately justified by the long view. . . ." He said nothing about Stalin's purges, even when old friends disappeared and his Jewish accompanist was refused entry to the USSR; he applauded the Nazi-Soviet Pact, dismissed the Hungarian revolution as a Fascist uprising, even argued that while the Smith Act was unconstitutional when applied against Communists, it was just what *Trotskyists* deserved. "Paul is inclined to be a bit arrogant sometimes when people don't agree with him," his wife once admitted in private, "especially politically. Not in any other field, as I think of it now. Only politically."

Nothing Robeson ever did or said abroad can excuse the appalling treatment he received at home during the early Cold War years. After he had been quoted as having said American blacks would never fight against Russia, a mob tried to kill him at a Peekskill, New York, concert in 1949. Theatres closed their doors. Networks blacklisted him. For eight years, the State Department denied him the right to travel because he refused on principle to say whether he had ever been a member of the Communist Party (according to Duberman, he never was). The FBI dogged his footsteps, tapped his telephone. In a move that Stalinist historians might have envied, the editors of *College Football*, a record book published in 1950, listed only *ten* members of the All-American team for 1918, rather than have Robeson's name subvert their pages. He refused to bend. Why didn't he stay in Russia where he belonged, Congressman Francis Walter demanded at a Washington hearing. "Because my father was a slave," Robeson thundered back, "and my people died to build this country, and I am going to stay here and have a part of it, just like you. And no fascist-minded people will drive me from it. Is that clear?"

It was, and he paid a fearful price for that clarity. In 1955, as the FBI turned its unwanted attentions upon Dr. King, Robeson began to show signs of manic depression. When on the upswing, he could not be dissuaded from talking about his "discovery" that the universality of the pentatonic scale (the five-note harmonics of the piano's black keys) was proof of the essential oneness of all peoples. When on the way down, he slashed his wrists, tried to drown himself, wandered away from home. Neither drugs nor fifty-four separate episodes of electroconvulsive therapy could permanently restore his equilibrium. Nor could the 1958 publication of *Here I Stand*, a slim manifesto affirming that his first loyalty was to his own community, win back the black masses whose hero he once had been. The new generation of students now sitting-in and freedom-riding and registering voters all across the South had barely heard of him.

A psychiatrist who saw him a few times during his last years remembered above all Robeson's profound sadness: "He was an 'innocent,' in the best sense," he concluded, "his motivational spring was 'compassion, not ego,' and therefore he felt devastated when others, less 'purely' motivated, cast him aside; he was a man 'fundamentally puzzled' at how his humane instincts and vision had run aground."

Essie died of cancer, in 1966. Robeson lived on for another nine years, a haunted, isolated invalid, looked after by his sister and by the son he had once been too preoccupied to spend time with.

American Heritage April 1989

"LOOKING FOR THE PRETTY NOTES": CHARLIE PARKER

THERE APPEARS TO BE NO LIMIT TO OUR INTEREST IN THE private lives of unhappy artists. As I write, a compelling best-seller details the swift rise and interminable disintegration of Truman Capote, and a cockeyed one makes more of Picasso's misogyny than of his painting; two new books chronicle the sour, sad life of Dorothy Parker; and in another, friends and enemies bicker over every one of Ernest Hemingway's battle scars.

Although our interest in drunks and neurotics and egomaniacs like these was at least initially piqued by their work, biographers customarily slight their art in the interest of their eccentricities. Complacent envy helps fuel our fascination with artistic gossip: Just think, we smile as we turn the page, how much better we would have done if *we'd* been given such gifts. So does the secret hope that in the course of reading about the supremely talented, we will somehow discover the trick that separates them from the rest of us.

There is no trick, of course—genius defies analysis and is non-transferable—and the danger is that such books yield lopsided portraits in which the art gets lost among the aberrations that lesser talents like to imitate.

The alto saxophone player Charlie Parker, for example, is still remembered as much for his gargantuan appetites and the relentless pace with which he wrecked himself as for having forever altered American music, influencing every performer who came after him, no matter what instrument he or she played. It was once fashionable to blame all of Parker's troubles on racial prejudice and the indifference he met from a public made uneasy by innovation. But that is too simple. As the jazz critic and historian Gary Giddins points out, "Racist and philistine societies are alike; every artist is unique," and it is Giddins's special achievement that the reader finishes his elegant biographical essay *Celebrating Bird: The Triumph of Charlie Parker* with a fresh appreciation of Parker's demanding music as well as a greater understanding of the troubled individual who made it.

Charles Parker, Jr., was born in 1920 in Kansas City, Kansas, and raised just across the Kaw River in Kansas City, Missouri. His father was a tap-dancer turned Pullman chef who drank too much and deserted his wife and son before the boy was eleven. His mother spoiled her only child while demanding much of him, insisting that he wear a suit and tie to school, and that he hold her hand whenever they went out together.

Abandoned by his father, smothered by his mother, "Charlie was always old," the first of his wives recalled. He had few friends, kept his own counsel. Then, at thirteen, he found an emotional outlet in music and his mother bought him his first saxophone. Barely an adolescent, he began to haunt the bars and bordellos that flourished just a few blocks from his home under the tolerant eye of Boss Tom Pendergast, steeping himself in the pulsing, blues-laced Kansas City jazz of which Count Basie became the most celebrated exponent. (It is a nice question whether history will ultimately give more credit to Pendergast for having helped produce Harry Truman or Charlie Parker.) No matter how esoteric and intricate Parker's playing became, he never lost his link with that joyous music: Jay McShann, the bandleader who gave him his first important job, remembers that Parker always "loved to see people patting their foot, loved to see the people *moving.*" He got the nickname "Bird," short for "Yardbird," while still a growing boy in McShann's band, when he insisted that the car in which he was riding pull over after hitting a stray chicken—a yardbird—so that he could have it fried up by his landlady.

He also married at sixteen, began to drink heavily and to use drugs—marijuana at first, then the benzedrine inhalers dissolved in cups of black coffee that allowed him to play without sleep, night after night. At seventeen, he was permanently hooked on heroin.

He stormed into New York at twenty-one, where his mesmerizing technique, his enthusiasm for complex and frantic tempos, fondness for dissonance, and ability to create fresh melodies out of the chord structure of familiar tunes frankly baffled older musicians: "We don't flat our fifths," said the Dixieland guitarist Eddie Condon, "we drink 'em." But to musicians of Parker's own generation, already experimenting more tentatively along the same lines, he seemed something like a prophet, pointing the way the music should go. Soon, one remembered, "there was everybody else and there was Charlie."

Parker abhorred the word "bebop" applied by others to what he played: "It's just music," he said. "It's trying to play clean and looking for the pretty notes." Nothing musical was alien to him: he memorized the work of avant-garde composers, but a friend also remembered leaving him transfixed in a Manhattan snowstorm late one night, unable to tear himself away from the thump and blare of a Salvation Army band. Another told of driving with him through the Swedish countryside when someone remarked idly that livestock loved music; Parker asked the driver to stop, assembled his horn, stalked into a field, and gravely played several choruses to a bewildered cow.

But when he was not playing, Parker once said, he was "always on a panic." He borrowed money constantly and rarely paid it back, loved and left a succession of wives and mistresses, nodded off on the bandstand, quarreled with colleagues, failed to turn up for work or refused to play, once crying, "They just came out . . . to see the world's most famous junkie." He was eventually barred from Birdland, the New York nightclub named in his honor.

He was never satisfied with his own work, and was put off by the mythology that already threatened to engulf him before he was twenty-five. The acolytes who followed him from bandstand to bandstand, lugging wire recorders which they turned on whenever he stepped forward to solo and clicked off the moment he had finished, embarrassed him, and he was appalled by worshipful musicians who emulated even his addiction in the hope that by sharing his habit they could somehow share his genius, too. He was helpless to stop them, though in his lucid moments he tried. "He kept drugs away from me," a younger saxophone player remembered, "but after we'd spent a lot of time together, he injected himself in my presence and said, 'This is something that I have to do. It's terrible but I'm stuck with it.' It was terrifying to watch my hero do that. He made it as revolting as possible, as though it were a lecture on what not to do." The lecture failed as often as not.

In California in 1946, where he found himself playing to audiences still more bewildered by his music than they had first been in New York, Parker's descent accelerated. He turned up for one recording session without having made his connection and on "Lover Man," recorded that day, Giddins writes, an uncharacteristically tremulous Parker played "as though the shore were always one stroke beyond his grasp." (Although Parker himself said the recording should have been "stomped into the ground," record producers released it, anyway—and admirers dutifully committed it to memory, note for querulous note.) That night, he twice wandered into the lobby of his hotel naked, then fell asleep while smoking, setting his bed ablaze. He was hospitalized, remained clean for a little while, then resumed his steady self-destruction.

By 1950, Parker was being hailed abroad as an important artist but was still largely ignored by the American press in favor of his great collaborator, John Birks "Dizzy" Gillespie, a born showman as well as a trumpet player of astonishingly inventive virtuosity whose dark glasses and goatee, hipster talk and cheeks that ballooned like a puff adder's whenever he played guaranteed good show-biz copy.

In 1952, the two innovators appeared together on a television variety show called "Stage Entrance." The kinescope made that evening is all that we have of Parker in action, and the "Downbeat" awards ceremony that precedes it provides an excruciating example of the kind of condescension often displayed toward jazz even by those who believe themselves its boosters. The critic Leonard Feather delivers a stiff little speech about brotherhood, then hands the host, Broadway gossip columnist Earl Wilson, wooden plaques to present to Parker and Gillespie. Wilson greets the musicians, offers up the plaques—making fun of Gillespie's nickname as he does so—and then asks whether "You *boys* have anything to say?"

For once, Gillespie is speechless. Parker, his face without expression, his voice low and icily polite, replies: "They say music speaks louder than words, so we'd rather voice our opinion that way."

During that voicing—an abbreviated version of the bop anthem "Hot House"—Parker's face remains impassive, his fierce eyes and the movement of his big fingers on the keys the only outward signs of the effort required to yield such brilliant, jagged cascades of sound.

When Parker died in New York on March 12, 1954, he was just thirty-four years old. The official cause was pneumonia, but he had simply worn himself out; the coroner estimated his age at between fifty-five and sixty.

When he got the news on a California bandstand, the alto saxophone player Frank Morgan remembers, he announced it to the audience, then took an extra-long break: "We proceeded to celebrate Bird's death by doing the thing that had killed him . . . [used] some junk. I think it would have been better if we'd realized that . . . it was the time to stop."

"You hear [Parker's music] perhaps unexpectedly," Giddins writes, "when you walk into a friend's house, or on the car radio, or worked into a film score, and you are struck by the relentless energy, the uncorrupted humanity of his music. It is never without direction.

This most restive, capricious of men is unequivocal in his art."

It is Parker's unequivocal art, not his equivocal life, that finally matters.

American Heritage December 1988

BAD MEN
AND LIARS

TARGETS OF OPPORTUNITY: AMERICAN ASSASSINS AND ASSASSINATIONS

SSASSINATION IS NOT AN AMERICAN PRACTICE OR HABIT,"
wrote Secretary of State William H. Seward on July 15, 1864,
"and one so vicious and so desperate cannot be engrafted into
our political system. This conviction of mine has steadily gained
strength. . . . Every day's experience confirms it." Nine months later,
John Wilkes Booth fired his bullet into the brain of Abraham Lincoln
and Seward himself lay seriously wounded, stabbed repeatedly in the
face and neck by Booth's accomplice, Lewis Powell.

In recent years we have learned again and again how wrong Seward was. Lee Harvey Oswald, Arthur Bremer, James Earl Ray, Sirhan Sirhan, John Hinckley—these are just the names of those who managed to hit their political targets over the past twenty years; if those who missed were included, the list would nearly double.

Such puny creatures seem incapable of altering history on their own, and so we search almost desperately for What Really Happened, for the Something or Someone that must be Behind It All. Even before Lincoln stopped breathing on the boardinghouse bed to which he was carried from Ford's Theater, a substantial number of Americans were persuaded he had been the victim of a vast plot directed by the leaders of the dying Confederacy. No one believed this more fervently than the man who directed the hunt for the assassin, Secretary of War Edwin Stanton, and it is one of American history's more absurd ironies that Stanton himself eventually became the prime suspect for a later generation eager to unearth a conspiracy.

A large body of literature has been published about Lincoln's murder, much of it purporting to show that one or another group of unindicted men somehow pulled the strings—the Vatican, perhaps, or the Radical Republicans. One enthusiast recently suggested that Booth may have been entirely blameless, that the real killer was Major Henry R. Rathbone, Lincoln's guest in the theatre box. Another hinted that

Mary Todd Lincoln herself might have been implicated in her husband's death; although the President left her a comfortable legacy, she was often in financial difficulty in her later years: "Could her continued impoverishment suggest blackmail?"

The library of books on the Kennedy assassination may already be even larger. A few have been sober and substantive, aimed at solving the troubling puzzles left in the Warren Commission's broad wake or answering new questions prompted by the sorry record of agency incompetence and cloak-and-dagger fumbling in the Caribbean that has emerged since that commission rendered its verdict.

But all too many books have been the work of deluded obsessives or of shameless cynics willing to exploit our worst fears with misrepresented or manufactured evidence for a quick profit. Among those who have been accused of complicity in the President's murder or its concealment: Lyndon Johnson, the KGB, the Pentagon, Cubans (both pro- and anti-Castro), the CIA, the FBI, the Mafia, the Dallas police department, "Texas oilmen," and exotic, top-heavy combinations of any and all of the above—almost anyone, it seems, but Oswald. These charges have had their impact: a *Newsweek* poll published two decades after Dallas showed that three out of four Americans believed "others were involved" besides the accused assassin; only 11 percent thought he acted on his own.

Two excellent books—William Hanchett's *The Lincoln Murder Controversy* and *Oswald's Game* by Jean Davison—should help put the focus back where it belongs, on the turbulent, embittered men who actually pulled the triggers. Both Booth and Oswald held distorted images of the world and of their own importance within it; each found in the murder of a President a dramatic part worthy of his most grandiose fantasies.

Professor Hanchett shrewdly demolishes in turn each of the tortuous plot theories that have flourished since 1865, sketches the fevered, anti-Lincoln atmosphere within which Booth acted, and offers the most plausible account we are ever likely to have of his real motivation. Booth did not act from professional frustration, as some have suggested; he was a good and successful actor, not a ham. But he was implacably attached to the Confederacy and persuaded that it was up to him to save it single-handedly. When his crackpot scheme to kidnap Lincoln and spirit him away to Richmond fizzled in 1865, he seems to have given up in despair, downing a quart of brandy at a sitting to blot out his shame. "But so goes the world," he wrote to his mother in apparent resignation in the early morning of April 14, 1865. "Might makes right."

In fact he may have had no fixed purpose to murder Lincoln until noon that same day when he strolled down to Ford's Theater to pick up his mail and learned that Lincoln and Ulysses S. Grant were expected at the evening performance of *Our American Cousin.* Sheer coincidence had now provided him with access to the object of his hatred—and by killing both Union leaders at once, he would at last be able, in his own words, to do "something decisive and great" to redeem the South—and himself. Had the President stayed away, as Grant did, Booth would likely be remembered now only by historians of the American stage.

In the book *Oswald's Game,* Jean Davison argues—persuasively, I think—that John Kennedy's assassin was different in at least one respect: had coincidence not brought the presidential motorcade beneath the sixth-floor window of the Texas School Book Depository five weeks after Oswald happened to land a job there, he would eventually have found someone else to kill. (He had, in fact, already tried to shoot the feckless right-wing general Edwin A. Walker, in the apparent belief that by removing him he would save the country from fascism, and he may have been on his way to have another try when he was arrested.)

It is impossible to do justice to Davison's crisp, commonsensical book in this space, but it retraces the flat, dispiriting trajectory of Oswald's entire life, beginning with a friendless boyhood spent in the care of his egomaniacal mother and already haunted by what a social worker described as "fantasies of being powerful, and sometimes hurting or killing people." Lee "wanted to be 'the boss' or not play at all," his older brother, Robert, remembered. "He was like mother in this respect." He was like her, too, in his relentless loathing for authority.

Nothing ever worked for Oswald—school, the Marine Corps, the Soviet Union, marriage, friendships, the dreary succession of menial jobs from which he was fired and which he disdained as unworthy of his talents. Even the Fair Play for Cuba Committee, whose pamphlets he noisily distributed on a New Orleans street corner, eventually thought it best to ignore his shrill, self-advertising letters. He was by every sane measure a wretched failure. Yet in his own mind he was a bold, resourceful freedom fighter: when he scrawled a phony after-the-fact journal meant to cast his defection to Russia in a more flattering light, he called it his "Historic Diary."

Davison points out that the Warren Commission did a remarkably thorough job of investigating Oswald's career but was never able to say precisely what finally impelled him to commit the melodramatic act that was its logical culmination. That failure she attributes to the fact that the commission members did not then know of clandestine American efforts to eliminate Oswald's revolutionary hero, Fidel Castro. But Castro did, and when he warned in September 1963 that "United States leaders" should not feel "safe" if they persisted in them, he indirectly provided Oswald with the heroic role he had been searching for: Oswald would become Fidel's defender.

Three weeks later Oswald turned up at the Cuban Embassy in Mexico City, seeking an entry visa. With him he brought a fat dossier he had compiled to impress the Cuban authorities with his all-round usefulness to the revolution: in it, he claimed (mostly falsely) to be a skilled translator, specialist in "street agitation," polished "radio speaker and lecturer," organizer, ideologist, soldier, and potential spy. (Once the Cubans saw all this, he assured his weary, Russian-born wife, he would be welcomed eagerly in Havana. "You laugh now," he told her when she seemed doubtful, "but in twenty years, when I am prime minister, we'll see how you laugh then.") As further evidence of his zeal, he loudly suggested that someone should kill Kennedy; that perhaps he would do it.

Castro himself is the source of this revelation: on separate occasions he told at least two witnesses about Oswald's threat, though he later denied having done so, probably for fear Americans might hold him even indirectly responsible for the death of their President. The Cubans turned Oswald away, in any case; the embassy official before whom he launched his tirade thought him either a madman or an American *agent provocateur.* And Oswald returned again to Texas and likely obscurity. Then, as with John Wilkes Booth a century before, fortune brought his victim within range.

The possibility of conspiracy is always disquieting. More frightening still is the reality of madness and of chance.

American Heritage April–May 1984

HENRY THE KID, A.K.A. BILLY

FOR ME, THE WORST HORROR OF ENTERING A NEW SCHOOL IN the fourth grade was Show and Tell. Each morning, just after Attendance, we were expected to hone our "communication skills" by giving a little talk on something that interested us. I had no communication skills to hone—terror made me sway alarmingly and caused my voice simply to disappear when called upon (no loss, since it also prevented me from summoning up the simplest words)—and I was convinced that nothing that interested me could possibly interest my new classmates.

After several days of this, the teacher gently suggested that I might try reading something aloud. I was obsessed with the Old West then, and chose Walter Noble Burns's *Saga of Billy the Kid,* published in 1926. Burns was a veteran Chicago newspaperman, weak on research but strong on storytelling, whose protagonist was a genuine hero, modest and misunderstood, an enemy of privilege and friend to the poor. Best of all, for my purposes, Burns wrote with shameless panache. Here, his hero shoots his way out of a burning house: "The Kid's trigger-fingers worked with machine-gun rapidity. Fire poured from the muzzles of his forty-fours in continuous streaks. . . . On he ran like a darting, elusive shadow as if under mystic protection. He cleared the back wall at a leap. He bounded out of the flare of the conflagration. Darkness swallowed him at a gulp. Splashing across the Bonito, he gained the safety of the hills."

Great stuff for a ten-year-old, and my fellow ten-year-olds agreed: even the girls clapped and cheered and begged for more. For several weeks—until I reached the last gaudy page—I was a smash at Show and Tell.

If I had then been able to read aloud from Robert M. Utley's *Billy the Kid: A Short and Violent Life,* my audience's attention might have wandered some, but they would have learned a lot more about what the Old West was really like. Utley is an old-fashioned scholar in the best sense, stubbornly unwilling to rearrange evidence to fit current historical fashion: his books about the old Indian-fighting army, for example, published in the late sixties and early seventies when seldom was heard an encouraging word about the westward movement, demonstrated that neither troopers nor tribesmen ever had a monopoly on villainy—or virtue.

Unimbellished facts about outlaws are hard to come by, and Utley's study is necessarily less full-scale biography than biographical sketch, but it nicely conveys the context in which the Kid's misdeeds can be understood. The Lincoln County War has been fought and refought in more than forty films, but, as Utley wrote earlier in *High Noon in Lincoln: Violence on the Western Frontier*, the actual events failed to follow any of the "formulas favored by screenwriters. The war was not a fight between sheepmen and cowmen, or stockmen and sodbusters, or big cattlemen and little . . . , or enclosers and fence-cutters, or vigilantes and outlaws, or corporate moguls and nesters, or Anglos and Hispanics, or feuding families. . . ."

It was instead "a war without heroes," fought strictly for profit by armies of hired guns. Lincoln County sprawled over 30,000 square miles, but the only real profits to be made in this mostly empty, cashless land were government contracts for beef and other provisions with which the Mescalero Apaches and the soldiers posted nearby to keep them quiet had to be supplied. "The House," an establishment run by a hard-fisted Lincoln merchant named John J. Dolan, held a monopoly until 1876, its grip fortified by friends at court, a malleable sheriff—and a band of paid enforcers called "the Boys."

Then John H. Tunstall arrived. An ambitious Englishman with no illusions about how to get ahead in his adopted country, he wrote home that "*Everything* in New Mexico that pays *at all* is worked by a 'ring,' there is the 'Indian ring,' the 'army ring,' the 'political ring,' the 'legal ring' . . . the 'cattle ring,' the 'horsethieves ring,' the 'land ring,' and half a dozen other rings." In partnership with the cattle king John Chisum and others, Tunstall determined to form a ring of his own, wrest power from Dolan and his minions, and thus "get the half of every dollar that is made in the county by *anyone.*" To back his play he hired his own gunmen, the Regulators, among them a beardless eighteen-year-old called "the Kid" by his mostly older companions.

His real name was Henry McCarty (William H. Bonney, the name under which he is still most often indexed, turns out to have been an alias), and he was a product of the New York slums, not the Old Frontier. His widowed mother, Mary, an Irish laundress, took him west with her at the close of the Civil War, first to Indiana, then Kansas, then to sunny New Mexico after she was diagnosed as tubercular. It was too late. She died in 1873 at Silver City. She had picked up a second husband, Bill Antrim, along the way, but once she was gone, he seems to have done little for her son other than to lend him the second of the three last names he used interchangeably.

Seeking reasons for the orphaned boy's precipitous slide into outlawry, his earliest biographers made much of his having been left too much alone at an impressionable age with the *Police Gazette*. More important, surely, was the fact that in a place where size and strength and bluster were highly prized, he was slender and softspoken and undersized—"really girlish looking," a boyhood friend recalled, with hands so small and supple they slipped easily through standard-issue handcuffs. His seems to have been an especially deadly instance of overcompensation.

Whatever its causes, he began his life of crime at fifteen by stealing a tub of butter from a rancher and got caught trying to sell it in town, then stole a bundle of clothes from a Chinese laundryman, got caught again, and managed to make his escape from jail by squirreling his way up the chimney and onto the roof.

He graduated to stealing horses and rustling cattle, broke out of two more jails—part of his legend, like that of the bank robber Willie Sutton in this century, had its roots in the extraordinary difficulty the law had just holding on to him—and in 1877 at Bonito he shot and killed his first man, a blacksmith and bully who, according to an eyewitness, had once too often chosen to "throw [him] to the floor, ruffle his hair, slap his face and humiliate him before the men in the saloon."

Utley's research shows that while he did not kill twenty-one men (one for each year of his truncated life, as boys of my generation fervently believed), he did account for four, and was present and firing enthusiastically when six others died. (That is not to say that he wasn't good at killing when circumstances required it: "Grant squared off at Billy," an admiring eyewitness to one of his authenticated killings recalled, "who when he heard the click whirled around and 'bang, bang, bang.' Right in the chin—could cover all of them with a half a dollar.")

The Kid's side would eventually lose the Lincoln County War: John Tunstall was murdered in the very first serious engagement, but his partners persevered and the fighting stuttered on for more than two years. There were chases, shoot-outs, and stand-offs, before the climactic five-day pitched battle along Lincoln's lone street in July of 1878 that ended with the daring escape from a burning building Walter Noble Burns described so lovingly.

In the interest of returning to some semblance of law and order, Governor Lew Wallace issued a "general pardon," but specifically exempted from it the young man who now called himself Bill Bonney because he was already under indictment for murdering a sheriff. The peace that followed was only relative, in any case: after a drunken parley in Lincoln, members of both factions, glassy-eyed with whiskey and good fellowship, happened upon a one-armed attorney who un- wisely refused to dance for their amusement. He was shot through the heart and left where he fell, his coat still burning from the powder flash, while all hands went off to an oyster supper. "There was really no malice in this shooting," a bystander later explained. "Life was held lightly down there in those days."

The Kid happened to have been a sober witness to the lawyer's shooting (alcohol was not among his vices), and struck with the gov- ernor what he thought was an ironclad bargain: in exchange for going through the motions of being arrested, fingering the attorney's killer, and providing information about other crimes and criminals, all charges against him were to be erased. He duly testified against others, then was told all bets were off: he would have to stand trial for murder himself. Disgusted, the Kid simply rode away from prison (thanks to a sympathetic lawman) and returned to cattle rus- tling.

Local stockmen, weary of their losses and with old scores to settle, helped elect a sometime bartender named Pat Garrett sheriff and sent him pounding after the Kid. On the night of July 14, 1881, Garrett shot him dead in the darkened bedroom of a ranch house in which he had taken refuge.

The first book about him was in the stores within a year. It is hard to see just what made his legend loom so large so fast. His youth had something to do with it. So did the eagerness of old allies to spin tales that reflected well on him and on their common cause. But beyond that he seems to have been genuinely amiable when he did not feel threat- ened. He was "happy go-lucky all the time," a victim of his rustling admitted. "Nothing bothered him."

"You appear to take it easy," a reporter told him once, as he smiled for the crowd that had turned out to see him momentarily locked up.

"Yes," the Kid replied. "What's the use of looking on the gloomy side of everything? The laugh's on me this time."

"He done some things I can't endorse," an old friend said. "But Kid certainly had good feelings."

American Heritage April 1990

INTO THE DARKEST CONTINENT:
HENRY MORTON STANLEY

IN THE SPRING OF 1891, NEARLY TWENTY YEARS AFTER HENRY Morton Stanley introduced himself to Dr. David Livingstone on the shore of Lake Tanganyika, Oxford awarded the grizzled, stumpy explorer an honorary degree. As he made his way forward to receive it, an undergraduate shouted out, "Dr. Stanley, I presume."

The subsequent laughter greatly embarrassed Stanley. His sense of humor was meager at best, and about himself, nonexistent, but there may have been more to his discomfiture than that, for no one, least of all Stanley himself, seems ever to have been entirely sure just who he really was. His achievements as an explorer of what he was the first to call the Dark Continent should have been enough to satisfy any man's ambition: In four expeditions between 1871 and 1889—and in the face of illness, intermittent warfare, the deaths of his companions and a hundred other obstacles—he explored Lake Tanganyika, circumnavigated Lake Victoria, paved the way for a British protectorate at Buganda, identified the Ruwenzori range as the legendary Mountains of the Moon, traced the twisting course of the Congo, established outposts, built roads, and—when Britain proved insufficiently enthusiastic about colonizing the lands watered by the great river—helped establish the Congo Free State under Leopold II of Belgium.

Yet, as John Bierman's biography, *Dark Safari: The Life Behind the Legend of Henry Morton Stanley*, demonstrates, none of his accomplishments was ever great enough to overcome his own self-loathing, soften his distrust of others, or slake his thirst for the warm approval that had been so conspicuously denied him as a boy. The authentic adventures that crowded his life are all vividly chronicled here, but it is his other life, the one he fabricated for himself to conceal the drab, dispiriting truth about his origins, that held my attention.

Stanley's illegitimacy seems to have been the central fact of his existence. At his birth at Denbigh, Wales, in 1841, the pastor of his parish church recorded him as "John Rowlands, Bastard." His father may have been the town drunk whose name the boy would jettison as soon as he could, or a local landowner who had paid the drunk to admit paternity, or yet another, still more transient lover—Stanley was never sure—but his slatternly mother never showed the slightest interest in him. Her early rejection, he remembered, was "so chilling that the valves of my heart closed, as with a snap."

They would rarely open again for long.

He was farmed out, first to indifferent relatives, then to utter strangers, and then was locked away inside an authentically Dickensian workhouse.

Abandoned children often reinvent their childhoods, idealizing absent parents or fantasizing for themselves wholly new ones. But few have ever done so for so long, or with such dogged consistency, as did the man who named himself Henry M. Stanley. When fame first came to him, he stubbornly insisted he had been born in America; later, as an old man, he would fabricate a brand-new boyhood for himself, one in which he was often ill-treated but always a hero.

He claimed that he broke out of the workhouse at fifteen, after beating the sadistic Master with his own blackthorn cane; in fact, he had been the Master's special favorite and simply left to live with an uncle. At sixteen, he went to sea as a deck hand and jumped ship at New Orleans. There, he would later write, he was taken in at eighteen by a benevolent cotton broker named Henry Stanley, who not only adopted him but bestowed upon him his own name. "In my earliest dreams and fancies," Stanley would write of this extraordinary moment, "I had often imagined what kind of a boy I should be with a father or mother. What ecstasy it would be if my parent came to me to offer a parent's love as I had seen it bestowed on other children. . . . My senses seemed to whirl about for a few half-minutes; and finally I broke down, sobbing from extreme emotion." Tragically, Stanley continued, his adoptive father died shortly thereafter.

In reality, Henry Stanley lived on into the 1870s, and no adoption ever took place, except in Stanley's rich imagining—indeed, Bierman offers evidence that the authentic Henry Stanley had done his best to rid himself of the importuning young man who clung to him with such alarming intensity.

In the end, Stanley simply commandeered the broker's first and last names, entered the Confederate army, was captured at Shiloh, then enlisted in the Union Army in order to avoid imprisonment and became an American citizen.

His middle name, Morton, was sheer invention, added later, in part to make his journalistic byline seem more impressive. Some of his early reporting was invention, too, and it seems miraculous that he got away with it; when he wrote at twenty-five that a cup of camp coffee poured for him while covering Indian warfare on the western plains was better even "than the best Mocha I ever drank in an Egyptian khan," for example, no one objected that he had not as yet been within a thousand miles of Egypt.

His first expedition to Africa in 1871 did more than merely make him famous. In finding Livingstone for the *New York Herald,* he seems also to have found, however fleetingly, the surrogate father for whom he had always yearned: basking in the famous missionary's paternal approval, Stanley wrote, "I have come to entertain an immense respect for myself and begin to think myself somebody, though I never suspected it before. . . . I get as proud as can be, as though I had some great honor thrust on me." When Livingstone died two years later, Stanley was disconsolate: "I loved him as a son," he told the missionary's daughter—and he would subsequently justify his own, sometimes bloody-minded African adventuring as part of a filial mission to carry on Livingstone's work, expunging the slave trade by introducing European commerce.

Action alone staved off Stanley's chronic depression: "When a man returns home and finds for the moment nothing to struggle against," he once wrote between expeditions, "the vast resolve which has sustained him through a long and difficult enterprise dies away . . . and then the greatest successes are often accompanied by a peculiar melancholy." And only Africa, as far as he could get from the white world in which he always felt himself an interloper, and where he was surrounded by blacks willing to follow his orders without question, could provide him with the distinctive kind of action he demanded.

Whenever even momentarily at rest, Stanley made trouble for himself, picking quarrels with the rich and well born, feuding with everybody from fellow journalists to fellow explorers. He gave offense as easily as he took it, was always restless, always aggrieved, always certain others were mocking him: At forty-four, he wrote that he had "not found one man—and I have travelled over 400,000 miles of this globe—who did not venture to say something unkind the minute I turned my back to him."

His distrust of women seems to have run still deeper. He professed to be too timid for courtship: "To propose and be refused," he told a friend, "would be my death. . . ." But in fact, he craved companionship and intimacy, pursued young women on both sides of the Atlantic with such single-mindedness that they were frightened off, then denounced them for their faithlessness. (He may also have had sexual relationships with at least two young men who later threatened him with blackmail, though the evidence is more suggestive than conclusive.)

In any case, in 1890, he finally persuaded Dorothy Tennant, the daughter of a British diplomat, to marry him. Though she was much younger than he, she seems to have treated him as more mother than wife, and he responded with a son's gratitude: it was an enormous relief, he told her, "not to be chilled and have to shrink back. Between mother and child, *you* know the confidence and trust that exist; *I* never knew it; and now, by extreme favour of Providence, the last few years of my life shall be given to know this thoroughly."

She persuaded him to renounce his American citizenship, become a naturalized Briton and stand for Parliament as the candidate of the right-wing Liberal-Unionists. He disliked even the minimal sort of flesh-pressing required of British politicians, loathed being "herded in the lobbies like so many sheep in the fold," could not abide having to listen to speakers he believed less well informed than he. But, despite recurrent malarial fevers that forced him to shroud himself in blankets on even the warmest summer days, he did enjoy working away at his relentlessly imaginative autobiography, and played happily with Denzel, the illegitimate Welsh baby he had adopted.

In 1899, Stanley was knighted by Queen Victoria. But by then sinister reports of Belgian cruelty—floggings, mutilations, butcheries—had already begun to leak out of the Congo. Stanley privately worried over the "moral miasma" that seemed to have encompassed the lands he had laid open to the Belgians, but in public he denied it all—and even paid tribute to King Leopold as Africa's Divinely appointed "redeemer."

The British Foreign Office would prove Belgian rule far more barbaric than the first reports suggested, but by then Stanley had been paralyzed by a stroke.

Toward the end, he asked his wife, "Where will they put me when I am—gone?"

"In Westminster Abbey," she assured him.

He was delighted: "Yes, they will put me beside Livingstone."

But in the end, even posthumous legitimacy was denied him. He was cremated, then buried in a country churchyard after the Dean of Westminster, evidently appalled by the horrors to which Stanley's explorations in the Congo had led, refused to grant him space near the man whom he had yearned to have be the father he had never known.

American Heritage April 1991

SCOUNDREL TIME: LILLIAN HELLMAN

V ANESSA REDGRAVE GAVE ONE OF HER MOST MEMORABLE PER-
formances in the title role of *Julia*, the film based upon the most
memorable chapter in Lillian Hellman's bestselling memoir,
Pentimento: her portrayal of the doomed heroine—cool, intelligent,
courageous—symbolized anti-fascism at its most selfless. Jane Fonda
was good, too, as Hellman herself: bright, earnest, spunky enough to
undertake a risky secret mission into the heart of Hitler's Germany on
her friend's behalf, later anguished at her powerlessness to save Julia
from the vengeful Nazis, or to find and care for her baby, left behind
in occupied Europe after her murder.

Both performances paled compared to that given by Lillian Hellman one evening as she talked about her dead friend on television.
Hellman looked like a ship's figurehead by then, her long, pouchy face
proudly bearing the chisel marks of a full life lived: too much alcohol,
too many cigarettes, too much blacklisting, too much Dashiell Hammett. The tragedy of her tale was underscored by her flat, tough,
survivor's voice and the apparent modesty with which she described
her fruitless postwar search for Julia's missing child. At the bitter
memory, tears glistened in her eyes. The interviewer choked back tears
of her own. So did I. So, I suspect, did a lot of other viewers.

We now know that the whole story was a lie, of course: Hellman
never undertook a mission into Germany. Nor did she seek to find
Julia's baby; there never had been one. Nor had she even known the
"real" Julia—the late Dr. Muriel Gardiner, a genuinely heroic veteran
of the Resistance, who escaped to America in 1939 and whose overly
talkative lawyer evidently told Hellman enough about his fearless
client to send her to her typewriter.

William Wright's biography, *Lillian Hellman, The Image, The
Woman,* is nearly as clumsy as its title, I'm afraid. But it sets forth the
facts of her life in sufficient detail to prove conclusively that whatever

else Hellman was—playwright, screenwriter, prose stylist, political radical—she clearly was a colossal liar, chronic and perhaps pathological.

"What a word is truth," Lillian Helman wrote in the preface to a one-volume version of her three memoirs (*An Unfinished Woman, Scoundrel Time,* and *Pentimento*). "Slippery, tricky, unreliable. I tried in these books to tell the truth, I did not fool with facts." Not only did she fool with them, Wright demonstrates, she invented them wholesale.

None of this is altogether new. Suspicions about Hellman's looseness with the truth surfaced well before her death in 1983, fueled by the inexplicable suit she brought against Mary McCarthy for having called her a liar on television. Other writers, Martha Gellhorn and Irving Howe among them, long ago picked apart those sections of her memoirs of which they possessed personal knowledge. But Wright is the first to have put the whole story together, and its cumulative effect is devastating.

Hellman commandeered Dr. Gardiner's life, he writes, in order "to enhance her own," and she seems to have done the same with many of the people she encountered. In fact, there are so many falsehoods and distortions in her autobiographical writings, so many convenient lapses of memory, that the reader can only sympathize with her biographer, whose job it became to discover the truth about a subject whose own account of any event, however trivial, to which she was the only surviving witness could not be trusted.

How did she get away with it for so long? She wrote beautifully, for one thing: John Leonard spoke for many when he said of the first volume of her memoirs that it shone "with a moral intelligence, a toughness of character, that inspires even as it entertains . . . the prose is as tough as an electron microscope."

And, as she went about reinventing her own past and settling old scores with ancient enemies, she was shrewd enough always to *seem* unsparing of herself. All sorts of personal flaws and frailities are confessed—shyness, lack of tact, naïveté about politics and money—but she somehow manages simultaneously to transform them into moral strengths, to make herself seem when faced with a hard ethical choice to have acted with greater, quieter courage than did those around her, who seem in her portrayal of them so much better equipped by nature or position to be brave.

In the spring of 1952, having exhausted the movie business as a source of dangerous enemies of the Republic, the House Committee on Un-American Activities moved back east in search of fresh pickings and bigger headlines among the writers and directors of Broadway plays. Hellman, already denied work by nervous Hollywood producers for her politics, was called to testify. (She and her lover, Hammett, undeniably suffered badly from the anti-Communist frenzy of the time; he was then serving six months in prison for contempt of a federal court, and she recently had been forced to sell her home in part to pay his legal bills.) She did not wish to go to jail; nor did she want either to plead the Fifth Amendment or to name the names of others. She hired as her attorney the young Joseph Rauh—just the sort of anti-Communist liberal she liked to denounce in other contexts—and together they agreed on an offer of partial cooperation: she would answer any and all questions about herself and her beliefs, she said, provided the Committee would not demand that she answer any questions about others. If they could not give her those assurances, she would reluctantly take the Fifth Amendment.

Her justly celebrated letter in response to the Committee's subpoena is one of the few inspiring documents to have emerged from that dark time: " . . . to hurt innocent people whom I knew many years ago in order to save myself," she wrote, "is, to me, inhuman and indecent and dishonorable. I cannot and will not cut my conscience to fit this year's fashions. . . ." When a witless Committee member unaccountably placed this eloquent letter in the hearing record, Rauh instantly passed out copies to the press. The result was a public relations triumph for his client, LILLIAN HELLMAN BALKS HOUSE UNIT, said the *New York Times*.

In retelling even this familiar story—which already reflected well upon her—Hellman could not resist polishing up the truth further to enhance her own luster. In *Scoundrel Time* she implied that she knowingly risked jail by taking her stand, that no witness had ever taken such a position before, and she reported that her testimony had been interrupted by an onlooker who shouted from the press gallery: "Thank God somebody finally had the guts to do it!"

All of this is suspect: Rauh says that he and his client were both confident before she wrote her letter that jail was not a real possibility; her expressed willingness to plead the Fifth Amendment once the congressmen denied her written request ensured that. Nor was Hellman by any means the first witness to offer partial cooperation with the Committee. Nor did anyone else present in the crowded hearing room see or hear the enthusiastic civil libertarian in the press gallery— who begins to shout at a dramatically opportune point in Hellman's chronicle, just as her interrogators are questioning her about her membership in the Party and she is giving answers that an uninterrupted reader might have found ambiguous. (Wright also argues persuasively that despite Hellman's frequent denials, her exquisite conscience did not dissuade her from remaining a Stalinist virtually all her life—unforgiving, unrepentant, and clandestine.)

"Lying," said Oscar Wilde, "the telling of beautiful, untrue things, is the proper aim of Art." It is one thing to recast facts to create fiction; that's what playwrights do for a living, after all. But surely it is another to invent and arrange facts, as Hellman did, so that they reflect especially well on their creator, then insist that they constitute what really happened. In doing that, she betrayed both past and present, all in the interest of accomplishing what had evidently become by the end of her life the highest aim of her dramatic art—to keep herself, the Heroine, always at center stage.

American Heritage September 1987

FEAR AND LOATHING: ROY COHN

JOSEPH McCARTHY'S FALL FROM FAVOR AFTER THE 1954 ARMY-McCarthy hearings was precipitous enough to satisfy all but his most unforgiving victims. Censured by his former colleagues in the Senate, snubbed by the White House, finally ignored even by the newsmen who had once fought to be first to carry his press releases, he grew persuaded that he was being hounded by triumphant Communists who had taken over the telephone company, and, when the tumblers of brandy and vodka he drank in relentless, suicidal succession began to produce delirium tremens, he screamed in fear of the writhing serpents he was sure surrounded him. "No matter where I go," he sobbed to a friend toward the end, "they look on me with contempt. I can't take it anymore. They're murdering me."

When McCarthy finally, mercifully, died in May of 1957, not yet fifty, Roy Cohn, the young investigator whose reckless arrogance had done more than anything else to start McCarthy on his downward slide, was among the pallbearers. Cohn had been revealed before the television camera's cold eye as surly, irresponsible, and untrustworthy, and he had finally been forced to resign his post. Unlike McCarthy, he had seemed to thrive on all the exposure, was already using his notoriety to build what turned out to be a thirty-year career as one of New York's preeminent political fixers. Part of his "mystique," he once said proudly, "depended on people thinking that I was getting away with every kind of shady deal."

Because effective fixers do their work behind closed doors, on untapped telephones, and are careful always to cover their tracks and commit as little as possible to paper, efforts to chronicle their careers rarely satisfy. Two books on Cohn further prove that rule. The core of *The Autobiography of Roy Cohn* is Cohn's own sketchy, self-serving version of his life, left unfinished at his death, then edited by Sidney Zion, the former newspaperman who bills himself as author. Since it was in Cohn's interest always to seem more powerful than he really was, it is impossible to know which of his gaudy tales to believe about judges bought and sold, politicians made or ruined, and the base motives that he claimed motivated all those who dared cross him, from Robert Kennedy to George Bush. A self-styled "flaming civil libertarian," Zion has also padded out his book with a number of stories intended, I think, to demonstrate his own generosity of spirit in having had Cohn for a buddy in the face of outraged friends; since, among other things, he got this book out of their relationship, these tales are not perhaps as persuasive as they might be.

Nicholas von Hoffman's *Citizen Cohn* is better, an attempt at a full life, but undercut by the inclusion of too many undigested passages from old newspaper and magazine articles, by the fact that a substantial number of the "several score" interviewees upon whom the author depended for his fresh material apparently preferred not to be identified, and by the author's own unfortunate fascination with the clinical details of the life Cohn led as a clandestine but desperately promiscuous homosexual amid yacht-loads of tanned young hustlers hired in Provincetown.

"Though Roy Cohn appears to have had no opportunity to develop the compulsive hatreds that lead many to adopt McCarthyism as a way of life," the journalist Richard Rovere wrote when Cohn was McCarthy's twenty-five-year-old counsel, "he is the sort of young man who takes things hard. . . . He has a perpetual scowl and studied toughness of manner. His voice is raspy, his manner cocksure enough to suggest vast insecurity."

He never lost that manner. Even at the end, his face ravaged by AIDS and rendered strangely masklike by a series of face-lifts, TV talk show hosts could count on him to act like the Cohn of old, interrupting his opponents, misrepresenting their views, or personalizing his attacks upon them whenever, as very often happened, he ran short of facts.

Von Hoffman at least suggests some of the sources of the lifelong insecurity that underlay this ceaseless aggression. Roy Marcus Cohn was born in the Bronx in 1927, the sole, adored offspring of an otherwise loveless marriage between Al Cohn, a soft-spoken Democratic judge, and Dora Marcus, a millionaire's noisy daughter whose dowry may have included enough of her father's money to buy her husband his seat on the bench. Two themes seem to have dominated this troubled little woman's long life: the belief that her husband was a failure because he was merely prosperous, and her determination that *her* son, with whom she would always live and whose life she would seek to run until her death in 1967, should be a spectacular success. "He was her crown prince," a relative remembered, " . . . she was the queen," and from the first, she taught him that rules applied to commoners, not royalty. While still a sixteen-year-old schoolboy, her boy was already using his father's influence to have his teachers' traffic tickets quashed, and many years later she was outraged when, after calling to explain that Roy had been out the night before and so would be just a bit late for the first day of his own trial for attempting to rig a grand jury, his attorney ordered her to get his client out of bed and to court on time, even if he was a little sleepy.

"People are forever asking me what I'd do differently if I had my life to live over again," Cohn wrote. "I disappoint them because I wouldn't change much. . . . I have no sense of over-riding guilt concerning my past, I look back with a clear conscience." He shed no tears over the reputations he helped ruin while failing to uncover a single Communist in government during his eighteen months at McCarthy's side, and he shrugged off repeated charges of bribery, collusion, thievery, tax evasion, as nothing more than harassment by ancient enemies. "I don't care what the law is, tell me who the judge is," he liked to say, and " . . . you trust and the next thing you need is a truss."

His single stated regret was that he and his young fellow counsel, G. David Schine, had ever undertaken their celebrated 1953 trip to Europe to purge United States Information Agency libraries of "more than thirty thousand works by Communists, fellow-travelers and unwitting promoters of the Soviet cause"—and he was sorry about that only because the press had portrayed him and his sleepy-eyed fellow crusader as ludicrous junketeers. (Even here, Cohn was still playing McCarthy's old game: in fact, at issue were not 30,000 "works" but 30,000 individual *copies* of books by 418 men and women whom the Committee's researchers had solemnly concluded were "Communist" authors—among them were W. H. Auden, Steven Vincent Benét, John Dewey, Edna Ferber, Arthur Schlesinger, Jr., even Bert Andrews, a devoutly conservative newspaper reporter, whose own anti-Communist zeal had earlier helped Congressman Richard Nixon nail Alger Hiss for perjury.)

Homosexuals were especially easy targets for McCarthy—and for his zealous young counsel: when Cohn and Schine checked into European hotels during their ill-fated excursion, they took turns insisting loudly on adjoining rather than double rooms, explaining tastefully to the baffled desk clerk, "You see, *we* don't work for the State Department." Cohn maintained public scorn for homosexuals to the end of his life, going out of his way to lobby against legislation on their behalf and, according to Zion, once turning away a delegation who hoped he would agree to defend a public school teacher fired because of his sexual orientation: "I believe," he told them, "that homosexual teachers are a grave threat to our children."

More than mere hypocrisy was at work here. Unable to escape the smothering mother he both loved and feared, a Jewish anti-Communist who first shot to prominence helping to prosecute Julius and Ethel Rosenberg for espionage, and a secret homosexual, Roy Cohn had a lot to prove, or thought he did. He always seemed eager to demonstrate that a Jew could be more ornately patriotic than any Gentile—in the early 1980s he was still leading his dinner guests in singing "God Bless America." Above all, he sought to dominate everyone he met, perhaps to show that *this* momma's boy was tougher than the next guy, whomever that next guy might be. At restaurant tables he routinely speared food off his client's plates without asking permission; one frequent lunch partner took to spitting on his own food as soon as it arrived in self-defense. Asked point-blank by a reporter if he was a homosexual, Cohn answered, "Every facet of my . . . aggressiveness, of my toughness, of everything along those lines, is totally incompatible with anything like that. . . ."

He was diagnosed as having AIDS in 1984 and shortly afterwards was brought at last before the disciplinary committee of the New York Bar. Defending him against charges that included having demanded a loan of $100,000 from a client in a divorce case, then refusing to pay her back, his partner was reduced to pleading that Cohn was "a man who loves people, loves animals. He once jumped into a river to save a dog in trouble." It didn't work. In the spring of 1986, with only weeks to live, he was disbarred.

Throughout his career, Cohn manipulated gossip columnists to keep him in the limelight he loved, and it seems fitting that the most succinct summary of that career may have been offered by Liz Smith of the *New York Daily News.* Despite his reputation, she said, Cohn was never really a great lawyer; "I think he was a great bully, who had connections and who frightened . . . people, and who was the greatest scrapper and fighter who ever lived. . . . He was totally impervious to being insulted."

And he never lost his power to bring out the worst in everyone. About the time he entered the hospital for the last time, I happened to attend a gathering of New York writers, several of whom were publicly identified with the cause of more enlightened treatment for AIDS victims. Party chatter among writers being no more elevated than it is among, say, construction workers, the causes of Cohn's condition were eagerly discussed.

"I never thought I'd be saying this about *anyone,*" said one best-selling novelist, well known for her generous support of humanitarian causes, "but I'm glad he's got AIDS. He deserves it."

"Couldn't happen to a nicer guy," agreed her no less celebrated, no less normally warm-hearted friend.

Everybody laughed.

That kind of merciless venom would not have surprised its target. Roy Cohn seems to have relished the special loathing his enemies reserved for him and, the evidence suggests, it seems more than likely that on some level he shared fully in it.

American Heritage July 1988

THE MAN OF GREAT SIMPLICITY:
ALGER HISS

ALMOST FIFTY YEARS AFTER WHITTAKER CHAMBERS FIRST
told a government official that Alger Hiss was a Communist,
and forty years after Chambers's charge was finally made public, Hiss wrote *Recollections of a Life,* billed by its publisher as "his long-awaited memoir." No one's frank memoir would be more welcome; many, even among those who believed Hiss innocent, also believe he had been unable to tell the whole story in court.

Chambers, a pudgy, rumpled, confessed ex-Communist, first tried to warn the White House about Hiss, then a minor State Department official, shortly after the Nazi-Soviet Pact was signed in 1939. Nine years later, on August 2, 1948, Chambers repeated his accusation before the House Committee on Un-American Activities.

The charge seemed wildly implausible, and Hiss, then forty-two and the president of the Carnegie Endowment for International Peace, was indignant in his denials. Lean and aloof, he was a graduate of Johns Hopkins and the Harvard Law School; had been a protégé of Felix Frankfurter and Oliver Wendell Holmes, Jr.; Secretary General of the conference that drew up the Charter of the United Nations; newly appointed to his prestigious post by John Foster Dulles.

He first testified that he had never even known "a man by the name of Whittaker Chambers," but then began grudgingly to equivocate, finally admitting a slight acquaintance with Chambers, but under a different name and several years earlier than his accuser alleged. Otherwise, he remained adamant, and dared Chambers to repeat his charges outside the legal sanctuary of the hearing room.

Chambers did so, on "Meet the Press," and three weeks later, Hiss sued him for libel. Chambers then produced documents that showed Hiss had been more than a Communist sympathizer; he had also provided classified State Department documents to Chambers, who had himself passed them along to the Soviets.

Hiss was indicted on two counts of perjury—for denying he had seen Chambers after 1937, and for denying that he had turned over classified papers to him. (He would likely have been indicted for espionage, too, had the statute of limitations not run out.) His first trial ended in a hung jury; a second found him guilty and he was sent to prison for forty-four months.

From that day to this, Hiss has consistently denied ever having done anything wrong. There is not room enough in this piece—or in this book, for that matter—to offer all the arguments and counterarguments involving oriental rugs and missing teeth, underground aliases and allegations of forgery by typewriter, that were central to this case, but I believe the most dispassionate, step-by-step account of it is still Allen Weinstein's *Perjury: The Hiss-Chambers Case*. Weinstein began his work suspecting that while Hiss may have been less than totally forthcoming about his friendship with Chambers, he had been innocent of both Communist sympathies and espionage, and he ended it nine years and 674 pages later convinced that Hiss had been guilty as charged. "There has yet to emerge from any source," Weinstein concludes, "a coherent body of evidence that seriously undermines the credibility of the evidence against Alger Hiss."

From the first, Hiss chose to portray himself as the blameless victim of reactionaries bent on discrediting "recent great achievements of this country in which I was privileged to participate," thereby making himself a rallying point for those liberals who, as Walter Goodman once wrote, "would not, could not concede that many New Dealers, including F.D.R. himself, had been slow in taking the Communists as seriously as they deserved to be taken. Those who . . . associated themselves with the sad cause of Alger Hiss made an error for which the liberal cause would pay in the next half dozen years," years during which zealots took the Hiss conviction as a license to look for more Hisses in places where none existed.

Because Richard Nixon, a member of HUAC in 1948, had always claimed more credit than he should have for trapping Hiss, the chronic mendacity that in turn trapped him in the 1970s lent a fresh if specious credence to Hiss's ancient denials: If Nixon was a proven liar, Hiss and his most ardent loyalists seemed to argue, those whom he had accused of lying must be truthful.

Hiss once vowed "never to write an autobiography . . . because I hold certain strong views about privacy." Unfortunately, in *Recollections of a Life* he has remained true to that pledge; it is a slender collection of reticent sketches, as well tailored but curiously distant as the man whom the jury chose not to believe almost forty years ago.

He reveals no more than is absolutely necessary, withholding even the maiden name of his second wife. One whole chapter is devoted to an aunt who read aloud to him as a child, another to a singularly uneventful summer he spent in France, still another to having read aloud to Justice Holmes, whom he served as secretary.

Chambers himself once described Hiss as "a man of great simplicity, and a great gentleness and sweetness of character," and on that point at least, Hiss himself seems to agree with his accuser. ". . . I just couldn't believe that anyone wouldn't love me, once I was there," he has said, trying to explain why he was so slow to gauge the trouble he was in when he first appeared to answer Chambers's charges, and he is still anxious for us to admire his rectitude; describing his post-prison career as a stationery salesman, he is careful to say that he was a success, even though "I didn't take my customers to lunch or give them whiskey or flowers at Christmas."

He remains unfailingly gallant—Alger Hiss must surely be the only person ever to remember Eleanor Roosevelt (who thought it "rather horrible" that Chambers, not Hiss, had been believed) as a woman of "quick-witted repartee"—and eerily unworldly: his best friends in prison, whom he describes as "affectionate family men, quick-witted, and . . . personable," were *mafiosi*.

Unsubstantiated theories about the case endlessly proliferate. Hiss and Chambers were lovers. Hiss took the rap for his wife or nobly failed to call as exculpatory witnesses other family members whose own private lives could not have stood the pitiless scrutiny of the courtroom. It was all a Communist trick; by sowing discord and suspicion, Chambers was still doing the Politburo's bidding. Hiss himself once produced a list of six more or less mutually exclusive explanations for why he had been singled out for persecution.

The case against him was "fabricated," he now says in the most all-inclusive explanation he has yet offered for his troubles, "by an unholy trinity bound together by the theology of anti-communism. . . . They were Richard Nixon, the power-hungry politician; J. Edgar Hoover, the ultimate bureaucrat; and Whittaker Chambers, the perfect pawn."

In his new book, Hiss continues to maintain that Chambers was a political paranoid and "psychopath," whose enmity stemmed from resentment that his homosexual attraction toward Hiss was not reciprocated (his accuser denied ever being so attracted). Now, something new has been added: Chambers was also a "cowed, timid creature . . . skulking and shambling," under the shrewd manipulation of Nixon and Hoover.

He attributes Nixon's malevolence to naked political opportunism, sparked by resentment of the "mild irritation" he himself displayed "at [the congressman's] manner" at their first meeting. (In fact, Nixon was at first an equivocal harrier, as mistrustful of Chambers as he was suspicious of Hiss until he had the documentary evidence in hand.)

Hoover's role, Hiss attributes to "personal vindictiveness against me because I had been one of the early New Dealers who had complained of his disloyalty to Roosevelt's policies, for which I believed he should have been forced out of office." This is apparently a brand-new notion; nowhere in the courtroom testimony, in Hiss's own previous book, or in any other account of the case available to me can I find so much as a hint of his having previously claimed to have been so outspoken a foe of the Director, and, since he was merely a lawyer for the Agricultural Adjustment Administration during the early New Deal, it is hard to see what would have motivated him to become one.

Nor does evidence elsewhere suggest that Hoover was a notably amenable co-conspirator. According to Weinstein and to Richard Gid Powers's biography, *Secrecy and Power: The Life of J. Edgar Hoover,* Hoover initially wanted to prosecute Hiss *and* Chambers. As always, the Director's first impulse was to defend the FBI; he resented HUAC's intrusions onto his turf, was angered when Chambers chose to cooperate with its investigators and other officials at the Justice Department rather than with his agents, and was so upset when the federal prosecutor let slip that the FBI had been unable to find the missing Hiss typewriter that he had G-men secretly search the prosecutor's files for evidence that he was "unfriendly toward the Bureau."

Alger Hiss is in his eighties now and nearly blind; younger people read aloud to him as he once did to Justice Holmes. But he is as eager as ever to wrap himself in the achievements of the Roosevelt administration whose reputation he did so much to damage: "In the New Deal, in the wartime State Department, for the nascent United Nations, I did what I could toward the common goal of a better world," he writes. "Since the war, in my adverse circumstances, the fact that I fought for my beliefs has been more than just a private good for me alone—I continue to meet people who take heart from what I stood for. I count as successful my efforts to live according to my goals and principles, and so I have no cause for bitterness or regret, nor have I ever felt any. . . . In the words of Job, I have pursued my goals 'in mine own ways.' In that I am content."

Sadly, the rest of us, who had hoped at last to hear from Hiss what really happened between him and Whittaker Chambers in New Deal Washington half a century ago, will also have to be content.

American Heritage November 1988

WRITERS
AND ARTISTS
──────── ★ ────────

"WRITING . . . IS THE GREAT INVENTION OF THE WORLD": ABRAHAM LINCOLN

B EFORE THE MOVIE VERSION OF ROBERT E. SHERWOOD'S *Abe Lincoln in Illinois* opened across the country in 1940, a special White House screening was arranged for Franklin Roosevelt, for whom Sherwood was then acting as speechwriter. The star, Raymond Massey, sat between Roosevelt and Sherwood, and after Lincoln's train chuffed slowly out of Springfield past his weeping fellow citizens and the lights came on, he remembered, FDR shook his head and muttered, ". . . and he wrote all those speeches *himself!*"

Roosevelt's envy was understandable. Lincoln did indeed write all those speeches—and all those letters and legal briefs, telegrams and presidential proclamations, as well. "Alone among American Presidents," Edmund Wilson once argued, "it is possible to imagine Lincoln, growing up in a different milieu, becoming a distinguished writer of a not merely political kind." Wilson was a little hard on the competition: Thomas Jefferson wrote elegantly on everything from architecture to English prosody, after all, and, between campaigns, the vigorous prose of FDR's own cousin Theodore helped pay the bills at Oyster Bay. And Lincoln's own literary forays beyond the realms of law and politics sometimes went alarmingly astray: here, for example, the author of the Gettysburg Address turns to verse to memorialize the same battle:

> In eighteen sixty three, with pomp, and mighty swell,
> Me and Jeff's Confederacy, went forth to sack Phil-del,
> The Yankees got arter us, and giv us particular hell,
> And we skedaddled back again, and didn't sack Phil-del.

But, as *Abraham Lincoln: Speeches and Writings 1832–1858* and *1859–1865*, the two volumes compiled by the editors of the splendid Library of America series, attest, Lincoln was unmistakably the greatest writer among our statesmen. Words were Lincoln's way up and out of the grinding poverty into which he had been born. If the special genius of America was that it provided an environment in which "every man can make himself," as Lincoln believed, pen and ink were the tools with which he did his self-carpentering.

"Writing," he once said, ". . . is the great invention of the world. Great in the astonishing range of analysis and combination which necessarily underlies the most crude and general conception of it— great, very great in enabling us to converse with the dead, the absent and the unborn, at all distances of time and of space. . . ." Lincoln still converses with us through his writing; his carefully crafted words still most memorably define the struggle through which he led us.

Professor Don E. Fehrenbacher, today's preeminent Lincoln scholar and twice the winner of the Pulitzer Prize, has winnowed through the 4,776 pages of Roy P. Basler's authoritative but daunting eleven-volume *Collected Works* to yield the 795 documents he considers most important to understanding Lincoln and his time. Everything you would hope to find is here—the House Divided speech, the complete Lincoln–Douglas debates, the magisterial first and second inaugurals, even the heartfelt if misinformed letter to Mrs. Bixby—but there is also much that will seem fresh to all but the most omniscient Lincoln enthusiast.

Lincoln liked to pretend a becoming naïveté about politics: "You know I never was a contriver," he once told a delegation of squabbling Republican leaders, presumably managing to keep his face straight. "I don't know much about how things are done in politics." In fact, he knew all there was to know, had learned it the hard way, maneuvering to excel among the Whigs of Illinois and, when *that* grand old party died, helping first to forge and then to lead to national victory an entirely new party. As his law partner William Herndon wrote, "That man who thinks Lincoln calmly sat down and gathered his robes around him, waiting for the people to call him, has a very erroneous knowledge of Lincoln." Still, what is perhaps most surprising about the documents that make up the first, pre-presidential volume is how much of Lincoln's life was taken up with the gritty mechanics of getting elected and staying ahead of his rivals. His letters are filled with knowing judgments on the motives of friends and enemies alike, judgments made all the shrewder because he understood his own ambitions so well: "Remembering that Peter denied his Lord with an oath after most solemnly protesting that he never would," he wrote an old Illinois ally on the eve of the Republican Convention that nominated him for the presidency in 1860, "I will not swear I will make no committals but I do think I will not."

To read Lincoln's prose, Fehrenbacher has suggested elsewhere, "is to see him in action, pursuing practical results, rather than ultimate truth," but he also was forced by history to confront thorny moral issues of a kind to which most politicians are mercifully immune, and he sometimes wrote just to puzzle out a position for himself before trying it on the voters. His "fragments" on Government and Slavery and the vagaries of the Divine Will are well known, but his refutation of *Slavery Ordained of God*, an 1857 book by the Reverend Frederick A. Ross which strained to provide theological underpinnings for the South's Peculiar Institution, was new at least to me:

> The sum of pro-slavery theology seems to be this: "Slavery is not universally *right*, nor yet universally *wrong*; it is better for some people to be slaves; and, in such cases, it is the Will of God that there be such."
>
> Certainly there is no contending against the will of God, but still there is some difficulty in ascertaining, and applying it, to particular cases. For instance we will suppose the Rev. Dr. Ross has a slave named Sambo, and the question is "Is it the will of God that Sambo shall remain a slave or be set free?" The Almighty gives no audible answer to the question, and his revelation—the Bible—gives none— or, at most, none but such as admits of a squabble as to its meaning. No one thinks of asking Sambo's opinion on it. So, at last, it comes to this, that Dr. Ross, is to decide the question. And while he considers it, he sits in the shade, with gloves on his hands and subsists on the bread that Sambo is earning in the burning sun. If he decides that God wills Sambo to continue a slave, he thereby retains his own comfortable position; but if he decides that God wills Sambo to be free, he thereby has to walk out of the shade, throw off his gloves, and delve for his own bread. Will Dr. Ross be actuated by that perfect impartiality which has ever been considered most favorable to correct decisions?

There is precious little of a personal nature in these pages. Lincoln was in truth the reticent, unconfiding man Herndon said he was, and most of his writing is sober and formal; little of the humor and vivid barnyard-and-backwoods imagery that enlivened his conversation ever made it to the page. But here and there, even during the grim war years, his writings reveal the human being behind the mask of Father Abraham.

"The lady—bearer of this—says she has two sons who want to work," he scrawled to an aide in 1861. "Set them at it, if possible. Wanting to work is so rare a merit that it should be encouraged."

Lincoln's legendary patience turns out to have had its limits: "It seems to me," he wrote on April 28, 1863, "Mr. [Francis L.] Capen knows nothing about the weather in advance. He told me three days ago that it would not rain again till the 30th of April or 1st of May. It is raining now & has been for ten hours. I can not spare any more time to Mr. Capen."

The President's frustration at George McClellan's too-gingerly ways and his forbearance at Joseph Hooker's boastful ones are familiar to anyone who has followed the Union's grim fortunes in the first years of the Civil War, but here he deals sternly with the "slows" that afflicted a lesser Union commander, Nathaniel P. Banks, in the autumn of 1862:

Early last week you left me in high hope with your assurance that you would be off [to command the Department of the Gulf, with orders to open up the Mississippi] . . . at the end of that week, or early in this. It is now the end of this, and I have just been overwhelmed and confounded with the sight of a requisition made by you, which I am assured, can not be filled, and got off within an hour short of two months! I inclose you a copy of the requisition, in some hope that it is not genuine—that you have never seen it.

My dear General, this expanding and piling up of impedimenta, has been, so far, almost our ruin, and will be our final ruin if it is not abandoned. If you had the articles of this requisition upon the wharf, with the necessary animals to make them of any use, and forage for the animals, you could not get vessels together in two weeks to carry the whole, to say nothing of your twenty thousand men; and having the vessels, you could not put the cargoes aboard in two weeks more. . . . You would be better off any where, and especially where you are going, for not having a thousand wagons, doing nothing but hauling forage to feed the animals that draw them, and taking at least two thousand men to care for the wagons and animals, who otherwise might be two thousand good soldiers.

Fehrenbacher's collection ends with a short note, written on one of the last two days of the President's life: "No pass is necessary now to authorize any one to go to & return from Petersburg & Richmond. People go & return just as they did before the war." As these rich and absorbing volumes again make clear, it was not merely the great armies Lincoln commanded but the words he mobilized that brought about that happy result.

American Heritage September 1989

"THE LOVELIEST HOME THAT
EVER WAS": MARK TWAIN

O F ALL THE RESTLESS WRITERS THIS RESTLESS COUNTRY HAS
produced, Mark Twain was by every measure the most peripatetic. The *Oxford Illustrated Literary Guide to the United States*
traces the wanderings of 1,500 literary figures across the American
landscape; its index lists no fewer than 114 cities and towns and crossroads that were important to Samuel Clemens during his 75 astonishingly prolific years—and that tally does not include any of his rambles
overseas.

Yet he managed to spend most of seventeen of those years in the
big curious house he built in 1874 at 351 Farmington Avenue in
Hartford, Connecticut. It was the happiest, most productive period of
his life: he wrote seven books during his Hartford years, including his
three masterpieces, *Tom Sawyer, Huckleberry Finn,* and *Life on the
Mississippi.* Here he reveled in his role as America's most celebrated
author, two of his three daughters grew to young womanhood, and his
untamable hair turned from red to gray. Today, restored to its High
Victorian exuberance, his house still evokes both the worldly success
for which the poor boy from Hannibal, Missouri, never stopped striv-
ing, and the affectionate family life he and his wife Olivia—known
always as Livy—worked almost as hard to foster.

Clemens once wrote of Hartford that "of all the beautiful towns it
has been my fortune to see this is the chief," but it was less the city's
beauty that persuaded him to settle there than the fact that it had a
literary neighborhood at what was then the western edge of town.
Here, on some 140 shaded acres known as Nook Farm, lived a stimu-
lating group of writers, most of whom Clemens already knew—among
them the playwright and actor William Gillette and the editor and
novelist Charles Dudley Warner, with whom Twain collaborated in
writing *The Gilded Age.* Harriet Beecher Stowe lived in a small brick

house right next door to the five-acre plot on which the Clemenses began to build their new home.

The most persistent legend about the house is that its three turrets and painted brickwork, its five carved balconies and long deep veranda were all meant somehow to evoke the gaudy Mississippi steamboats on which Clemens had served as pilot. There is no documentary evidence that this is what he or the architect, Edward Tuckerman Potter, had in mind. True, Potter was known for the ingenuity with which he incorporated into his designs the idiosyncrasies of his clients; when he was commissioned by Mrs. Samuel Colt, the widow of the Hartford firearms manufacturer, to design a downtown church in her husband's memory, for example, he managed to include in it stone capitals carved to resemble parts of the revolvers that had first made Colt a millionaire, and a steeple topped with a cross formed of two fused rifles.

But Clemens claimed to have been bewildered by the building process and to have left at least the day-to-day supervision of it to his patient, pregnant wife. "I have been bullyragged all day," he wrote to his mother-in-law as the house was being finished, "by the builder, by his foreman, by the architect, by the tapestry devil who is to upholster the furniture, by the idiot who is putting down the carpets, by the scoundrel who is setting up the billiard table (and has left the balls in New York), by the wildcat who is sodding the ground and finishing the driveway . . . by a book *agent*, whose body is in the backyard and the coroner notified. Just think of this going on the whole day long, and I am a man who loathes details with all my heart!"

Still, if he did not intend that his home look something like a steamboat, the analogy clearly came to delight him: one of his favorite parts of the house was the shady octagonal balcony just off the third-floor billiard room. Here he had a hammock strung from which he liked to look down into the green tops of his trees or admire the clouds mirrored in the stream that wandered off through the meadows below; he called this retreat his "Texas deck."

The local newspaper thought the house "one of the oddest looking buildings in the state ever designed for a dwelling, if not in the whole country," and it became a tourist attraction for Hartford visitors, who stood in knots along the street on weekends hoping for a glimpse of Mark Twain, and admiring the more intrepid boys who ventured all the way up the driveway to the door with their autograph books.

The inside of the house, with its nineteen rooms and five baths, was less eccentric than opulent, especially after the first floor was remodeled and redecorated by Louis Comfort Tiffany and his firm of Associated Artists in 1881. The entrance hall set the tone for the rest of the room. Its floor is white marble, highly polished; the carved wood-work and dark red walls and ceiling are elaborately stenciled in silver gilt; a Tiffany window (now lost) glowed above the fireplace, itself framed by ornate wood panels carved to order in Lockwood de For-est's workshop at Ahmedabad, India, where similar works were turned out for the homes of Andrew Carnegie and other self-made million-aires. A narrow, pierced-brass border, also made at Ahmedabad, sur-rounds the fireplace opening itself, and when Clemens learned how much it cost he ordered the wall behind it painted bright red so that visitors could not fail to admire its intricacy. Nothing he had ever seen in Europe, he once told his wife, could compare with "the perfect taste of this ground floor with its delicious dream of harmonious col-or. . . . It is the loveliest home that ever was." Before he was through, he spent some $130,000 to build and furnish this splendidly appointed stage set, against which Samuel Clemens could play Mark Twain.

A staff of six was required to run the house, headed by Livy's Irish maid, Katy Leary, and the black butler, George Griffin, who turned up to wash the windows not long after the Clemenses moved in and stayed with the family throughout their time in Hartford. He was a shrewd and resourceful man, a deacon of his church, and especially adept at inventing tactful ways of turning away visitors who arrived unannounced and expecting to be ushered right in to see Mark Twain; he sometimes slept in a room of his own on the third floor.

Among the features of the house its owner liked best was the imposing library mantelpiece which he had brought home intact from a Scottish castle. When it was uncrated and proved too tall for the room, he had the top sawed off and its crowning cluster of cherubs installed separately just above the door. Above the hearth was a brass plate, designed by Tiffany and inscribed with a quotation from Emer-son: "The ornament of a house is the friends who frequent it."

Clemens's house rarely went unornamented. The Nook Farm colo-nists did not lock their doors, wandering in and out of one another's homes as mood and weather suited. This was not an unmixed blessing. In her old age, Harriet Beecher Stowe grew increasingly vague and restless, and the family was sometimes startled to hear old songs sung in a dry, almost disembodied voice drifting out of the darkened parlor into which their aged neighbor had ghosted to sit at the piano. Mrs. Stowe was also fond of flowers and liked to surprise Livy with bou-quets of them, often torn up by the roots from the Clemenses' own greenhouse when the gardener wasn't looking. Livy hung scissors there for a time in the hope that her visitor would at least snip the blossoms rather than destroy the plants, but the bright-eyed old lady's fervor could rarely be controlled.

"The Clemenses are whole-souled hosts," their close friend the Boston critic William Dean Howells once wrote home from Hartford, "with inextinguishable money and a palace of a house." Overnight visitors stayed in the Mahogany Room, really a guest suite complete with paneled bathroom and a canopied bed so grand that Howells called it the Royal Bedchamber. His small son was still more impressed: a cake of red soap, the first the boy had ever seen, rested on the bathroom sink. "Why, they've even got their soap painted," he told his father, and the next morning when he looked out and saw George readying the dining room for breakfast, he hurried back to Howells's bedside: "Better get up, Papa. The *slave* is setting the table!"

Clemens shone at dinner. An imported music box the size of a sea chest provided continuous music—the Wedding March from *Lohengrin*, the Pilgrim Chorus from *Tannhäuser*, and seven other favorites. The kitchen, presided over by a black cook named Marge, served up the rich dishes of that day: canvasback duck, fillets of beef, cherubs molded in pink or green ice cream. But the guests—among them William Tecumseh Sherman, Edwin Booth, Matthew Arnold, and the journalist and explorer Henry M. Stanley—came primarily to see and hear their famous host perform, and he was happy to oblige, prowling the long room between courses, puffing a black cigar and waving his napkin for emphasis as he told long stories which so convulsed George that he sometimes had to retreat into the pantry to recover.

The stories pleased his daughters, too, who often sat on the staircase to listen. But they had heard many of them before, and one would sometimes say to another, "Father is telling the beggar story; they must have reached the meat course."

There were three Clemens girls: Susy, who was three when the house was completed in 1874; Clara, born just weeks before the family moved in; and Jean, born in 1880. (An infant son, Langdon, had died of diphtheria not long before the house was begun, and the elder Clemenses' special joy in their new home may have been intensified by a sense that it represented a new start after that tragedy.)

Susy was her father's favorite; she was lovely—yellow-haired, introspective, and gifted. He wrote sentimental verse about her as a baby:

> *In slip of flimsy stuff all creamy white,*
> *Pink-belted waist with ample bows,*
> *Blue shoes scarce bigger than a house-cat's ears—*
> *Capering in delight and choked with glee. . . .*

And when she was thirteen, she wrote a brief but perceptive biography of her father. "We are a very happy family!" it begins. "We consist of papa, mama, Jean, Clara and me."

Only Susy was given a room of her own; Clara and Jean slept together in the nearby nursery. But the vivid presence of all three girls now permeates the restored house: toys very like those with which they must have played lie scattered across the nursery and schoolroom, but thanks to family letters and the reminiscences of Clara Clemens and others, nearly every other room also has its association with the three little girls who once ran in and out of them—including even their parents' bedroom with its massive Venetian bed; Clara and her sisters relished being at least slightly ill, she recalled, because then they were allowed to spend the day beneath its blankets, playing with the big removable cherubs that topped the bed posts.

Clemens tried without much success to find a comfortable, quiet place in which to work within the house. The schoolroom had originally been intended as his study, but the noise the girls made in the adjacent nursery and the distracting views from its windows kept him from serious work, and he retreated upstairs to the billiard room. It was quieter there, but the views were even better, and even with his back to the windows he found he could only "work *at* working" in Hartford: most of his writing was done in an isolated studio at Quarry Farm, his in-laws' summer place north of Elmira, New York, where he took the family every year. Still, he spent much of his time away from the girls on the top floor of the house, his presence betrayed to those downstairs only by the distant clicking of billiard balls and the faint smell of cigar smoke.

The drawing room was meant for formal entertaining, but the girls were given their dance lessons there, too, Susy and Clara gravely watching their whirling images in the floor-to-ceiling mirror. Sometimes their father sat at the piano, performing the spirituals he had learned from slaves as a boy in Hannibal, swaying on the bench as he sang—"Rise and Shine and Give God the Glory, Glory, Glory" was a favorite; so was "Swing Low Sweet Chariot." He fixed his eyes on the chandelier, Clara remembered, and "his fingers stretched straight out over the keys so that each time a chord was struck it seemed as if a miracle had happened."

But the family most often gathered in the crowded, friendly library, a fountain gently splashing in the adjacent glassed-in conservatory, filled with greenery and flowers. They played at big-game hunting: Clemens himself was the elephant, scrambling on all fours among the oriental carpets with one or another small huntress on his back.

"George was the lion," he wrote, "also the tiger; but preferably the tiger, because as a lion his roaring was over-robust and embarrassed the hunt by scaring Susy." There were quiet times here, too. Clemens loved to read aloud after dinner, alternating Shakespeare sonnets with the girls' own doggerel to their intense pleasure, and he was often asked to tell them a ritualistic bedtime story in front of the fireplace, made up as he went along and always incorporating in strict order all the items on the cluttered mantelpiece, beginning at the right with the portrait of a cat wearing a ruff and ending on the far left with an impressionistic watercolor of a young woman whom the girls named "Emeline." "In the course of time," their father noted, "the bric-a-brac and the pictures showed wear. It was because they had so many and such violent adventures in their romantic careers."

The girls staged more public dramas here, as well. Just after Christmas in 1889, they put on a home-grown production of *The Prince and the Pauper*. Some two hundred friends attended. The backdrop was a curtain hung over the arched entrance to the conservatory. Livy had written the script and helped make the costumes. Susy played the Prince; neighbors' children were given supporting roles. When one small member of the cast fell ill at the last minute, Clemens himself eagerly stood in, managing to spill a pitcher of water and devising other bits of business to keep the audience laughing—and its attention firmly focused on him.

Christmas, Clara wrote, was a time for "royal preparations"—so elaborate, in fact, and so time-consuming that her father once called it "the infernal Christmas suicide." The stairwell, door frames, and several of the mantelpieces—there are eighteen of them in the house— were wound with evergreens; a ten-foot fir filled the library alcove, strung with gilded walnuts and garlands of popcorn and cranberries, and lit by candles in the evenings while George stood by with a bucket of ashes just in case. There was a frenetic round of Nook Farm parties; scores, sometimes hundreds, of gifts were exchanged. The doors to the Mahogany Room were kept closed for weeks; behind them, Livy wrapped and tagged packages and prepared some fifty Christmas baskets of food and wine which her husband and her older daughters distributed from the family sleigh on Christmas Eve. That night, before the girls pinned their stockings to the mantelpiece in the school-room, their mother recited " 'Twas the Night Before Christmas," and at least once Clemens made an appearance dressed as Saint Nicholas, stomping around the room—its lamps discreetly lowered to add to the illusion—and suggesting that the girls thank him in advance on the chance that they might be displeased when they opened their presents the next morning. They were rarely displeased. Their parents stayed up most of the night making sure of that—once, an upright piano was somehow spirited up the staircase and into the schoolroom to astonish Clara, then just six.

Such cheerful lavishness ended abruptly in 1891. The cost of running the Hartford establishment finally proved crushing, and a series of disastrous business ventures had forced Clemens so deeply into debt that no new book or lecture could dig him out. Even Mark Twain's wealth had finally proved extinguishable. He moved his family to Europe, where they could live more cheaply. He did not want to leave his home, the only real home he'd had since Hannibal: "Travel no longer has any charm for me," he wrote. "I have seen all the foreign countries I want to see except heaven and hell." But he had no choice. The Clemenses would never again live together at 351 Farmington Avenue.

Nothing was ever the same for any of them. It was as if the strains that had always existed within the family could only be contained inside the familiar walls of their old house. It had never been easy to be the wife of Samuel Clemens; even in Hartford, Livy had suffered occasional periods of nervous prostration. These now intensified and no European spa seemed able to dispel them. Nor was it easy to be the child of such a celebrated man: "Mark Twain's daughter!" Susy once said. "How I hate that name." His daughters all adored him, but their adoration was always alloyed with fear. "He was a constant surprise in his varied moods which dropped unheralded upon him," Clara remembered, "creating day and night for those about him." She and her sisters loved to be with their father, she added, and his sudden rages were rarely aimed at them, but they preferred, even as little girls, to visit him in pairs—the prospect of witnessing one of his lunges from joy to anger and back again was too unsettling for any one of them to endure alone.

Five years after the family left for Europe, Susy—now twenty-four—came back for a visit and the locked house was opened for her. She fell ill and was put to bed (probably in the Mahogany Room where her mother had once wrapped her Christmas gifts). In England on July 15, 1896, her father was handed a cable that told of her death from spinal meningitis. "It is one of the mysteries of our nature," he wrote later, "that a man all unprepared, can receive a thunder-stroke like that and live." In his grief, he blamed himself: "My crimes made her a pauper and an exile."

Livy became a semi-invalid. Jean began to suffer from epileptic seizures and from psychological torments that at least twice drove her to try to kill her mother's elderly maid, Katy Leary. (Clemens's youngest daughter would finally drown in her own bath in 1909.)

Neither Clemens nor his wife could bear to think of living in the house in which Susy had died; they sold it in 1903 for a fraction of what it had cost twenty-nine years before. Livy died later that same year. Clemens survived until 1910. Only Clara outlived him to become the eccentric but vigilant guardian of his papers and his reputation.

Almost everything has changed since the Clemens family left Hartford nearly a century ago. The modern city has moved in on all sides. The clear stream that once ran past the house has been diverted underground; a big featureless high school, inevitably named for Mark Twain, has obliterated the homes of some of his neighbors and sprawls across the meadows where his daughters gathered wildflowers.

But the house itself remains what Samuel Clemens said it was. "To us," he wrote after Susy's death, "our house was not unsentient matter—it has a heart, and a soul, and eyes to see with; and approvals and solicitudes, and deep sympathies; it was of us, and we were in its confidence, and lived in its grace and in the peace of its benediction. We never came home from an absence that its face did not light up and speak out its eloquent welcome—and we could not enter it unmoved."

When this article appeared in the December issue of Gourmet *for which it was commissioned in 1984, I was startled to find that all mention of what happened to the Clemens family after they went abroad had been expunged. I called my editor to find out what had happened. "Oh," she said, "we just thought it was a downer at Christmas."*

MOM AND PAPA: ERNEST HEMINGWAY

B IOGRAPHIES OF WRITERS OFTEN DISAPPOINT. ALBERT CAMUS once described life in the literary arena with bleak accuracy: "One imagines black intrigues, vast ambitious schemings. There are nothing but vanities, satisfied with small rewards."

In some ways, Ernest Hemingway's tumultuous life is an exception to that rule. Everything about him—his talent as well as his rewards and vanities—was outsized. His sixty-one years were so crowded with noisy sideshows—wars, travels, feuds, safaris, fishing trips, boxing matches, bullfights, marriages, affairs, hard drinking—that it sometimes seems astonishing he found the time to write anything at all. Yet virtually all of it reappeared in his work. He was, as Alfred Kazin has noted, "the most extraordinary appropriator," able to make nearly everything he ever saw or felt or survived part of his pages. And although thirty years have now passed since he shot himself, our interest in him has never flagged. Professor Carlos Baker's official biography, *Ernest Hemingway: A Life Story*, appeared in 1969; it is a solid study—scholarly, admiring, readable—but it has turned out to be only an island in the stream of Hemingway books, all seeking to separate what really happened to the writer from his own vivid versions of it. Memoirs have been published by old friends and old enemies, by hangers-on and members of the family; academics have picked over his syntax, quarreled over his sexual orientation, assessed and reassessed his output.

Peter Griffin's *Along with Youth: Hemingway, the Early Years* is the first of a projected three volumes. It focuses on the writer's earliest experiences—boyhood summers in upper Michigan, World War I, his romance with the nurse Agnes Kurowsky (who is shown to have been more serious about him than had previously been thought)—all of which would later inspire much of his best writing. And it includes intriguing new material: chatty but revealing letters to Bill Horne, a close friend from Chicago newspaper days; love letters from his future wife, Hadley Richardson; and five unpublished short stories, wildly uneven but already filled with evidence of his early determination to write about "real people, talking and saying what they think."

But perhaps more important, it offers a few suggestive clues as to what went so terribly wrong at the end. Hemingway's suicide stopped a long sad decline into despair and paranoia and miserable health. "What does a man care about?" he had asked a few weeks earlier. "Staying healthy. Working good. Eating and drinking with his friends. Enjoying himself in bed. I haven't any of them." But he had in fact been talking of ending his own life for years before he fell ill. The conventional wisdom has been that it was the example of his father's suicide in 1928 that he had finally been unable to resist emulating. That may, in part, be true; but as Griffin reveals, Hemingway was already considering doing away with himself at the age of twenty-one, nearly a decade before his father's death. His anxious fiancée wrote then to talk him out of it, her alarm perhaps enhanced by the memory of her own father's suicide. "Remember," she told him, " . . . it would kill me to all intents and purposes. . . . You got to live first for your, and then for my happiness. . . . You mustn't feel so horrible unworthwhile, dear Ern . . . . " Hemingway's sister Ursula, and his brother Leicester, evidently came to feel similarly worthless; both of them would also commit suicide.

Common sense suggests that the cause of all this self-destruction must lie in the life Hemingway led with his parents and five siblings in the fashionable Chicago suburb of Oak Park at the century's turn. He once joked to a young friend that there were "heaps" of skeletons in the Hemingway closet, and he threatened one day to write a novel that would reveal them all. It is a pity he never did, for in trying to piece together what happened to him in Oak Park we are left to guesswork. Griffin is almost too responsible a sleuth, content to amass his evidence without openly making a case. Still, thanks to his labor, our guesses are better informed than they once were.

Hemingway's father—named Clarence but known to everyone as Ed—was a big, stolid physician, a taciturn man's man who spent as much time as he could on his own, hunting and fishing and walking in the woods, or locked in his own attic turret with his collection of pickled specimens ranged along the walls—snakes, salamanders, toads, and a human fetus, all bleached white by alcohol.

The real power in the house was Hemingway's mother, Grace. She was tall, bosomy, overconfident, a failed artist. (She had made her debut as a contralto at Madison Square Garden, then gave up all thought of a professional career because, she claimed, the footlights hurt her eyes.) She found solace in strict teetotal religion and in cloying self-dramatization that bordered on madness.

She seems to have loved her eldest son precisely as long as she could control all that he did, could see him as a projection of herself. Her big, leather-bound "Memory Book" of his first years is filled with examples of how devoted he is to her: "He sleeps with Mama and lunches all night. . . . He is so strong and well and loves his Mama so *tenderly* . . . and cries with such heart broken sorrow when we all put on our things in the morning." One of his favorite games, she noted, was " 'Kitty' where Mama be the Mama kitty and strokes him and purrs."

But when he broke away from her and began to act on his own— and especially when he coupled that natural desire for independence with a lively interest in girls and a gift for writing as undeniable as it was all-consuming—her love seems to have been transformed into something very like hatred.

Here she explains to her son on the occasion of his twenty-first birthday just what he must do to win back her love:

> The account [of maternal feeling, which she says he has overdrawn] needs some deposits. . . . Interest in Mother's ideas and affairs. Little comforts provided for the home. A desire to favor any of Mother's peculiar prejudices, on no account to outrage her ideal. Flowers, fruit, candy or something to wear, brought home to Mother with a kiss and a squeeze. The unfailing desire to make much of her feeble efforts, to praise her cooking, back up her little schemes. A real interest in hearing her sing or play the piano, or tell the stories that she loves to tell—a surreptitious paying of bills, just to get them off Mother's mind.
>
> A thoughtful remembrance and celebration of her birthday and Mother's Day—the sweet letter accompanying the gift of flowers, she treasures it most of all. These are merely a few of the deposits which keep the account in good standing.

That account would never be reopened. Hemingway's fame only depleted it further. His mother loathed his writing; it seemed to her "a doubtful honor," she told him when *The Sun Also Rises* first appeared, to have written "one of the filthiest books of the year."

Personal success for Hemingway was tainted, then, from the first. The better he did, the more ungrateful he was made to seem, the more "unworthwhile" he was made to feel. He dutifully supported his mother after his father's death—an event for which he believed she was mostly to blame—and he even tried to remember to write her on her birthday and to praise her for the mediocre paintings she turned out as an old lady in the vain hope of building an artistic reputation of her own. But he could not stand to visit her. And she never grew less envious of him. "Some critics and professors consider Ernest's books among the finest of our times," she told an interviewer in 1951, the last year of her life, "but I think the essays he wrote as a schoolboy were better." Those essays, of course, had been written under Grace Hemingway's own fierce and unforgiving guidance.

American Heritage February 1986

AT HOME WITH THE SAGE OF
BALTIMORE: H. L. MENCKEN

O NE DAY TOWARD THE END OF HIS LIFE, H. L. MENCKEN IS SAID to have come upon his own obituary in the files of the Baltimore *Sun*. He read it through and, to the intense relief of its anxious author, pronounced it satisfactory. Then he asked that one more line be added: "As he got older, he got worse."

On the evidence of *The Diary of H. L. Mencken*, edited by Charles A. Fecher, that seems literally to have been true, and it is perhaps understandable that Mencken asked that the journal he kept during his last active years be sealed until a quarter of a century after his death, and then be opened only to serious scholars. After that anniversary arrived, it took the trustees of the Enoch Pratt Free Library in Baltimore, to which Mencken had entrusted his papers, five more years to rule that the interests of history outweighed the author's informally expressed wishes and decide to publish it—and another three for Charles Fecher, the editor of the library's quarterly *Menckeniana*, to winnow out the present substantial volume from its 2,100 double-spaced pages.

The diary begins in November 1930 when Mencken was fifty-five and ends in November 1948, seven years before his death. The twenties had belonged to Mencken; never in our history has a single critic or journalist wielded more gleeful power than he did then, using the Baltimore *Sun, Smart Set,* and *The American Mercury* to loose gaudy onslaughts on everything from Prohibition and fundamentalism to democracy itself—"the theory that the common people know what they want and deserve to get it, good and hard." His language was always more ornate than his ideas: "I am strongly in favor of liberty and I hate fraud," he once told a biographer who asked for his credo, and he stubbornly believed that government best which governed least, whatever the circumstances.

That view did not sit well with the generation that grew to maturity in the grip of the Great Depression, and Mencken's reputation was still another victim of the Great Crash and its grim aftermath. By 1933 the readership of the *Mercury* had so dwindled that he felt called upon to resign as its editor. The next year, FDR—the man Mencken routinely dismissed as "Roosevelt Minor" and loathed most in American political life—assumed the presidency. By 1935, Mencken had fallen so far from favor that a Cleveland writer could caustically mention "the late H. L. Mencken," and then add: "What? You say Mencken isn't dead? Extraordinary!"

Mencken simply didn't seem funny any more; for better or worse, the thirties demanded reform, the very idea of which was anathema to him. "It has . . . been assumed on frequent occasions that I have some deep-lying reformatory purpose in me," he confided to his diary. "That is completely nonsensical. It always distresses me to hear of a man changing his opinions, so I never seek conversions. My belief is that every really rational man preserves his major opinions unchanged from his youth onward. When he vacillates it is simply a sign that he is stupid. My one purpose in writing I have explained over and over again: it is simply to provide a kind of katharsis for my own thoughts. They worry me until they are set forth in words. This may be a kind of insanity, but at all events it is free of moral purpose."

"Mencken sets down many true sayings but spoils his case by overemphasis . . . ," the novelist Hamlin Garland wrote in 1934. "I finished [a book of his essays] with a sense of being entertained as by a 'cut-up' at a dinner table. It is like being thumped on the head with a boy's wind-blown bladder filled with dried peas. This comes ultimately to be a bore. The fact is, Mencken in private life is a quiet and peaceable citizen. This lessens the ferocity of his prose."

The quiet and peaceable routine of Mencken's daily life should not have surprised anyone. The lives of writers are rarely eventful and Mencken was always, as the critic Carl Bode has written, "the happy prisoner of his origins." After his wife's death in 1935, he lived alone with his bachelor brother August in the Baltimore row house at 1524 Hollins Street in which he had spent his boyhood, resolutely tapping away for most of almost every day at his vast correspondence (nearly every letter received was answered by nightfall), or working on one or another of the several books upon which he liked to labor simultaneously—the fourth edition of *The American Language* and two supplements to it, *Treatise on Right and Wrong*, *A New Dictionary of Quotations*, *Happy Days*, *Heathen Days*, *Newspaper Days*, *A Mencken Chrestomathy*, *Minority Report*, plus seven more autobiographical volumes (now locked away in a safe at the Pratt Library, to be opened—and presumably published—in 1991). He worked so hard in part because he hoped to be rediscovered by the post-FDR generation. "On the ultimate fate of my writings I sometimes speculate idly," he wrote in 1942. "At the moment, with the Roosevelt crusade . . . in full blast, my ideas are so unpopular that it is impossible . . . to print them. But when the New Deal imposture blows up at last, as it is sure to do soon or late, they may have a kind of revival."

He did take time off to make his way downtown from time to time, to the offices of the *Sunpapers* to offer the (mostly unwanted) editorial advice for which he was still paid a salary, and he met each week with other lovers of German music at the Saturday Night Club to play the piano, devour seafood and pilsener beer, and smoke his noisome Uncle Willie cigars.

What surprises the reader of Mencken's diary is not the relative drabness of the everyday life it chronicles, then, but the drabness with which most of it is set down. Here and there are flashes of the wit that had once enlivened even his most bombastic writings: he pronounces the findings of Dr. Joseph B. Rhine, the extrasensory perception enthusiast, "so worthless they have been hailed as masterly by Upton Sinclair," and recalls shaking hands with his enemy in the White House and being reluctantly "bathed in his Christian Science smile." But for the most part the writing is uncharacteristically flaccid, the tone often merely peevish.

Publicly, as the diary's editor writes, Mencken was always "utterly unafraid," happy to take on anyone and anything, and he was invariably cocky and good-humored when visitors came to call. But, on the evidence of his diary, Mencken seems at least during the latter part of his life to have been privately anxious about almost everything—encounters with "low-grade" Jews and "dreadful kikes"; wartime incursions into his neighborhood by poor blacks ("blackamoors," all of whom are "essentially child-like") and "[f]ilthy poor whites from Appalachia and the Southern Tidewater" ("lintheads" who "live like animals, and are next door to animals in their habits and ideas"); and the constant and entirely baseless threat that the federal government was poised to crush him because he opposed American participation in the war—which he believed to be a product of British propaganda combined with Rooseveltian duplicity.

"It is astonishing how little the war impinges upon me," he wrote in 1944.

I am, of course, rooked like everyone else by excessive taxes, and now and then some eatable that I like is unprocurable (or procurable only by giving up an enormous number of ration points); but in general I am hardly affected by the great effort to save humanity and ruin the United States. . . . The American people are now wholly at the mercy of demagogues, and it would take a revolution to liberate and disillusion them. I see no sign of any such revolution, either in the immediate future or within the next generation. When the soldiers come home it will become infamous to doubt—and dangerous to life and limb.

Above all, he was apprehensive about his own health. Perhaps because his father had died at forty-four, he seems to have been haunted hourly by the prospect of his own sudden death and planned to append a full medical history to his already voluminous autobiography on the assumption that his readers would share his fascination with it. "So far as I know," he writes, "no one has ever set down such a record of himself," and he went still further, gathering affidavits from doctors and hospitals to supplement his own encyclopedic notes. The reader can only be grateful to the editor for his decision to leave out of the published version fully two thirds of Mencken's querulous hypochondriacal musings; the remaining eighteen-year tally of ailments, real and imagined, is numbing enough, page after page of aches and pains and mysterious twinges, each of which at the time evidently seemed to herald imminent doom.

Nothing much seemed to please him any more. The end of the war brought no joy. Even the pleasure he might otherwise have derived from the death of Franklin Roosevelt (who had possessed, he wrote the next day, "every quality that morons esteem in their heroes") was spoiled for him when the passage of the presidential funeral train through Baltimore forced the Saturday Club to miss "its usual post-music beer-party for the first time in forty years." (Mencken did take some comfort from the supposed plight of the President's widow: "The case of La Eleanor is not without its humors. Only yesterday she was the most influential female ever recorded in American history, but tomorrow she will begin to fade, and by this time next year she may be wholly out of the picture.")

The diary ends on November 15, 1948. Eight days later, his worst fears were realized when he suffered a stroke which destroyed his ability to match words with ideas and made it impossible for him to write. He lingered on for seven silent years, watching as Hollins Street and the great world beyond it continued inexorably to change, unable ever again to achieve the katharsis that had once transformed his fears and crotchets into art.

American Heritage December 1989

WINSOME FOR WAR:
DOROTHY THOMPSON

W HEN DOROTHY THOMPSON'S LAST COLLECTION OF COL-
umns, *The Courage to Be Happy*, was published in 1957 and
got a generally friendly review from the *New York Times*, its
author professed to be disappointed. "It's a magnificent testimony to
my character—of the 'whether you agree with her or not' variety—,"
she complained to her editor, "but it seems to be my fate always to be
judged as a conscience and a character rather than as a mind and a
writer."

No praise, however fulsome, fully satisfies any author, of course,
but Thompson had a point, and, despite the efforts of her exhaustive
biographer, Peter Kurth, to include an assessment of her thought and
her writing alongside the events of her crowded, peripatetic life in his
American Cassandra: The Life of Dorothy Thompson, it is still primarily
her conscience and character that hold our interest.

It is hard, more than half a century after the fact, fully to grasp the
journalistic power Dorothy Thompson exercised during the prewar
years. "She can do more for any cause than any other private citizen
in the United States," *Time* reported in 1937; among American
women, only Eleanor Roosevelt was said to be more influential.
Thompson's column, "On the Record," appeared in 170 newspapers
three times a week and had 10 million readers. She had her further
vigorous say every week on NBC Radio, every month in the *Ladies'
Home Journal*, and between deadlines she swept back and forth across
the continent sounding her alarms in person. Her subject, in print and
from the podium, was almost invariably the same: Adolf Hitler meant
precisely what he said in *Mein Kampf*, and the future of civilization
depended upon stopping him in his tracks.

Her single-mindedness wearied even her admirers. "She was always one-ideaed," an old friend remembered, "and difficult either to
work or play with, unless the idea she had was shared by her playfel-

low." Her fellow columnist Walter Lippmann privately compared her to the Statue of Liberty: "Made of brass. Visible at all times to the world. Holding the light aloft, but always the same light. . . . Capable of being admired but difficult to love."

But she got results. "Day by day," wrote her friend the novelist Dorothy Canfield Fischer, "with a clang like that of a powerfully swung hammer, she beat upon [the] general confusion of mind till the will to defend democracy was forged."

The zeal with which she produced that righteous dim came naturally to Dorothy Thompson. Born in 1893, she grew up in a succession of threadbare Methodist parsonages in upstate New York. The Reverend Peter Thompson, the English-born father she adored, was himself a slight, frail man, over whom his wife and two daughters constantly fussed, but his message was unfailingly cheerful and robust: "It is our privilege to be winsome for Christ," he assured his flock, and when for six months his family was forced to subsist largely on rice and apples, he got them through it by reminding the children that Asians throve on rice and "the heathen . . . admirable people in some respects, [are] able to teach us many things."

He was very nearly everything to his daughter; his example would remain with her all her life, the benchmark against which she measured both the world and herself and found both wanting:

> . . . [M]y . . . childhood was bathed in warmth and light, which was nothing but the irradiation of a beautiful personality, a man whose sole being was warmth and light: my father. His intimate belief in the goodness and justice of God, his unconquerable faith in the inherent decency of men, made him a creature radiating cheerfulness, even gaiety, turning every misfortune into a challenge or an only half-rueful joke. . . . His was the liberal spirit. Liberal in the sense that we use the word when we speak of "liberal arts." Humane, rooted in humanity, caring for human beings, not as producers, or consumers, or workers, or employers—but as human souls.

Her mother died when Dorothy was seven, after exacting a death-bed promise to "always care for your sister and your father." She did her earnest best to fulfill that pledge, waiting at the door each afternoon for her father to return from his pastoral calls so that she could brew his tea and fetch his slippers, just as her mother had—and was rewarded for her fidelity by his remarriage to the church pianist, a hypochondriacal interloper who seems from the first to have loathed her eldest stepchild and whose loathing the little girl returned in full measure.

At fifteen, Dorothy was shipped off to Chicago to live with two aunts, ostensibly so that she could enjoy big-city "advantages," actually because her stepmother could no longer abide her assertive, adolescent presence. In later years, Thompson professed to have been delighted by this sudden move and the new vistas it opened to her (and she must in fact have felt some genuine relief in escaping the tensions of the parsonage), but her younger sister recalled that at the time she went "about in a sort of daze. She felt that Father had deserted her at last."

Dorothy Thompson would later credit her father with having taught her a host of things that comprised the core of her beliefs throughout her career: the sense that "the world was a continual struggle between good and evil, virtue and sin," that "progress was furthered only through creative individuals, whose example and achievement leavened and lifted the masses . . . ," above all, perhaps, the conviction that *she* could be one of those creative individuals, could do anything she wanted to do, in fact, once she set her mind to it.

But her father's meek acquiescence in her exile also seems to have taught her other lessons, unacknowledged but no less formative. She evidently never stopped believing that her beloved father would some-how have managed to keep her with him had not her already fierce independence led her to neglect his needs. "Oh, my dear father!" she wrote in her diary years after his death in 1921, "I was never a comfort to you and you live in me like the truth of a thought. I wanted to grow up, amount to something, do something for you, make you proud of me." All her life she would remain torn between her drive to make her own, utterly autonomous way and her guilt at failing to be "a comfort" to those she loved but left behind.

Outwardly, she would display startling self-confidence throughout her life. Even as a child she had been thought by some too full of herself, too voluble, too "sassy" and "highty-tighty." She exhausted her teachers in junior college, and at Syracuse University she established a reputation for rapid-fire talk on every imaginable topic, scared off male suitors ("She knew too much," one remembered. "A fellow felt inferior"), and formed ardent attachments with other women who shared her determination to find new roles to play, free of what she called *"artificial* repressions, conventions or traditions."

After college, she stumped western New York for Woman Suffrage, tried social work in the slums of Cincinnati and writing advertising copy in Manhattan, and fell in love, first with a much older woman,

Gertrude Franchot Tone, a wealthy Niagara Falls suffragist and paci-
fist (and the mother of the actor Franchot Tone), who encouraged her
to believe that she was "a daughter of the gods," and then with a
married man, Wilbur C. Phillips, founder of the philanthropic National Social Unit Organization for which she worked for a time as
chief publicist.

In 1920, she fled to Europe to forget Phillips—and to see if, at
twenty-seven, and with precious little experience, she could make her
own way as a journalist. "[M]en are brutes," she confided to a friend
before she embarked, "nothing will make you happy except what you
can find in yourself... *nothing* else matters *much* except keeping your
own self respect and having satisfactory work." Her attitude toward
men would eventually mellow, but her other priorities were already
set for life.

Her first big story fell into her lap—on the basis of shipboard chats
with members of a Zionist delegation, she talked the London office of
the International News Service into believing that "I know more about
Zionism than anyone else," and got assigned to cover an international
conference on Palestine. Soon she was scouring Europe for stories,
first under the fond tutelage of Marcel Fodor of the Manchester *Guardian,* whose devotion to her survived her refusal of his marriage pro-
posal.

She brought to reporting inexhaustible curiosity and unending
energy—a colleague recalled her as "the blue-eyed tornado"—as well
as a talent for making events in exotic Europe comprehensible to
stay-at-home Americans, and a gift for placing herself at the center of
the story. It was "a wonderful, risky unforgettable time," she later
wrote. She survived riots, covered coups, wangled interviews with
everyone—Ataturk, Trotsky, Masaryk, Richard Strauss, Romain Rol-
land—and befriended many of them. When news of a Polish uprising
took her by surprise at a Vienna dinner party, she liked to remember,
she boarded the night train for Warsaw, still in her evening gown and
slippers and holding a ticket paid for with a late-evening loan from
Sigmund Freud.

Eventually, she was made bureau chief of the Philadelphia *Ledger*
and *New York Evening Post,* with headquarters in Berlin, a salary of
$50 a week, and nine countries to see to. The once-staid *Ledger* had
recently been bought by Cyrus H. K. Curtis, who was willing to
provide what he called "unlimited funds" to beat the competition
overseas. Thompson was not the first American woman to run an
overseas bureau—Sigrid Schultz, who had been reporting from Germany since 1918, was already in charge of the Chicago *Tribune* office

when she arrived—but she soon made herself the most celebrated, reporting on German affairs with such brisk authority that John Gunther declared her "the best journalist this generation has produced in any country." Still, "[t]his isn't enough for me," she told a friend. "It's not what I really want. I'm nothing in my own country. I want to be something there—something no woman has been yet."

Tall, fresh-faced, and striking, with a big, resolute jaw and brilliant blue eyes, Thompson was a distinctive presence among her trench-coated male competitors, and a number of them pursued her without success. "Yes, dear," she was supposed to have told an especially ardent Austrian begging for a kiss, "but right this minute I've simply *got* to get to the bottom of this Bulgarian business."

"She never used sex-attraction to get her story," George Seldes recalled, but she was not above using the *fact* of her femaleness. Once, when she raced to the telegraph office in Prague to file a dispatch, found she had no money, and could not persuade the telegrapher to extend her credit, she wrote out a telegram addressed to the Czech foreign minister, Edvard Beneš (whom she barely knew): "Beloved: Will you bring pressure to bear to have the officials in this post office fired?" She signed it "Sweetie." Her wire went right through.

Among her most persistent suitors was Joseph Bard, a darkly handsome Hungarian Jew with philosophical pretensions, then embarked upon a trilingual treatise, *The Mind of Europe,* that never quite got finished. "He looked like an Egyptian prince," Thompson remembered, "his hair lay on his head like burnished wings. . . . Something emanated from him. . . . Tenderness . . . beauty . . . one felt always shy before it. A little blinded." Her friend Rebecca West was less impressed. Bard was "not an unkindly soul," she remembered, "but the equivalent of a hairdresser, with a naive passion for fancy vests."

In any case, he talked her into marrying him in 1923. "Delirious with love, I was," she explained later, "delirious with youth and love, together, and yet in the midst of it that blackness over my heart, that certainty of apprehension: This man will let me down; I shall break my heart over this."

He did let her down, living off her salary and seducing her woman friends while accusing her of devoting too little time to him. She stuck with him for four years, nonetheless, having persuaded herself that no matter how he treated her it was her duty to nurture his creativity, to provide him with the same sort of comfort she had somehow failed to provide for her father: " . . . it is my one consciousness of worth," she wrote, "—the feeling that there is in me a source of strength renewed from some deep inner spring, some rich abundance of nature, which others who have talent to give it form can draw upon." Then, she herself strayed, spending a single drunken night with the flamboyant one-eyed reporter Floyd Gibbons. Her husband demanded a divorce. ("The double standards you know," Bard's next wife recalled. "What a man did in those days didn't matter. But for a woman of Dorothy's high moral standards—shocking!")

The divorce came through in 1927, the year she fell in love with another man of whose creative genius she was still more certain— Sinclair Lewis, then the most celebrated writer in America, already the author of *Main Street, Babbitt, Arrowsmith, Elmer Gantry.*

The marriage that began the following year, one of the most spectacularly unhappy in American literary history, may also be the most exhaustively chronicled—Mark Schorer's *Sinclair Lewis: An American Life,* Vincent Sheehan's *Dorothy and Red,* and Marion K. Sanders's *Dorothy Thompson: A Legend in Her Own Time* have all gone over the same ground, and it is not her latest biographer's fault that he adds little to their harrowing battlefield reports.

Lewis was distant and demanding, very often drunk and vituperative, and by turns proud and envious of the wife whose celebrity grew as his own creative powers waned. For her part, Thompson came to detest her husband's sodden self-pity, could not bear to sit by and watch him drink himself to death, and, despite the fact that she did not wish to lose him through failing to be a source of everlasting succor— as she was convinced she had somehow lost her father and her first husband—was unwilling either to cut back on the work that gave meaning to her life or to curtail the ceaseless travel that work demanded. "You will have to choose," Lewis told his wife once while she was away. "I can't stand this. I haven't a wife."

She hadn't much of a husband, either. Lewis disappeared for days at a time, coldly ignored their only child, Michael, was routinely rude to her friends, and to her in front of her friends: a guest remembered her struggling to continue a conversation about European affairs while Lewis crouched beneath the dinner table, bellowing that he could not stand to hear another word about "the Situation." Sex was never among his priorities—"I exist mostly above the neck," Lewis once admitted—while Dorothy Thompson flourished everywhere: "She was the most obviously sensual woman I have ever met," remembers a friend who did not first set eyes on her until she was in her late fifties, and, while she professed never to have allowed "Lust" to make her lose her head, it turned it a good many times.

"I prefer men [to women]," she once told a friend. "But better keep off this subject. Nowadays every time one opens one's mouth a psychoanalyst peers into it." But she also had affairs with women, and her lengthiest liaison during her marriage to Lewis was with Christa Winsloe, the beautiful, divorced Baroness Hatvany of Budapest, author of *The Child Manuela*, the novel about a girls' school upon which the film *Mädchen in Uniform* was based.

In her journal, Thompson worried over her feelings for the baroness with the same theatrical intensity with which she would later brood over world events:

> There's something weak in it, and even ridiculous. To love a woman is somehow ridiculous. *Mir auch passt es niche. Ich bin doch heterosexuel* ["Anyway it doesn't suit me. I *am* heterosexual"]. Even according to the very simple sexual Freudian definition which determines the matter by the location of the orgiastic sensation. Like Marguerite in *Faust*, the womb throbs—not something else, more surface. All this petting is nothing without the deep thrust to the heart of one.
>
> Well, then, how account for this which has happened again, . . .

She never did quite account for it, evidently, but she continued the relationship for more than three years, reveling in what she called "This incredible feeling of sisterhood" while assuring her husband that he needn't worry, "I ain't thata way," until her pansexual lover abandoned her—for Ezio Pinza.

H. L. Mencken's published diary includes an account of an all-too-characteristic weekend at Twin Farms, the Lewises' summer home near Woodstock, Vermont, during which a perpetually drunken Lewis deliberately drove his car into a ditch, smuggled a bottle of rye into his desk, and then, after he had downed it, could not be dissuaded from angrily demanding that his wife uncover the liquor supply she kept hidden from him. "He craves whiskey," Mencken concluded, "and when he gets the chance he drinks it straight, drink after drink. . . . He is in a sad mess, and his poor wife is a tragic figure."

Later, when Thompson was leading her interventionist crusade, Mencken's chronic misogyny would force him to alter his opinion. He clearly disliked both the fact that Thompson *had* ideas and that they differed so completely from his: "Ignorant bitch," he would then say of her. "Shrieking hurricane. . . . Poor Red Lewis, stuck with that."

That was more or less what Lewis hoped posterity would think, and he was often ungallant about the woman who, for all her faults, had been prompted in her dealings with him largely by the simple impulse to keep him alive. He caricatured her most mercilessly in one of his least memorable novels, *Gideon Planish*, as "Winifred Homeward the Talking Woman . . . an automatic, self-starting talker. Any throng of more than two persons constituted a lecture audience for her, and at the sight of them she mounted an imaginary platform, pushed aside an imaginary glass of water, and started a fervent address full of imaginary information about Conditions and Situations that lasted till the audience had sneaked out—or a little longer."

Lewis himself finally sneaked out in 1937, but Thompson refused to grant him a divorce until 1942, reluctant to admit even to herself that she had again somehow failed to provide sufficient selfless support to a man she loved, and she continued to look after both Wells Lewis, the son of Lewis's first marriage (killed in Europe in 1944), and their own son, for whose alcoholism and instability she would berate herself to the end of her life.

During the early years of their marriage it amused Lewis to say that if he were ever divorced, he would name Adolf Hitler as co-respondent. Certainly, it was Hitler who ensured that his wife would no longer be known primarily as Mrs. Sinclair Lewis.

In November 1931, she interviewed the would-be Fuehrer and was unimpressed:

> When finally I walked into Adolf Hitler's salon in the Kaiserhof Hotel, I was convinced that I was meeting the future dictator of Germany. In something less than fifty seconds I was quite sure I was not.
>
> It took just about that time to measure the startling insignificance of this man who has set the world agog.
>
> He is formless, almost faceless, a man whose countenance is a caricature, a man whose framework seems cartilaginous, without bones. He is inconsequent and voluble, ill-poised, insecure. He is the very prototype of the Little Man. . . .

The Little Man himself was enraged by her scornful dismissal of him and shortly after he came to power, following a series she wrote for the *Jewish Daily Bulletin* in New York warning of what the Nazis were planning for the Jews, he ordered her expelled from Germany.

She wept as her train pulled out of Berlin, her arms filled with roses from the reporters assembled to see her off, and she never lost her love for the Germany she had known before the Nazis commandeered it. But her expulsion made her an instant celebrity. She set forth on a thirty-city tour as soon as she got home, warning that "Germany has gone to war already and the rest of the world does not believe it," and was soon offered her own column in the *New York Herald Tribune.*

This, Thompson believed, was the real beginning of her career. After fifteen years of reporting events, she was now free to help shape them.

Her politics were always distinctively her own. Having visited the Soviet Union and lived in Nazi Germany, she had learned to distrust "collectivism" of any kind, and declared herself faithful to what she called the "aristo-democratic . . . liberalism of the Founding Fathers," of which she had her own characteristically grandiloquent definition:

To be a Liberal means to believe in human freedom. It means to believe in human beings. It means to champion that social and political order which releases the greatest amount of human energy; permits greatest liberty for individuals and groups, in planning and living their lives; cherishes freedom of speech, freedom of conscience and freedom of action, limited by only one thing: the protection of the freedom of others.

To be a Liberal did *not* mean to be a supporter of the New Deal, in which she professed to see signs of incipient fascism. It was all very well for FDR to proclaim that "this generation of Americans has a rendezvous with destiny," she wrote, but "this generation had better not make any blind dates," and she opposed the Wagner Act, the Federal Writers' Project, and Social Security (because, she said, it violated "my constitutional right to be insecure"). Roosevelt himself once dismissed her as "the oracle of Wall Street."

At the same time, she deplored what she called "roughshod capitalism," and its mindless focus on material gain at the expense of individual worth.

She had been brought up to believe that mankind's real problems—and the answers to them—were finally spiritual. "There is only one effective revolution," she said in 1937, in words that might have been spoken by her circuit-riding father, "and that is the revolution represented by the evangelical idea of conversion: that men see where they have been wrong; that a light dawns upon them; and that they change their ways."

She made it her task to help them do just that. Nazism was everything she had been taught to despise. It was "the apotheosis of collective mediocrity," she wrote, bullying, bigoted, evil, godless.

In its joyful destruction of all previous standards; in its wild affirmation of the "drive of the Will"; in its Oriental acceptance of death as the fecundator of life and of the will to death as the true heroism, it is darkly nihilistic. Placing will above reason; the ideal above reality; appealing, unremittingly, to totem and taboo, elevating tribal fetishes; subjugating and destroying the common sense that grows out of human experience; of an oceanic boundlessness, [Nazism]—that has been my constant conviction—is the enemy of whatever is sunny, reasonable, pragmatic, common-sense, freedom-loving, life-affirming, form-seeking, and conscious of tradition. . . . [I]t cannot be appeased; it can only be opposed.

Thompson opposed it more implacably than any other prominent American journalist, at a time when public opinion was overwhelmingly against increased American involvement in European affairs. Sometimes weeping with indignation at Nazi perfidy and frustration at the timorousness of the democracies in the face of it, she sat at her typewriter beneath a hand-lettered sign that read:

GOD PROTECT US

FROM

TRAITORS AT HOME

AND

TYRANTS ABROAD

and took it upon herself to stiffen the American spine. No one intimidated her. She took on Charles Lindbergh when other interventionists quailed at attacking the aviator who was still America's greatest hero, and after Father Charles Coughlin patronized her as "Dotty" on the radio, she routinely referred to him as "Chuck" in her columns. At a German-American Bund rally in Madison Square Garden, she laughed and shouted "bunk" from the front row of the press gallery so loudly that the rattled Brownshirt at the microphone ordered her ejected.

Nor was she afraid to face head-on the issue about which most of her colleagues kept timidly silent—Hitler's threat to Europe's Jews. Ignoring death threats and hate mail accusing her of being "Jewry's protégé," she campaigned for their rescue and publicly identified herself with their plight. Once, when her New York host told an anti-Semitic joke, she stormed from the table, saying, "I will not remain in the same house with traitors to the United States."

"The crisis is not a Jewish crisis," she wrote after *Kristallnacht*. "It is a human crisis."

To help meet it, she urged the Roosevelt administration to adopt a coordinated political strategy with other nations to shelter Hitler's victims.

But whether any comprehensive plan will be proposed at all by any body of responsible people; whether any really grandiose attempt will be made to deal with this problem, depends in the final show down, on whether there is a will anywhere in the world to deal with it. . . . [W]e are moved not merely by pity for the exiles, but by the need to re-affirm our own beliefs, to take a stand for them, to re-capture the ground which our indifference has lost, lest all our pre-cepts become hollow dogmas to which, at last, not even lip service will be given anywhere.

For the most part, lip service was all she got. Although her exhortations helped push Roosevelt into convening the 1938 conference at Evians-les-Bains, the Intergovernmental Committee on Refugees created by it was feeble at birth and moribund the moment the war began.

As her fame spread, Thompson grew increasingly imperious and eventually came to be seen by many—including herself in the end—as the personal embodiment of the struggle against Nazism. At the height of her fame, young John Hersey saw her as "an overpowering figure in a Wagnerian opera, a Valkyrie, deciding with careless pointing of her spear who should die on the battlefield." She did not demur when introduced over the radio as "a cross between Harriet Beecher Stowe and Nurse Edith Clavell," and when a friend told her she had "spoken like an angel," she nodded gravely in agreement, then added "and every word was true." A visit to embattled England in 1940 was something like a royal progress: she addressed the House of Commons, lectured the Admiralty on naval strategy, toured bombed-out areas of London, had tea with the Queen: "We sat for nearly three-quarters of an hour together," she told a friend when she got home, "just the two of us, the Queen and I. We talked of everything that two women would talk about—I can't, of course, repeat it."

"I am living," she wrote, "on quantities of adrenalin[e], self-distilled from the fury I feel for appeasers, for the listless, apathetic and stupid people who still exist in this sad world!" That fury, often further fueled by Dexedrine to keep her energy from flagging, infused every-thing she said or wrote or broadcast. One critic said she had "discov-ered the secret of perpetual emotion." Another suggested that *Let the Record Speak*, a collection of her columns, be retitled *Let the Record Shout* because her "prose style . . . reproduces with extraordinary fidelity the effect of having someone bellowing in your ear." The nervous sponsor of her radio program tried to soften the impact of her views with reassuring theme music—"Love Sends a Little Gift of Roses," played by Phil Spitalny and his All-Girl Orchestra.

It is difficult for us to understand just why Thompson was so often attacked for being overwrought during the prewar years. Her apocalyptic tone, with its unequivocal moral judgments, its elbows-out style and thickets of exclamation marks, seems just what those apocalyptic times demanded. For we know, as neither she nor her contemporary critics could possibly have known, that Nazism was still more radically evil than she thought, that the nightmare about to befall Europe would be worse than even she could dream. Read today, her opinions seem not so much shrill or even prescient as self-evident: *of course* there would be no "free rides to freedom" for America; democracy certainly would "not be preserved by geography or by the insistent chant, that no matter where else it is raining, it is bound to be sunny here—if not today, then tomorrow"; Hitler was indeed a "psychopath" and Munich a temporary peace, "established on betrayal" and sustainable only by "further betrayal."

And, while it may have been gracelessly self-aggrandizing to call herself Cassandra, as she did in a 1939 column that sonorously called the roll of past prophecies that had proved all too accurate, she was in fact far more often right than wrong during the prewar years, and that American opinion swung slowly but inexorably toward the hard fact that Hitler could not be beaten without American help was due in no small part to the relentlessness with which she foretold what was coming and what was at stake.

In the end her single-mindedness cost her her job. In October 1940, after helping to foster Wendell Willkie's Republican candidacy for President, she suddenly deserted him in favor of FDR, afraid that even Willkie would in the end prove unable to withstand the isolationist wing of his party. The Republican publisher of the *Herald Tribune* refused to renew her contract.

She went to work for the *New York Post* and shortly thereafter fell in love again, this time blissfully. He was Max Kopf, a strapping, amiable Czech émigré painter of mediocre portraits and religious scenes. She fretted that her celebrity would drive him away: "My experience of intimate personal things has been very bitter," she warned him. "For it is hard for a man to be constantly shoved aside by the crowd."

She needn't have worried. Calling her "my Great Woman" and "Sweet Majesty," he jettisoned his third wife to marry her in 1943. Their marriage was vigorously physical—"When I make love the house shakes," Thompson gleefully confessed to a startled friend as she approached sixty—and whenever she came home from her travels, she knew she could count upon finding the bed made, the house clean, dinner in the oven, her drink chilled and waiting. Dorothy Thompson had found herself the perfect wife.

She would need him during the years to come, as she applied her old moral indignation to new and more elusive targets, some of them a good deal closer to home. While most Americans were preoccupied with winning the war, Thompson was already exercised over the kind of peace that should follow it. In 1943, she denounced the Allied policy of unconditional surrender as a "barbarity," sure to prolong the war by discouraging decent Germans from suing for peace. She took a dim view of what she called the "Hollywoodizing" of the war, too: "If I have to read another ad in which a wounded soldier tells me that he is fighting for fluorescent lighting I will go on strike." And as the fighting ended she angrily opposed those who attributed Nazi crimes to some unique flaw in the German character.

> The Germans are in many ways *like us* [she wrote after visiting Dachau in 1945]. . . . I have heard over and over again the words, "Such things never happened before anywhere else in the world." But do people say, "Such things never happened before in *Germany*"? For that it is also true. These monstrous crimes happened in our own civilization; in a white, European civilization, Christian for centuries, among a people in no way inferior to other western peoples in the things of which our society is especially proud: science, technology, organization, production and a high standard of living. . . .
> If only one could say, and dismiss it with that, "These people are savages." They are—but they are a new and terrifying kind of savage. . . . For modern man has set himself up in his own image; or rather he has set up his own creations as the image of God. He is "functional." . . . Hitlerism is not a unique, isolated phenomenon, but a terrible example and warning. It is a symptom of universal moral crisis which even in cries for revenge and reprisal emits the animal-like cries of Nazism itself.

Flushed with victory, Americans did not wish to be told they were in any way like the Germans. Nor did they much like her criticism of the Nuremberg Trials as hypocritical. Or her sympathy with German civilians struggling to survive. Addressing a Town Hall audience in New York, Kurth writes, she warned of mass starvation if something were not done:

> "To drive the point home," she remembered, "I suggested that it would be more humane to re-open the gas chambers for German

children," and to her horror—"just at Christmastime, perhaps in commemoration of the Babe of Bethlehem"—"the response was a scattered applause. The vicarious spectacle of the famished bodies and charred bones of Nazi victims had only turned the applauders into vicarious baby-killers themselves."

In 1947, the *Post* dropped her column. "Politically," a friend remembered, "she was like a great ship left stranded on the beach after the tide had gone out."

Yet with her audience steadily shrinking, and her passionate certainty about things fully intact, she continued to set her own independent course for another eleven years. As always, her views were consistent only in the stubborn conviction with which she proclaimed them. She took out after progressive education and big-city "sophisticates," saw less to fear from Joe McCarthy than from Moscow's agents in America, and was disappointed when Harry Truman refused to declare a national day of prayer that she was convinced would keep the Soviets from expanding further into Europe.

In 1948, she persuaded herself that men had proved themselves unworthy of world leadership; only women could bring about genuine peace. "Gentlemen beware!" she began "A Woman's Manifesto" that her own editors at the *Ladies' Home Journal* found "nauseating" in its "earth-motherish" tone:

I come . . . not to beseech but to warn. I come humbly, but without fear. For I am pushed forward by the hosts of the mothers for whom you first groped in the dark, and without whom you now wander in the dark. . . . Gentlemen we would relieve you of your fears. But first you must lay aside your guns. You cannot talk to your mothers with planes and atomic bombs. You must come into the room of your mother unarmed.

When her writings were made to serve as the central document of a short-lived international women's peace group, the World Organization of Mothers of All Nations (WOMAN), Thompson was flattered, but refused to get deeply involved; she was, she said, altogether too "apocalyptic" for committee work.

She further alienated old allies by opposing creation of the State of Israel, which, she predicted, would ensure "perpetual war" in the Middle East. The "extermination of the European Jews could not be laid at the door" of the Arabs, she wrote. "I should be opposed to it if I were a Jew with the undimmed memory of the dispersion of my own people in mind. I should not want any Arab to sit beside the waters of Babylon and weep because he remembered Zion. . . ."

Thompson's prewar efforts on behalf of European Jews were quickly forgotten by many American Zionists; false rumors were spread that she was an alcoholic, on the take from Ibn Saud, a prisoner of her new husband who was secretly a Nazi. Thompson was understandably embittered—"What a world," she wrote a friend, "when even the *Jews* have gone crazy"—but she refused to give an inch, helped found the pro-Arab American Friends of the Middle East, and stubbornly served as its president for five years, mostly, she confessed later, out of anger at how her record had been distorted.

Only the death of her third husband silenced her. A month after Maxim Kopf's death in 1958, weary and grieving, she finally gave up the column she had turned out three times a week for twenty-one years. She attempted an autobiography but never got much beyond her childhood, which she remembered as uniformly sunny, suffused with the memory of her beloved father. "Certainly my life had its essential pattern fixed before I was 12," she wrote. In comparison, the years afterward seemed largely to have lost their meaning:

> Odd that I never really knew what I wanted to "do" with my life except live it, and not work from 9 to 5 in an office, at a "job." Journalism was only a means to an end—to see, to learn, if possible to *be*. The means swallowed the end and the search for freedom became a (voluntary) slavery. I find today that the "success" I had means nothing to me whatever. I wonder *exactly* what went wrong.

She died in 1961, disappointed that her tireless effort to spread something of her father's warmth and light could not finally stop the world from growing steadily more cold and dark.

A slightly shorter version of this piece appeared in *New York Review of Books* August 16, 1990

THE TOUGH GUY: THOMAS HART BENTON

WHEN THE FILM MAKER KEN BURNS ASKED ME IF I'D LIKE to write a documentary film about the painter Thomas Hart Benton, I signed on with enthusiasm for Burns's work but serious qualms about the subject he had chosen. There really is no accounting for tastes, but Benton's art has never appealed to me much—too broad, too sentimental, too self-consciously heroic. More important, from the viewpoint of a potential scriptwriter, aspects of Benton's personality struck me as both distasteful and inexplicable: short and chesty, he insisted loudly on his own "genius," felt compelled to hide his genuine sophistication behind down-home pronouncements about art calculated to appeal to the smallest of small-town minds, and appears to have been frightened all his adult life of homosexuals, who, he believed, were somehow universally bent on destroying him.

You needn't like your subject to write adequately about him, but it is very nearly impossible to do so when you are utterly baffled, as I was, by what motivates him, and I actually thought briefly of backing out. But in the course of our work we were fortunate to have the knowing counsel of Henry Adams, curator of the Nelson-Atkins Museum of Art in Kansas City, Missouri, whose solid, richly illustrated biography, *Thomas Hart Benton: An American Original,* had recently been published. Adams admires Benton and makes a strong case for the importance of his art, but he never loads the dice, and his careful research offered us fresh evidence which, while it does not excuse Benton's most puzzling excesses, helped make them understandable.

The outlines of Benton's career are familiar enough. Born in Neosho, Missouri, in 1889 and trained in Chicago and Paris, he was an avid and eclectic modernist in New York during the 1920s, then turned his back on his contemporaries and their enthusiasms in favor of all-American themes and Italian renaissance techniques and returned to the Midwest where, with Grant Wood and John-Steuart Curry, he led the regionalist movement and became for a time the best-known painter in the country. After World War II his art was eclipsed by a new, no less distinctively American school of painting—Abstract Expressionism. Benton lived and painted on until 1975, long enough to see representational art return to critical favor. "The human figure is coming back into fashion," he told a reporter not long before the end, "and what are those sons of bitches going to do now? They never learned how to draw."

Benton was as well known for his bombast as he was for his art. He liked to pretend that this public role had been thrust upon him, but in fact he reveled in it and in the headlines it engendered: "Like movie stars, baseball players and loquacious senators," he once exulted, "I was soon a figure recognizable in Pullman cars, hotel lobbies, and night clubs. I became a regular public character." "I paint sometimes," he admitted on another occasion, "to get people to criticize my work."

Along the way, Benton quarreled with just about everybody, spouting off to the newspapers, as one friend said, whenever he had a tumbler of bourbon in his hand and a reporter within earshot: Academicians and abstractionists, clergymen and Communists, critics and collectors, all felt his scattershot wrath, but he reserved his most savage attacks for homosexuals.

In 1912, he gave up a potential teaching job in Kansas City and fled to New York, in part because, he said, he had been appalled by an art institute party to which a handful of visiting vaudevillians came in drag. "Now listen," he later explained, "I had been to Paris and I'd never seen anything like that. It shocked the hell out of me. . . . That was something I was absolutely innocent about and I couldn't stay there."

In 1935, before fleeing *back* to Kansas City, he loosed a poisonous farewell blast at the Eastern art world which had failed to grant him the unmixed accolades he was certain he deserved. Homosexuals, he charged, with their "lisping [voices] and mincing ways," had fatally perverted the New York art world: "If young gentlemen, or old ones either, wish to wear women's underwear and cultivate extraordinary manners it is all right with me. But it is not all right with the art which they affect and cultivate. It is not all right, when, by ingratiation or subtle connivance, precious fairies get into positions of power and judge, buy, and exhibit American pictures on a base of nervous whim and under the sway of those overdelicate refinements of taste characteristic of their kind." Kansas City, he was now sure, would be free of their influence: "The people of the West are highly intolerant of aberration. . . . Power, in smaller places, is . . . subject to the scrutiny of strong prejudice."

But in Benton's fevered imagination, there was apparently no hiding place even there. Five years later—and at the height of his fame—he gratuitously attacked the staff of the museum where he taught as members of "the third sex . . . even in Missouri we're full of them . . . pretty boys . . . ballet dancers . . . who hate my pictures and talk against them." Not surprisingly, he got himself fired.

Even those closest to him knew something was odd about this obsession. "Tom did a lot of quite unnecessary talking about fairies taking over the art world," his sister, Mildred, remembered. "He had this violent hatred of homosexuals. There must have been some terrible urge in him that made him do it. His hatred wasn't natural."

Henry Adams traces the roots of Benton's homophobia—and of the crusty belligerence with which he often greeted even his admirers—back to the troubled Missouri boyhood his paintings made appear idyllic.

His father, Meceneas Eason Benton—"M.E." to his cronies—was a squat, combative, hard-drinking populist lawyer who billed himself as the "Little Giant of the Ozarks" and served four noisy terms in Congress. To him, artists were "mincing, bootlicking" panty-waists: "That I should even think of becoming an artist gave him a sense of outrage," his son remembered. "Such a thing was unthinkable. It would never do for a Benton to descend so low." Young Tom was meant for politics and the law, like his father and Missouri's first senator, the swaggering great-uncle after whom the boy was named.

His mother, Lizzie Wise Benton, was nineteen years younger than M.E., a pious, handsome, high-strung woman with lofty social and artistic ambitions who swooned when crossed and came both to loathe her husband's touch and to scorn his countrified constituents. In Washington, the Bentons were known as "Beauty and the Beast."

Their marriage was soon a war, with young Tom as the prize. "The hopes of both parents," Adams writes, "were centered on . . . Tom. Three other children were born to the couple . . . but for both Tom and his parents they were just afterthoughts." M.E. found he could annoy his wife satisfactorily by taking the boy hunting and fishing and speechmaking among his backwoods friends; his mother got hers back by encouraging young Tom to draw and paint, nurturing the remarkable gift for sketching he first displayed at six.

The boy came to see all the attention lavished upon him as somehow his due. "Tom was very sure that he was always right," Mildred remembered, "and he was very talkative. At meals, my father would sometimes send him away from the table because he insisted on 'What I think,' and 'What I do,' and 'What I will do,' and it was always, as my father said, 'I,' 'I,' 'I.' My father called him 'Big I.' "

Torn between his parents, he fought to establish an identity of his own. Always small and slight for his age—as an adult he would stand less than 5 foot 3 and still sometimes bought his clothes in the boys department—he was frequently forced to prove his toughness against small-town boys who ridiculed his girlish hobby and the sissified big-city clothes his mother insisted he wear: "It don't pay me no mind," he would say, no matter how hard he was hit.

Lizzie Benton would eventually win the war for her son's first loyalty. Tom came to see himself as her protector within the household; he became an artist; and, when his parents eventually separated, he sided with his mother.

But the battle left lasting scars that dangerously distorted his perception of the world. The father's contempt for art and artists as somehow unmanly remained stubbornly alive within the son, and was further reinforced when he discovered that all three of the older men who did the most to encourage him to stick with art in the face of his father's opposition had been homosexuals. (One of them made a drunken attempt to seduce him while he was still an art student—an event which Benton recounted in *The Intimate Story*, a fragmentary unpublished autobiography upon which Adams draws for the first time; the off-hand tone in which the artist describes this betrayal is belied by his compulsion to include every distasteful detail. Clearly, it deeply affected him.)

If M. E. Benton's boy were ever to feel comfortable in the world his father despised, he had to prove himself utterly different from his fellow artists, to expunge every remotely feminine trait from his own make-up, and to deride anyone else who weakly let his softer side show. "He had a great persona of a hard-drinking tough guy who happened to be an artist . . . ," his friend the novelist Dan James remembered. "His pride was to be able to drink with anybody and fight with anybody and fuck with anybody, and so forth. A real *he-man*."

There was a good deal that was desperate in that life-long performance but, newly armed by Henry Adams with the sad facts of Benton's youth, it is now possible for us to see in the leathery boastful old man who inhabits our film something of the confused little boy who struggled to find his own way between the contrasting worlds of his mismatched parents.

American Heritage July 1989

THE DARING CAMERA GIRL: MARGARET BOURKE-WHITE

M Y GRANDFATHER, CONNECTICUT-BRED, WAS A SAVER. NOTH-
ing was willingly discarded—stamps, golf clubs with shattered
handles, coins, clippings, top hats, toys from his childhood,
and, toward the end of his long life, even the aluminum trays in which
TV dinners came, scoured out, nested, and tied with twine in bundles
of a dozen.

He saved magazines, too, neat stacks of them at the top of the attic
stairs, covered with cloth to keep off the dust. Every issue of the
National Geographic was piled there. So was every copy of *Life*, and
during one early visit I gravely decided that I would read through both
runs in chronological order. I couldn't stay with the *Geographic;* the
early issues seemed drab and dispiriting, their gray glimpses of ruins
and animals and remote tribes long superseded by better views in color
published elsewhere.

But *Life* was irresistible, and as I eagerly lugged armloads of the
oversized magazines up and down the stairs while my grandparents
napped after lunch, I had the almost guilty sense that I was being
allowed to look directly into the world my father and mother had
known but I had not. *Life* would let me catch up.

The cover of the very first issue—November 23, 1936—hooked
me, four huge pylons of the Fort Peck Dam, the largest earthen structure in the world, freshly built by the PWA but photographed somehow as if they had been out there in Montana since Eden. The picture
essay inside held me, too. It was one of the first picture essays ever
published in America, I now know, a portrait of the people who had
built the dam and lived in the tiny, short-lived boomtown of New
Deal.

Cover and essay were both by Margaret Bourke-White, and as I
turned the big, crackling pages of subsequent issues, I began to see that
her pictures were often more vivid, more dramatic, more monumental

than those made by her colleagues. At her best, she had the eerie power to make her vision of people and events *become* our memory of them. Even now, I cannot hear the word "Buchenwald," for example, without recalling her frieze of numbed, staring survivors still trapped behind barbed wire; the apparently perpetual misery of South Africa continues to bring to my mind's eye her portrait of two weary young black miners, pouring sweat, photographed at the bottom of a gold mine.

Her aim, she once wrote, was to help "expand the pictorial files of history for the world to see. Just one inch in a long mile." That was for public consumption. In her diary she was more frank: "I want to become famous and I want to become wealthy," she wrote in 1927, long before she was either. She certainly became famous, almost as much for the fearlessness with which she tackled assignments then thought best left to men—industry, war, political chaos—as for the pictures she brought back.

As *Margaret Bourke-White,* a biography by Vicki Goldberg, demonstrates, her real life was every bit as vivid and theatrical as her pictures—or her legend. She went everywhere, photographed everything, slept with (almost) everybody. (How *People* would have loved her!)

Bourke-White's hyphenated credit was her own idea, combining her mother's maiden name with her father's last, and she herself seems to have been an amalgam of her curious parents' qualities. Her mother was a driven perfectionist who encouraged her daughter to inquire into things, to be fearless, but also hemmed her in with eccentric strictures: no potatoes, no funny papers, no *friends* who read funny papers. Her father, an inventor, was grim, too; he often sat for hours without speaking, absorbed in his projects. "Work, work, work," he once told Margaret in an uncharacteristically voluble moment. "That's the watchword, that's the cry . . . that's what we know to be our salvation."

Margaret revered him, and shared his fascination with the world of machinery, the "secret world," Goldberg writes, that he had shown her, "and that other girls had never seen." He died when she was seventeen, leaving her bereft but determined to live up to his watchword, "YOU CAN."

She was a shy girl, bright but humorless, who hid her shyness beneath a distinctly unconventional exterior; while in high school she announced she would be a herpetologist (her father had also been a naturalist) and attended classes with snakes wound around her arms. It is perhaps not surprising that she was respected rather than liked by her classmates. (Later, working for *Life*, she walked a matched pair of Afghans for a time, kept two full-grown alligators in her studio, and had her tailor run up camera hoods in colors to match her designer outfits.)

She began making photographs in college, first in the cottony style of the Pictorialists, then, truer to her late father's vision, seeking out a stark, abstract beauty in the gears and smokestacks and open-hearth mills of the Machine Age. (For the first issue of *Fortune*, she managed to find handsome patterns even in the heads of hogs moving along a packing-house assembly line.)

Always the picture, the work, was everything. For *Life*, she dangled from helicopters, faced down mobs, survived a submarine sinking. When Nazi bombs blew in all the windows in the American Embassy in Moscow, burying her beneath a mound of broken glass, she gingerly rose and ran out for her equipment, after leaving signs on all the highest heaps of shards saying "PLEASE DON'T SWEEP UP GLASS TILL I GET BACK WITH CAMERA."

Once, when she was faced with a complicated portrait sitting, the journalist Ralph Graves volunteered to change each of several flash bulbs for her after every shot. Twice, totally focused on her subject, she forgot Graves was at work, firing off the flash and burning his hand. She apologized. But when her subject assumed an interesting new pose, she did it again. The flash seared Graves's hand a third time. "She turned to look at me," he remembered, "with an extraordinary expression: profound regret that she had done it to me again—coupled with absolute triumph that she had got the perfect picture at such little cost."

Others paid the cost of her pictures quite often. Her assistants got little thanks; the vital charm with which she persuaded her subjects to cooperate with her—to "*obey*" her, she once said—was rarely wasted on them.

She was a combination, as Goldberg writes, of "concrete and tulle," utterly unblinking about power and how a handsome young woman might get it in a man's world. Although she became a heroine to young women—there was even a comic book about her exploits, meant to inspire little girls—for her, Sisterhood was powerless. Women were unimportant if you wanted to get ahead.

Men were different. Her looks and charm helped her get assignments—though her biographer concludes that a quid pro quo was rarely if ever exacted. Bourke-White's romances were conducted on her own time. She was striking rather than beautiful, more energetic and intense than amusing, but her impact on men was devastating.

When the young Dwight MacDonald was assigned to work with her and went to meet her at Grand Central Station, he dropped his suitcase when he first saw her, spilling all the clothing it contained across the floor of the waiting room. Emperor Haile Selassie of Ethiopia once found himself eagerly carrying her camera bags.

When starting out, she deliberately wore low-cut blouses, then leaned pliantly across prospective clients' desks to point out the pictures in her portfolio. "What a lucky lady I am," she wrote in her diary in those days. "I can do anything I want with these men, and through it all I like them."

That seems clear, although whether it was the men themselves or the power she so effortlessly wielded over them that meant the most to her is difficult to tell. She married and left two men (the second was the novelist Erskine Caldwell), each of them like her father in his moody remoteness, neither of them able to accept the fact that her work came first. And she had affairs, long and short, with a truly startling number of others—so many, according to her biographer, that when she refused publicly to kiss one long-time lover who had taken her to the London airport, he seriously "wondered if she was fearful of narrowing her options on the transatlantic flight."

She was certainly not the only roving photographer to whom seduction seemed a part of the job description. "Property of Robert Capa, great war correspondent and lover," was scrawled inside the helmet that photographer wore on the Italian front during World War II, and he worked hard at making good on both pledges. So did a good many of his imitators.

The difference, of course, was that Bourke-White was a woman who excelled in a field dominated by men, a fact which fascinated the press—long before she worked for *Life* she was being written up under headlines such as "THIS DARING CAMERA GIRL SCALES SKYSCRAPERS FOR ART"—as much as it later infuriated her male colleagues.

With an artist's lusty ego, she sometimes seemed to fancy that the world itself was intent upon posing for her. In 1943, she rode along on a bombing run over Tunisia. When anti-aircraft fire began to explode around the plane, the pilot took evasive action. Bourke-White assumed the bomber's plunging, twisting flight had been arranged for her benefit, and as bursts of flak came closer, the crew listened to her exult over the intercom: "Oh, that's just what I want, that's a beautiful angle! Roll me over quick. Hold me just like this. Hold me this way so I can shoot straight down!"

Her early work had romanticized the machinery her father had taught her to love and, although Depression and war had encouraged her to see human beings as more than props added for scale, the composition continued to come before anything else. Lee Eitington, a former *Life* reporter, remembered working with her to capture one of her most celebrated pictures, a long, silhouetted line of Sikh refugees fleeing Pakistan on foot at the time of India's partition in 1947: " 'We were there for hours. . . . She found a group she liked. She told them to go back again and again and again. They were too frightened to say no. They were *dying.* " Eitington protested. Bourke-White told her to give them some money. "That wouldn't help them. These people just needed to move on. That's why she was such a good photographer. People were dying under her feet. . . . She thought herself a great humanitarian, but when it came to individual people. . . ."

"Work is a religion to me, the only religion I have," she once wrote, echoing her father. "Work is something you can count on, a trusted, life-long friend who never deserts you."

But it did desert her at the end and there was little to take its place. She fought gallantly against Parkinson's disease for seventeen years, unable for most of that time even to grip her camera. It was a lonely struggle; one man, who saw her often over a three-month period while writing a television script about her, recalled seeing no other visitor in all that time.

Finally, only her bright, inquiring eyes remained mobile inside her rigid body and she died in August of 1971. A little over a year later, so did the weekly *Life*.

American Heritage October 1986

THE SUFFERER: EDWARD R. MURROW

IN CHICAGO ONE LONG-AGO SUNDAY AFTERNOON, I SAT WITH MY parents in front of the family's brand-new television set, with its small, round-cornered screen, and watched the first of a new kind of program on CBS. It was called "See It Now," and while most of what was shown during that first half-hour has faded from my memory, two things remain vivid. At one point, a pair of monitors simultaneously showed New York Harbor and the Golden Gate—both a little wobbly, as I remember, and in black and white, of course, but each unquestionably *live*. (No technological achievement since—not even the sight of the first Moonwalkers, eighteen years later—has ever seemed to me so miraculous.)

Beyond that, there was the extraordinary presence of the baleful host, squinting into the camera through a writhing, blue-gray scrim of cigarette smoke, his voice, low, authoritative, a little weary, conveying the sense that there was very little in the world he hadn't seen or heard or thought before.

From that moment, whatever Edward R. Murrow told me, I believed, and whenever he was scheduled to appear, I watched, wondering sometimes just what sort of man he really was.

Murrow: His Life and Times, the mammoth biography by A. M. Sperber, has trouble answering that question. To be fair, another biography, *Prime Time: The Life of Edward R. Murrow,* written by one of Murrow's former CBS colleagues, Alexander Kendrick, got no closer to the man behind that extraordinary voice. And part of the problem lies with Murrow himself. In her index, under "Murrow, Edward R., personality and character of," Sperber lists "charm," followed by "as child," "conscience," "death wish, self-destructiveness," "guilt and sense of sin," "loneliness and isolation," "as maverick," "need for security," "pessimism and fatalism," "reticence, guardedness, private-ness," "self-distrust," "shyness," and "temper." Not an easy man to get to know.

Still, Murrow's tale is worth your time; I can't imagine anyone who remembers him and the events through which he and we lived together not being moved by it.

Murrow had a reporter's healthy cynicism about politicians and political rhetoric, but a stubborn naïveté about what might be done for the public good through radio and television. He was "a sufferer," his wife remembered, and his late colleague Charles Collingwood once suggested that what he suffered from most was his belief "that we live in a perfectible world."

Murrow was born on a North Carolina dirt farm in 1908, the descendant of Dissenters—southern Quakers who opposed slavery and supported the Union. He was a Big Man on Campus at the University of Washington (where he swapped "Edward" for the hated "Egbert"), and became a bigger one, as president of the National Student Federa-tion, assistant director of the Institute for International Education, and as European director for CBS—all before the age of thirty.

His reporting of the rise of Hitler and the early days of the Euro-pean war made him famous—and helped make broadcast journalism more than a novelty. Murrow was a tireless and brave reporter; Ger-man bombs blasted three CBS offices out from under him in London, and direct orders from New York could not keep him from going along on bombing runs over Germany. (A friend once asked him why he ran such risks: "I have a peasant's mind," he said. "I can't write about anything I haven't seen.") He assembled an extraordinary re-porting team—William L. Shirer, Collingwood, Eric Sevareid, Larry Le Seur, Cecil Brown—who were proud to be known as "Murrow's boys."

But above all, he had an extraordinary ability to make distant listeners see what he was seeing. Here, he looks across London from a rooftop while the bombs fall:

I think probably in a minute we shall have the sound of guns in the immediate vicinity. The lights are swinging over in this general direction now. You'll hear two explosions. There they are! That was the explosion overhead, not the guns themselves. I should think in a few minutes there may be a bit of shrapnel around here. . . . Earlier this evening we could hear occasional—again, those were explosions overhead. Earlier this evening, we heard a number of bombs go

sliding and slithering across, to fall several blocks away. . . . Now you'll hear two bursts a little nearer in a moment. There they are!
    That hard stony sound.

"You burned the city of London in our houses and we felt the flames . . . ," Archibald MacLeish told Murrow in 1941. "You laid the dead of London at our doors and we knew that the dead were our dead . . . were mankind's dead . . . without rhetoric, without dramatics, without more emotion than needed be . . . you have destroyed the superstition that what is done beyond 3,000 miles of water is not really done at all."

Murrow's time in London was only the start of his broadcasting career; working in television during the two decades that followed the war, he set standards of eloquence, concision, and probity to which young reporters still aspire. But the London years clearly marked the high point of his life. Most of what came after disappointed him, in large part because the institutions for which he worked were never so interested in reporting hard facts as he was.

His most memorable TV documentaries—the defense of Lieutenant Milo Radulovich, unjustly dismissed from the U.S. Air Force as a security risk; the devastating portrait of Joseph McCarthy; pioneering programs on the plight of migrant workers and the fatal link between cancer and smoking—reaped armfuls of awards for him and for his network. But the criticism they drew also made the executives of that network nervous, and its sponsors wary: toward the end of his time with CBS, he and his partner, Fred W. Friendly, were paying out of their own pockets to advertise "See It Now" in the *New York Times*.

Sperber's book offers a good deal of evidence for what the CBS staffers who formed the clandestine "Murrow is not God club" always knew—that he had his share of quirks. He was tortured by black depressions; had a series of affairs (with Marlene Dietrich, among others); and took himself so seriously that as a young man he pretended to be two years older than he was, and consciously tried to spread wrinkles across his unmarked brow because, he said, he wanted people to know that he thought a lot. He was uncomfortable with fame, and never overcame the mike fright that made his legs shake and sweat stream down his neck; the unfiltered Camels on which he pulled with such ferocity—up to ninety a day—helped steady him.

He also himself helped further to blur the already shadowy line between news and entertainment. He is best remembered for "See It Now," but he was also the host of a far more popular weekly program called "Person to Person," in which he chatted with celebrities—from Marilyn Monroe to Norman Vincent Peale, Sherman Adams to Gypsy Rose Lee—while being shown through their homes. The closest current parallel is, well . . . "Life Styles of the Rich and Famous." (Murrow's efforts to be informal were painful to watch. Herbert Bayard Swope wrote him that he thought there was something odd about all these apparent strangers calling him "Ed." "Mr. Murrow" would be more fitting. Swope was right.)

It was a muddled confrontation with his boss, Frank Stanton, over programming practices on *this* show, not one of his uncompromising documentaries, that sparked his final break with the network. (Stanton, anxious to assure viewers in the wake of the quiz show scandals that CBS would sin no more, had promised henceforth to begin each "Person to Person" interview with a solemn disclaimer saying the program had been rehearsed. Murrow felt his integrity had been called into question.)

He then accepted John Kennedy's offer to serve as director of the United States Information Agency, hoping to bring a new boldness and honesty to its overseas broadcasts—and made a whole new set of superiors nervous. *The March*, a USIA film on the 1963 Civil Rights March on Washington, for example, came under heavy fire from within the administration for lacking "balance." "I am unrepentant . . . ," Murrow told an aide. "It is a good film, and anyone who believes that every individual film must present a 'balanced' picture, knows nothing about either balance or pictures." Murrow also found Robert Kennedy's penchant for gumshoeing tiresome; according to the author, Murrow once found a stranger going through his desk at the USIA. He slammed the drawer shut on the man's hand, trapping him, then let him go, and told him—among other, more colorful things—to "tell Bobby if he wants to know something, he can ASK JACK!")

Cancer, the inevitable product of all those hundreds of thousands of cigarettes, drove Murrow to retire in January 1964, and spread swiftly from his lungs to his brain. He lived just over a year. A friend remembered calling upon him at home toward the end; he was wasted, unable to stand, wearing a red stocking cap to hide the signs of surgery and radiation, but he watched the TV screen with something of his old intensity as an administration spokesman offered the official version of prospects for victory in Vietnam. "They're out of their *minds*," he said, covering his face with his bony hands. "They're lying. How can he *say that?*"

At the end of his last official speech as director of the USIA, defending the principle of truth-telling even when discussing our worst flaws, he reminded his listeners that appearances finally didn't count for much. "At the end of the day," he said, "it's what we *are* that matters."

American Heritage February 1987

COMBATANTS

★

STANDING BY EACH OTHER, ALWAYS: U. S. GRANT AND WILLIAM TECUMSEH SHERMAN

O N AUGUST 8, 1885, THE CROWDS THAT LINED THE ROUTE OF Ulysses S. Grant's funeral procession from New York City Hall to the vault at 122nd Street and Riverside Drive numbered well over a million. "Broadway moved like a river into which many tributaries poured," a spectator wrote. "There was one living mass choking the thoroughfare from where the dead lay in state to the grim gates at Riverside opened to receive him."

Somewhere in that living mass stood a slender, alarmingly pale young man wearing smoked glasses to disguise himself. His name was Ferdinand Ward and, although he had been the late President's business partner, he had no right to be there, had bribed the warden, in fact, to let him out of the Ludlow Street Jail just long enough to see the canopied hearse pass by before being locked up again to await the trial that eventually sent him to Sing Sing for grand larceny.

Ferdinand Ward was also my great-grandfather and, I'm afraid, had little if any redeeming social value (at least I've discovered none while beginning research for a book about him). Nor was a penny of the millions he was convicted of misappropriating ever passed on to any of his embarrassed descendants.

But he did indirectly leave one extraordinary legacy to the country as a whole—*Personal Memoirs of U.S. Grant*. Without my nefarious ancestor, Grant would never have written his magnificent account of the Civil War; it was only the President's last-ditch desire to return his bankrupt family to solvency that persuaded him to undertake the writing of it, despite the throat cancer that killed him just a few days after he had finished the manuscript.

"I am reading Grant's book with a delight I fail to find in novels," William Dean Howells told its publisher, Mark Twain, in 1886. "I think he is one of the most natural—that is *best*—writers I ever read. The book merits its enormous success, simply as literature." In our own time, John Keegan has called it "Perhaps the most revelatory autobiography of high command to exist in any language." Certainly, it is revelatory of its author. Grant wrote his memoirs precisely as he fought the war: with complete clarity and unrelenting drive and without a hint of boast or bluster.

That same year, D. Appleton & Co. got out a new edition of *The Memoirs of William Tecumseh Sherman.* The first edition, published in 1875, had sparked criticism from southerners with raw memories of what Sherman had done to them and from Northern officers who felt themselves wronged by what he said about them. Sherman corrected a handful of factual errors, added appendices of letters from his critics, and a new chapter on his prewar experiences in California, but he apologized for nothing he had written. He was a "witness," not a historian, he explained, and

> [in] this free country every man is at perfect liberty to publish his own thoughts and impressions, and any witness who may differ from me should publish his own version of facts in the truthful narration of which he is interested. I am publishing my own memoirs, not *theirs,* and we all know that no three honest witnesses of a simple brawl can agree on all the details. How much more likely will be the difference in a great battle covering a vast space of broken ground, when each division, brigade, regiment, even company, naturally and honestly believes that it is the focus of the whole affair! Each of them won the battle. None ever lost. That was the fate of the old man who unhappily commanded.

Sherman himself commanded happily. "To be at the head of a strong column of troops, in the execution of some task that requires brain," he wrote, "is the highest pleasure of war—a grim one and terrible, but one which leaves on the mind and memory the strongest mark; to detect the weak point of an enemy's line; to break through with vehemence and thus lead to victory; or to discover some key-point and hold it with tenacity; or to do some other distinct act which is afterward recognized as the real cause of success. These all become matters that are never forgotten."

Read together, the memoirs of Grant and Sherman provide both an unrivaled account of the war they won and an indelible record of one of the most providential friendships in our history.

"We were as brothers," Sherman wrote. "I the older man in years, he the higher in rank." They were opposites in some ways: Grant was short, slouchy, phlegmatic; Sherman tall, rail-thin, and voluble—"boiling over with ideas while discussing every subject and pronouncing on all," one of his soldiers recalled. But both were Ohio boys, undistinguished in civilian life, unmoved by the thought of overthrowing slavery, utterly realistic about what had to be done to win a war and free of the vainglory and backbiting that undid so many Union commanders.

And each was in the other's debt. "He stood by me when I was crazy," Sherman once said of Grant, "and I stood by him when he was drunk; and now we stand by each other always." Grant's memoirs never touch upon alcohol or the rumors about his fondness for it. (Mark Twain privately lamented that he'd never told the General, "Put the drunkenness in the memoirs—and the repentance and reform. Trust the people.") Sherman dutifully recalls his fury at the newspaper stories declaring him "crazy, insane and mad" that nearly destroyed his career in 1861, although he is less than forthcoming about the genuine nervous collapse that lay behind them.

In any case, each man bolstered the other's confidence. Sherman first won Grant's gratitude by the selflessness with which he supported him during his siege of Fort Donelson: "At the time he was my senior in rank," Grant remembered, "and there was no authority of law to assign a junior to command a senior of the same grade. But every boat that came up with supplies or reinforcements brought a note of encouragement from Sherman, asking me to call upon him for any assistance he could render and saying that if he could be of service at the front I might send for him and he would waive rank." Grant's victory at Donelson, in turn, provided Sherman with hope of an eventual Union triumph, what he called "the ray of light which I have followed ever since."

The two men stood together at Shiloh and in the aftermath, when Grant resolved to leave the army after Henry Halleck relegated him to the empty post of second-in-command, it was Sherman who talked him out of it: ". . . you could not be quiet at home for a week when the armies were moving. . . ."

No one moved armies more relentlessly than Grant, but even Sherman quailed when, after repeated failures in the Vicksburg campaign, he resolved to plunge into enemy territory, cutting himself off from his base of supply and risking attack from hostile forces whose size he could not estimate. Sherman privately urged retreat. Grant gently overruled him: "The problem for us was to move forward to a decisive victory," Grant recalled. "No progress was being made in any other field, and we had to go on." They did go on, Sherman kept his qualms to himself and, when the rebel stronghold fell, made sure everyone knew that "Grant is entitled to every bit of the credit for the campaign; I opposed it."

". . . [T]he chief characteristic in your nature is the simple faith in success you have always manifested," Sherman told Grant, "which I can liken to nothing else than the faith a Christian has in his Saviour . . . I knew wherever I was that you thought of me, and if I got into a tight place you would come—if alive."

Lincoln brought Grant east to take overall command, saying, "[he] is my man and I am his the rest of the war." Together, he and Sherman took on the task of completing the Confederacy's dismemberment. This time, it was Grant's turn to back his lieutenant's plan for a march from Atlanta to the sea, a plan so daring that even Lincoln was timorous for a time. "I never had a doubt of the result," Grant told Sherman when he reached Savannah, and he ended his letter: "I subscribe myself, more than ever, if possible, your friend, U.S. Grant."

In offering his thanks for the same victory, Lincoln went on to ask "But what next?", then cheerfully answered his own question: "I suppose it will be safe if I leave General Grant and yourself to decide."

Sherman's account of the war is less successful than Grant's: he stops and starts, offers too much detail about some things and too little about others, and too often reins in his distinctive prose. But the authentic Sherman—implacable, agitated, at his most eloquent when most angry—is still present in the letters and dispatches with which he frequently interrupts his narrative. His response to a letter from the city fathers of Atlanta who had dared protest his order that the city's inhabitants leave their homes is characteristic—and expressed Grant's views as well as his own:

> You might as well appeal against the thunder-storm as against these terrible hardships of war. They are inevitable, and the only way the people of Atlanta can hope once more to live in peace and quiet at home, is to stop the war, which can only be done by admitting that it began in error and is perpetuated in pride. . . . I want peace, and believe it can only be reached through union and war, and I will ever conduct war with a view to perfect and early success.

In the end, success came later—and at far greater cost—than either Sherman or Grant would have liked. But without Grant's belief in the inevitability of that success, without Sherman's belief in

Grant—and without Lincoln's self-confident willingness to let these two friends fight the war as they saw fit—it might never have come at all.

American Heritage November 1990

THE PATRIOT: ROBERT E. LEE

A NORTHERN GIRL, THE STORY GOES, WATCHED ROBERT E. LEE ride past her house on his way to Gettysburg. "Oh," she said, "I wish he were ours!"

Time's alchemy has *made* him ours, of course, all of ours; but that always baffling process seems especially mysterious in his case. For Lee was, after all, the most effective commander in the bloodiest war ever waged against the United States. More than 500,000 Americans died in the conflict his skilled generalship helped prolong; when the fighting stopped, 16,000 boys lay beneath the sloping lawns of his confiscated mansion at Arlington. Yet Lee has become an American hero, not just a Southern one. No other Confederate leader has been so transformed.

The secret lies, at least in part, in the dramatic peacemaking role he played during the five brief, busy years left to him after Appomattox. Others have looked for it there, notably Marshall Fishwick, whose *Lee After the War* was published nearly thirty years ago, and Thomas L. Connelly, whose more recent *The Marble Man* shrewdly traced the making of the Lee legend. Now, in *Lee: The Last Years,* the novelist and historian Charles Bracelen Flood offers a crisp new account of the end of Lee's life, some of it based on previously unpublished family papers.

Just twenty weeks after the Confederacy's collapse, weary, jobless, ailing, and under indictment for treason (he was never tried), Lee accepted the presidency of Washington College at Lexington, Virginia, an institution so small and threadbare that its trustees had at their disposal only $50, borrowed from a tobacco farmer. Lee never repented of his decision to follow Virginia out of the Union; he simply moved beyond it. "True patriotism," he explained, "sometimes requires of men to act exactly contrary, at one period, to that which it does at another." But the motive that compels them "the desire to do right"—remains the same.

That motive now compelled him to adopt a new cause: he would set the young an "example of submission to authority." Having lost the war, he sought to show his worshipful students (many of whom had fought under his banner), and the South at large, how to triumph in peace. He swore renewed allegiance to the United States, and by that act alone brought tens of thousands of his former soldiers peaceably back into the Union and won for himself widespread admiration in the North. Henry Ward Beecher raised funds for him; Northern industrialists including Cyrus McCormick made generous gifts to the college. He revamped the classics-steeped curriculum, once thought to be the only proper training for a Southern gentleman, to include subjects such as engineering and chemistry, which he believed were vital if the South was to be properly rebuilt. Taken to see a woman whose prized tree had had its branches shot away by Federal artillery, he urged her, "Cut it down, my dear Madam, and forget it." Attempts to embroil him in politics failed, though the *New York Herald* endorsed him for President on the grounds that he was a much better man in every way than U.S. Grant.

Lee was the object of constant idolatry that would have warped a lesser man. Vacations spent traveling in hopes of easing the heart ailment that eventually killed him in 1870 became triumphal progresses, with delirious crowds at every crossroads. Lean veterans of his campaigns knocked at his door, begging for just one more glimpse of their old commander. Women adored him. "The man who stood before us, was the embodiment of a Lost Cause, was the realized King Arthur," wrote one, who first saw him poised on the staircase of a roadside inn. "The soul that looked out of his eyes was as honest and fearless as when it first looked on life. One saw the character, as clear as crystal, without complications or seals, and the heart, as tender as that of ideal womanhood."

Lee delighted in such attention. A Lexington man watched him chat with two blushing girls while his war horse, Traveller, pranced and pawed beneath him—a spirited effect the old general was secretly producing with a "dexterous and coquettish use of the spur."

Each afternoon at four, Lee dressed in his old gray uniform—its insignia carefully cut off—and rode off into the surrounding hills. Even then he was rarely alone. Riding through deep woods one day, he met a mounted farmer. Lee noded pleasantly. The stranger identified himself as one of the general's old soldiers and said, "General Lee, I am powerful glad to see you, and I feel like cheering you." Lee said he saw no point in that; they were alone together, after all. The farmer replied that he couldn't help himself and, waving his hat, shouted, "Hurrah for General Lee!" again and again until his old commander trotted out of sight.

Everyone who ever saw Lee appears to have rushed right home to jot down his impressions. From all these stories he emerges as unswervingly patient, kind, and calm. He neither drank nor swore, prayed often and long, was inexhaustibly loving with his embittered invalid wife and revered by his three daughters, who took turns rubbing his hand while he dozed. (None of his daughters ever married: "To me he seems a Hero," one wrote, "all other men small in comparison.") Wealth did not tempt him; an insurance agent who offered him an enormous sum just for the use of his name was briskly turned away: "I cannot consent to receive pay for services I do not render." Lee never forgot Grant's generosity toward his men at Appomattox, and once dressed down a professor who did: "Sir," he said, "if you ever speak again disrespectfully of General Grant in my presence, either you or I will sever his connection with this university." His views on race were surprisingly enlightened for a man of his time and place: He never owned a slave himself and freed the last of those who had belonged to his wife's family during the war. While he did not believe in extending the franchise to blacks, he invariably treated them with courtesy, and once, when a freedman stunned the local congregation by seeking communion alongside whites, Lee quietly knelt near him at the chancel rail.

Lee was a fierce and able warrior, but he also offered Americans a larger lesson: that one can lose, as well as win, with grace. He seems finally to have come to regret his soldierly past. "The greatest mistake of my life was taking a military education," he told a member of the faculty, and whenever his students and those of the neighboring Virginia Military Institute marched together to a drum's beat, he made a point of marching out of step.

New York Times Book Review November 22, 1981

LOOKING BACK WITHOUT ANGER: EDWARD PORTER ALEXANDER

T HE PUBLICATION OF *Fighting for the Confederacy: The Personal Recollections of General Edward Porter Alexander* is in at least two ways an astonishment. First, it is not a reprint but a brand-new book by one of the South's ablest soldiers, 124 years after Appomattox. Porter Alexander of Georgia, the best artillerist in Robert E. Lee's Army of Northern Virginia, saw as much of the war as any man on either side, and was central to the action at First Manassas, the Seven Days, Fredericksburg, Sharpsburg, Chancellorsville, Spotsylvania, Cold Harbor, and during the last retreat from Petersburg.

More surprising still is the compelling, intensely personal style in which it is written: Alexander's book is relaxed and engaging, lacking utterly in the self-importance which mars the memoirs of a good many soldiers with weaker claims to distinction than his, and refreshingly candid about his own frailties and those of some of the Confederacy's most revered commanders.

In 1907, the old soldier published *Military Memoirs of a Confederate.* It is sober, magisterial history—Douglas Southall Freeman believed it "the best critique of the operations of the Army of Northern Virginia"—from which most traces of Alexander's personal experience were carefully expunged in the interests of objectivity. The newly published book was actually written first, at the urging of his wife and daughter, and was meant only for his descendants. The tattered manuscript, divided among ledger books and loose pages, was long thought simply to be the first draft of his published history, and the historian Gary W. Gallagher has done a genuine service in reassembling and editing it for publication.

Porter Alexander was just thirteen in 1848, when he heard from an old man who liked to take him fishing that some Southern hotheads were already talking of secession: ". . . I remember well the spot in the road where we were," he wrote, "& the pang which the idea sent through me, & my thinking that I would rather lose my gun—my dearest possession on earth—than see it happen." When it did happen, he was already the co-inventor of the wig-wag system of semaphore and among the most promising young West Pointers in the Federal Army, stationed with his new bride in Washington Territory. A friend, Lieutenant James L. McPherson, urged him to stay put: the Southern cause was hopeless, he assured him, and by staying on the Pacific coast he would "not be required to go into the field against your own people."

Alexander still had no wish for his native state to leave the Union, but "[a]s soon as the *right* to secede was denied by the North," he explained, "I strongly approved of its assertion & maintenance by force if necessary. . . . The Confederacy was raising an army. The only place for me was in that army."

"What I want," he told his old comrades when asking them to send him their recollections for a history of James Longstreet's corps he never quite got around to writing, "is not the general facts that everybody knows but the *details.* " It is his own remarkable memory for such details that enables us vividly to experience something of what he experienced: the mud daubing that drifted down to spoil his dinner of "sliced up meat and dished up vegetables" after a Federal shell tore through Wilmer McLean's log kitchen near Bull Run; the "loud spat" of a shell fragment hitting his horse's neck in the Wilderness; the savor of the "two thick camp biscuits, each with a slice of fat bacon in it," on which he gnawed while waiting for the surgeon after a bullet smashed his shoulder in front of Petersburg.

Alexander's memory enabled him to summon up whole scenes, unabridged and peopled by soldiers who *sound* like soldiers. After First Manassas, for example, he came upon a sergeant major dragging a frightened little man in civilian dress out of the woods and marching him before Colonel Ellerbe Cash of South Carolina. As Alexander rode up, the colonel "had drawn his revolver & was trying to shoot the little citizen who was dodging behind the big sergeant major as Cash turned his horse about & tried to get at him, poking at him with the pistol & swearing with a fluency which would have been creditable to a wagonmaster. 'You infernal s. of a b.! You came to see the fun did you? God damn your dirty soul I'll show you,' & he spurred his horse to get around the sergeant major."

Alexander asked Cash what was going on.

" 'He's a member of Congress, God damn him,' said the colonel. 'Came out here to see the fun! Came to see us whipped & killed! God damn him, if it wasn't for such as he there would be no war. They've made it & then come to gloat over it! God damn him, I'll show him.' "

The colonel's intended target, Congressman Alfred Ely of New York, had failed to escape with his sight-seeing companions after their carriage overturned during the Federal rout. Alexander told Cash to hold his fire; unarmed prisoners were not to be harmed. The colonel wheeled his horse and ordered the sergeant major back into the thicket: ". . . go & hunt the woods for Senator [Lafayette Sabine] Foster [of Vermont]. He is hiding here somewhere. Go & find him & God damn you, if you bring him in alive, I'll cut your ears off." Luckily for Senator Foster, he was not in the neighborhood, and Alexander saw that Congressman Ely was shipped intact to Richmond.

He made no bones about having taken pride in his work: he remembered Fredericksburg, Chancellorsville, and Gettysburg best, he wrote, for the "rare and beautiful opportunities" they afforded him for blowing apart the advancing enemy.

And he remained matter-of-fact about the horrors he witnessed: "I saw in a pile three of [the] Hampton Legion killed by a solid shot. One of them had his arms raised & extended exactly as if he were aiming his musket. The shot had passed through his body from side to side just below his arm pits. Evidently he was aiming when struck, for had his arms been down they would have been cut off. It would seem as if the shot not only killed but stiffened at least the muscles of the arms in the positions in which they were."

But many of his most eloquent memories had little to do with combat. More than three decades after Chancellorsville, he still recalled a tin cup filled with coffee, brought to him there by one Captain Parker: ". . . to this day, I never drink a cup of real, good coffee, but the picture comes up of the good captain approaching in the fire light with the cup in his hand, & I hear his gentle voice & he sits down by me under a tree & while I am cooling & drinking it he explains in his short quick sentences where the coffee came from, & exhibits one or more little buckskin bags full of ground coffee & sugar already mixed . . . all taken from the bodies of the dead, left by the enemy in his retreat."

Alexander's memoir is refreshingly free of the cloying sanctity with which his contemporaries often sought to cloak their shortcomings:

It is customary to say that "Providence did not intend that we should win," but I do not subscribe in the least to that doctrine. Providence did not care a row of pins about it. If it did it was a very unintelligent

Providence not to bring the business to a close—the close it wanted—
in less than four years of most terrible & bloody war.

. . . I think it was a serious incubus upon us that during the whole
war our president & many of our generals really & actually believed
that there *was* this mysterious Providence always hovering over the
field & ready to interfere on one side or the other, & that prayers &
piety might win its favor from day to day. One of our good old
preachers once voiced it in a prayer. . . . "Oh Lord! Come down we
pray thee & *take a proper view of the situation,* & give us the victory
over our enemies." But it was a weakness to imagine that a victory
could ever come in even the slightest degree from anything except
our own exertions.

Not even the exertions of Robert E. Lee were immune from
Alexander's dispassionate eye. An ardent gunner, who believed it "always better to lie down & shoot at them coming a half mile than to
have them lie down & shoot at you," he sometimes found Lee's celebrated audacity trying. Among the errors to which his commander's
excessive boldness drove him, he believed, were his decision to stand
and fight at Sharpsburg (where only George McClellan's timorousness saved him from disaster) and "in taking the aggressive at all" at
Gettysburg. The intensely human commander whom Alexander describes in action is both more interesting and less uniformly virtuous
than the Lee of legend: flinty in the face of human suffering, he
cannot bear to see a mule mishandled, does not easily admit even
trivial errors, and exhibits during moments of great tension an angry
jerking of the head that the wary members of his staff called "snap-
ping at his ear."

Alexander never regretted having cast his lot with the doomed
Confederacy, but he is not notably sentimental even about that. As the
end approached, he told his wife that rather than submit to the imprisonment he was sure would follow a Confederate surrender, he planned
to flee to Brazil, then about to go to war with Paraguay, win a commission in its army, and then send for her and the children: ". . . judging
from the map," he added, ". . . for once I would be on the winning
side." (He surely would have been. In the war that followed, Brazilian
forces were joined by those of Uruguay and Argentina, and more than
half of Paraguay's population died.)

Lee thought Alexander's hiring himself out to a foreign power a
poor idea. Brazilian diplomats were not encouraging. In the end,
Alexander returned to his wife without telling her he was coming:

"But although she thought me far on my road to Brazil, she knew the rush of my feet up the stairs the moment she heard it, & as I opened the door she was in the middle of the room advancing to meet me."

American Heritage March 1990

THE (SLIGHTLY) TARNISHED ANGEL
OF THE BATTLEFIELD: CLARA BARTON

EARLY BIOGRAPHIES OF THE GREAT, INDEPENDENT WOMEN OF the nineteenth and early twentieth centuries were most often written by admirers so ardent that their pages of unrelenting praise now defy reading. "Sensitive by nature, refined by culture," wrote the anonymous author of one biographical sketch of Clara Barton in 1876, "she has nevertheless taken unaccustomed fields of labor, walked untrodden paths with bleeding feet and opened pioneer doors with bruised fingers, not for her own aggrandisement but for that of her sex and humanity."

True enough. There have been few more impressive, more courageous, more resourceful women in the history of any country: Barton richly deserved the nickname "Angel of the Battlefield" given to her by the Union men for whom she cared during the Civil War. She created the American Red Cross and ran it for twenty-two years, helped persuade the United States to abandon its instinctive distrust of international treaties and sign the Geneva Convention, brought help to the helpless from Antietam to Armenia, and ceaselessly advocated equality for women all the while.

But it is a little startling to learn that the author of that fulsome tribute to Clara Barton, prepared for inclusion in a woman's encyclopedia edited by Susan B. Anthony, was Clara Barton herself, writing under the guise of "an old friend." This and much more is revealed in Elizabeth Brown Pryor's *Clara Barton: Professional Angel.* Based largely on the extraordinary thirty-five volume diary her subject kept for more than four decades, it shows how complex and contradictory Barton really was, and traces the roots of her subject's curious personality to her no less curious childhood.

Barton was born in 1821, the youngest by far of five children of a Massachusetts sawmill owner. "I had no playmates," she remembered, "but in effect six fathers and mothers." Her real mother seems to have been at least half-mad, storing vegetables until they had begun to decay before serving them to her family, never sleeping past 3:00 A.M., cursing so often and so vehemently that a small granddaughter, taken in to see her laid out in her coffin at last, was most struck by the fact that during the entire visit the old lady "never swored once." Barton's eldest sister was wholly mad, kept in a locked room with barred windows, in fact, from which she once escaped just long enough to attack a relative with an ax. Both her brothers were charming but erratic, and so unscrupulous in business that Barton lived in constant fear of their arrest; one would later kill himself.

Perhaps understandably, the little girl identified most closely with her fond, steady father, whose generous local philanthropies she admired and whose stories of service in the Indian wars under "Mad" Anthony Wayne she never tired of hearing. She did not play with dolls and was proud that she could "throw a ball . . . like a boy and not a girl," could "drive a nail, strike it fairly on the head every time . . . [and] tie a square knot that would hold."

But her father's genuine affection alone was not enough to instill in her a sturdy sense of her own worth; all her life, she would feel deserving only when in the service of others, would crave the kind of serious individual attention and unstinting praise she felt her turbulent, distracted family had failed to give her. "Instead of feeling that my childhood gave me time for recreation or play," she wrote, "it seemed to me like time wasted, and I looked anxiously about for some useful occupation." She found it beginning at the age of eleven, nursing her brother David through an illness that would last two years, cheerfully applying and removing leeches every day. When he recovered, she felt no elation, only a sense that she no longer had an important role to play, and cast about the neighborhood for others she might help to heal.

Attractive and tiny—she stood barely 5 feet when full grown—she turned away at least three suitors as a young woman, and instead of marrying began seeking new needs to fill, first as the founder of a New Jersey public school so successful that a man was appointed to oversee her work, then as a clerk in the U.S. Patent Office, one of the very first female employees of the federal government.

But it would take the Civil War to engage all of her fierce energy. She was not, legend to the contrary, the first woman to shoulder the task of supplying Union soldiers, but she was certainly the best known.

Despite her genteel upbringing, Barton was never a prude: when she learned that soldiers appreciated tobacco and whiskey at least as much as blankets and bandages, she happily complied: "You would smile at the sight of the half yard slabs of plug lying this moment on my table, waiting for Dr. Sidney's Basket of Whiskey to arrive . . . ," she wrote a member of the family. "*Dainty gifts,* you will say, but all necessary my dear Coz—this I conceive to be no time to prate of moral influences"; and, while stationed on Hilton Head off the South Carolina coast in 1863, she seems to have conducted a passionate romance with a married colonel.

Nonetheless, she worked exclusively behind the lines at first, fearful that if she went to the battlefield she might be thought a camp follower; it was her beloved father, on his deathbed, who encouraged her to go to the front. Her place, she came to see, was "anywhere between the bullet and the hospital," and even her harshest critics never plausibly questioned her bravery: her face sometimes blue from gunpowder, she ministered to the wounded and dying at Cedar Mountain, Second Bull Run, Chantilly, South Mountain, and at Antietam, where, when rebel artillery seemed sure to hit the field hospital and all the male surgical assistants fled, she stood her ground, holding the rolling operating table steady so the surgeon could complete his work. "I wrung the blood from the bottom of my clothing," she recalled, "before I could step, for the weight about my feet."

But if her courage was incontrovertible, her accounts of her wartime experiences were not: she could not resist exaggerating her genuine achievements, claiming she had spent five days on one battlefield when she'd gone home after two, for example, and that patriotism had kept her from accepting her Patent Office salary for the duration, when she'd actually lobbied hard to keep receiving it.

The war was the high point of her career—for the rest of her days she reveled in the praise of the increasingly elderly veterans she continued to call "my boys"—but it was only the start of her career of service. She dreaded inactivity above everything—"I must not rust," she said—and undertook a postwar lecture tour so strenuous that she collapsed and was sent to Europe to recuperate. There, she threw herself instead into the work of the International Red Cross, to which she dedicated all but the last few years of her life.

From the first, her great cause and her own celebrity were inextricably linked in her own mind. "I must attend to all business myself," she said; she made all decisions and dispersed all funds, so regally autocratic that even her most loyal subordinates took privately to calling her "the Queen" and the "Great I Am." She invariably led her staff into disaster areas herself, coming to the aid of victims of the Johnstown flood, the Galveston hurricane, famine in Russia, the fighting in Cuba—where, at seventy-seven, she found herself once again bent over a campfire, making gruel just as she had done almost thirty years earlier.

She preferred her assistants to be "meek, patient, faithful," a perfect description of her closest aide, Dr. Julian Hubbell, a far younger man so worshipful that he called himself "her boy," who took up medicine only because she asked him to, and did not complain even when she coldly drove off the young woman he had hoped to marry. Notwithstanding the devotion of Hubbell and other unswerving allies, Barton always saw herself as alone and embattled; all criticism, no matter how mild, she believed proceeded from base motives: "The paths of charity are over roadways of ashes," she wrote, "and he who would tread them must be prepared to meet opposition, misconstruction, jealousy and calumny. Let his work be that of angels, still it will not satisfy all." It did satisfy European royalty, and she took great pride in a wicker satchel full of jeweled decorations that rarely left her side and provided her with tangible evidence of their admiration.

She last took the field in 1903, when typhoid devastated the little Pennsylvania town of Butler. A local man remembered seeing her at work there: "She stepped out into the dark, wild night, with her small staff . . . a little colored girl went before her with a lantern . . . we pictured the light going on and through the night until it should stop over the stricken town . . . and the suffering people there would look upon it as the light of a great soul. . . ." That was just how she would have liked them to look upon it. The Red Cross would remain a one-woman show so long as she was its head; she had often said that "When the people got hold onto the Red Cross they would be uncontrollable."

The people finally were. In 1900, Congress had granted the Red Cross a charter aimed at making it more efficient and systematic. Led by Mabel Thorp Boardman, an able member of the new board who yearned to become Barton's successor, dissidents charged that the old lady was egocentric, capricious, careless with finances. She defeated them soundly in 1902, and had herself proclaimed president for life at eighty-one; "victory after victory was won," she wrote, ". . . our foes were slain at our feet."

But her enemies rose again and eventually prevailed: the Red Cross was wrested from her and reorganized in 1904, after a Senate probe of her handling of funds fully exonerated her of any wrongdoing. She went on to found the National First Aid Society, but things were never the same, and at her home at Glen Echo, Maryland, she comforted herself by conducting rambling conversations with long-dead allies through a medium: she noted proudly in her diary that Lincoln, Grant, and Kaiser Wilhelm I all continued to support her work from the spirit world.

In the end, for all her vanity, she remained true to her calling. She was still caring for indigent relatives at eighty-five, rising at dawn and marching to the barn to milk her cows, her best-loved decorations pinned to her calico dress. Shortly before her death from pneumonia at ninety-one in 1912, she apologized for having groaned with pain in her sleep: After all the uncomplaining soldiers she had nursed, she told the faithful Hubbell, "Here on a good bed, with every attention, I am ashamed that I murmur."

American Heritage April 1988

"GLORIOUS WAR!": GEORGE ARMSTRONG CUSTER

E VAN S. CONNELL'S BEST-KNOWN NOVEL, *Mrs. Bridge*, PUB-
lished in 1959, is a portrait of a Midwestern wife and mother of
the 1940s whose complacent certitudes inexorably isolate her
first from her own children, then from the increasingly uncertain
world beyond her tidy Kansas City neighborhood. Toward the end of
the book, her son and daughters gone, her husband dead, Mrs. Bridge
finds some solace in a family album containing snapshots of the single
European trip she and the late Mr. Bridge had managed to take:

> "I don't know whether this will interest you at all," she would say
> to guests, picking up the album in both hands, and as she deposited
> it on her visitor's lap she would say, "now just look at them until you
> get bored, but for heaven's sake don't feel obliged to go through them
> all." And she would then hover nearby, anxious to know which
> pictures were being looked at. Often she would still be unable to sit
> still; she had to look over the visitor's shoulder, reaching down now
> and then to say, "that's the famous old cathedral you're always hear-
> ing about." Or, "That's the ocean, of course." Or, "This was taken
> from the steps of the National Gallery, and right there—directly
> behind the man on the bicycle is where we ate lunch."

Mrs. Bridge is both funny and appalling, a mosaic of shrewdly
observed, flatly rendered details—her awful discovery of a girlie magazine while putting away her son's folded shirts, her too adventurous
attempt to bake pineapple bread for her husband on the cook's day
off—whose dispiriting pattern she never discerns but which the reader
cannot miss.

In recent years Connell has produced two eclectic historical essays—*A Long Desire* and *White Lantern*—in which he employs something of the same technique, spinning colorful versions of explorers'

adventures and scholarly feats out of seemingly disassociated facts, but embellished now with his own observations. Now, he has published *Son of the Morning Star: Custer and the Little Bighorn*. Like *Mrs. Bridge*, it is filled with wonderful detail. Readers interested in Western history will certainly not be bored by it, though they may be baffled and frustrated. For, despite the energy and elegance of Connell's writing and the diligence of his research, this volume, like Mrs. Bridge's photograph album, remains finally a collection of raw material for a moving story its compiler evidently could not find a coherent way to tell.

The book begins and ends on the Custer battlefield, but in between it twists and turns back upon itself as bewilderingly as the Little Big Horn. Nearly everything Connell gleaned from his reading seems to be included, and he read a great deal: his bibliography lists upwards of 420 titles. There are disquisitions on every imaginable aspect of the Plains Indian Wars of which it was the most memorable event; of the lives led by the various tribes against which those wars were waged; and of the myths that have grown up over the intervening decades. Among a thousand other things we learn that roasted puppy tastes like porpoise; that Sitting Bull's name more properly signifies "a wise and powerful being who [has] taken up residence among them"; that life for the troopers between punitive expeditions was so empty that they got up battles between colonies of red and black ants (the red ones were fiercest, the author reports).

Much of this material is riveting, if tangential to the story of the Custer fight. There is, for example, the tale of Mrs. Nash, a 7th Cavalry laundress at Fort Abraham Lincoln who married several troopers in succession over a number of years. While her final husband, a private named Noonan, was away on a scouting expedition, she fell ill and died. Friends preparing the body for burial discovered she had been a man. When Noonan returned and heard this astonishing news, the grieving husband bravely maintained for a time that his wife had been of the proper sex, then shot himself.

Connell's eye for telling detail is as sharp as ever, though he too often vitiates the raw power of his observations with arch and anticlimactic commentary; like Mrs. Bridge, he can't resist peering over the reader's shoulder, pointing up the obvious. Again and again, however, he does spot the little vivid things that traditional historians rarely see but which can help make the difference between literature and mere scholarship. Describing the Medicine Lodge Creek conference, for instance, a gaudy in-gathering of some five thousand Indians of the Southern Plains tribes for peace talks in 1867, he notes that "after Missouri Senator John B. Henderson finished embracing various Indians his nose was yellow, one cheek retained a red streak, and the other cheek had several green tattoos." He reports that one of the verminous soldiers' brothels that stood on the mudflat across the Missouri from Fort Lincoln was called "My Lady's Bower"; that Comanches especially liked sugar and, when they could get it, used half a cup in every mug of coffee they drank; that Custer's favorite staghound, Blucher, was a casualty of his 1868 assault on Black Kettle's Cheyenne village on the Washita. (Excited by all the noise and action, the big overeager dog "decided to join the Indians," Connell writes, "and got an arrow through the ribs.")

The Indian wars were grim, and the author spares the reader nothing. Even the *sound* of scalping is described: "a peculiar popping," he says, "evidently similar to the noise of bubbles or blisters popping." Indians traditionally mutilated the dead, and Connell provides a grisly field guide by which the reader can tell just who did what: the Sioux slashed throats, he reports; the Cheyenne cut arms; everybody liked to take home a bright tattoo. According to one elderly woman who claimed to be an eyewitness, two Cheyenne women paused on the battlefield to pierce the eardrums of Custer's corpse with a bone awl because he had been unable or unwilling to hear Indian warnings to those who dared venture into their sacred Black Hills. And whites often replied in kind: troopers routinely tore down Indian burial scaffolds, scattering the bones of the dead in search of beaded relics; the genitals of men and women killed in raids on their villages were sometimes carried away as souvenirs.

Connell understands, too, the special power of the understated language of ordinary people to evoke extraordinary scenes and explain extraordinary events. "We walked on top of their internals," remembered one veteran who had helped bury soldiers after the Fetterman Massacre in 1866, "and did not know it in the high grass." A Sioux warrior named Paints Brown recalled that Custer's trooper had carried "lots of money and we took it. We knew what the silver was, but the paper we didn't know. And the children played with it, they made little teepees out of it, and put about one hundred dollars in bills together and made toy shawls, and some of it was bloody." Asked by a member of a court of inquiry to account for the special ferocity with which the Sioux and their allies had fought Custer's invading army, Captain Frederick Benteen answered, "We were at their hearths and homes, their medicine was working well, and they were fighting for all the good God gives anyone to fight for."

The reasons for Indian resistance were never really very puzzling. Almost everything about Custer still is. What sort of man was he?

What made him hurry his command so gaily toward disaster? He was, of course, the flamboyant author of his own legend, and he struggles hard to stay at the center of this puzzling, crowded book despite the presence of enough lesser characters to people twenty rich novels. (Some years ago, Thomas Berger fashioned an especially elegant and mordant one, *Little Big Man*, from much the same material.) Connell approaches Custer from all angles, packing in all the data he can muster: we get everything from a list of the wedding presents he received to a partial catalogue of the black marks he ran up at West Point. Most revealing are the snippets of the letters he and his adoring wife Elizabeth wrote to one another.

It is clear that he was never the paladin she and her (mostly civilian) contemporaries believed he was; he was too haughty, mercurial, self-important for his own troops ever to have shared that view. Only Custer could have managed to make a heroic incident out of the fact that he had inadvertently shot and killed his own mount while out hunting buffalo, as he did in his lush autobiography, *My Life on the Plains.* He was never the eye-rolling hysteric that he became on screen in the 1960s, either, though one brief passage from a letter home, new at least to me, hints at the nakedness of his ambition: Fred Grant, the amiable son of the President, was to be in Elizabeth's vicinity; she should meet him at the depot and invite him home, Custer told her, but first she was to "have his father's picture hung in the parlor. . . ." The more evidence Connell piles on, the more paradoxical Custer becomes. He obviously exulted in battle. "Oh, could you have but seen some of the charges that we made!" he wrote Elizabeth from the Virginia front in 1863. "While thinking of them I cannot but exclaim, 'Glorious War!' . . . I gave the command 'Forward!' And I never expect to see a prettier sight."

But once the heady clangor of the fighting was over, he could display great tenderness. He wept openly whenever he parted from his wife, and before burying one of his men, he delicately slit his pockets rather than reach into them: "I cut a lock of [the dead man's] hair and gave them to a friend of his from the same town who promised to send them to his wife. As he lay there, I thought of that poem: 'Let me kiss him for his mother . . .' and wished his mother were there to smooth his hair." Custer kept a pet field mouse in an empty inkwell, letting it out in the evenings to scurry up his arm and bury itself in his red-gold curls, and he once altered his regiment's line of march into Indian country in order not to disturb a nest of meadowlarks.

Despite his labors, the best explanation Connell can finally offer for what happened to Custer and his men in the valley of the little river the Indians called the Greasy Grass is that "in a tight situation his response was instantaneous and predictable: he charged."

American Heritage April 1985

OLLIE AND OLD GIMLET EYE:
SMEDLEY BUTLER

A S I WRITE, THE EARNEST IMAGE OF MARINE LIEUTENANT Colonel Oliver North has faded from our TV screens, but a volume of his testimony before the Joint House-Senate Intelligence Committee still tops the non-fiction paperback best-seller list, a videocassette of the highlights of his appearances has materialized on the shelf of my local rental store, 200,000 copies of an Oliver North coloring book have been shipped, there is talk of an autobiography, a mini-series.

Half a century ago, another Marine was admired for the same qualities North seems to some to exemplify: plain speaking, aggression, impatience with channels. His name was Smedley Darlington Butler and his politics became very different from North's, but he, too, eventually found that untrammeled zeal of the sort that lets Marines take a hill and bring back their dead under fire is often out of sync with civilian life.

Hans Schmidt's *Maverick Marine: General Smedley D. Butler and the Contradictions of American Military History* is a sturdy, scholarly study of the old soldier, nowhere near as lively or colorful as its subject but instructive, nonetheless.

Born a Quaker in 1881, the son of a Pennsylvania congressman, Butler volunteered for Cuba at sixteen, faced his first hostile fire in the Philippines—where, before setting a thatched village on fire, his battalion paused to sing a chorus of "America"—was shot through the chest and awarded the Congressional Medal of Honor during the Boxer Rebellion, and later landed with the Marines in Honduras, Santo Domingo, Mexico, Nicaragua, Haiti, and France.

Thin and wire-tough, with a raptor's nose and a glare so fierce his men called him "Old Gimlet Eye," Butler led not one but three expeditions to Nicaragua between 1910 and 1912. His Marines helped overthrow the Liberal anti-American regime of José Santos Zelaya (which had dared execute two Yankee mercenaries caught fighting alongside rebels), intervened again to shore up Zelaya's conservative successors, and helped establish the Guardia Nacional, the armed constabulary that much later pushed Anastasio Somoza into power. Butler was proud to call himself "the main 'guy' " in these "Punic Wars."

Years after he had moved on, Nicaraguan mothers kept small children quiet by saying, "Hush, Major Butler will get you." He had little affection for the foreign civilians who came under his control. The poor Haitians whose destinies he directed after helping to seize their island were "savage monkeys" to him, and "Those who wore shoes," Butler said, "I considered a joke." When he shared a room with Sudre Dartiguenave, the pliant politician he had personally picked to be Haiti's president, Butler occupied the bed and the head of the Haitian government slept on the floor.

His bravery was never questioned. In Haiti, he led a Marine company against Fort Rivière, the final, hilltop redoubt of the *cacos*—"or bad niggers as we would call them at home," Butler said—who had chosen to resist. Butler, one private, and a sergeant named Ross L. Iams together scrambled up the slope, bullets pecking into the ground around them, and reached the foot of the wall, to find that the only way in was a storm drain through which the defenders were keeping up a steady fire. "I had never experienced a keener desire to be some place else," Butler remembered. "My misery and an unconscious, helpless, pleading must have been written all over my face. Iams took one look at me and then said, 'Oh, hell, I'm going through.' "

Sergeant Iams shouldered his way into the drain with Butler and the private right behind him. The startled defenders somehow missed all three, and before they could reload, the Marines were among them. Fifty-one were shot dead; twenty-nine inside the fortress, the rest as they jumped from the parapet and tried to flee into the jungle. Total Marine injuries: two teeth knocked out by a hurled rock. No prisoners were taken; no Haitian survived.

"We were all imbued with the fact," Butler wrote of the countries which he was ordered to "pacify," "that we were trustees of a huge estate that belonged to minors." And he was entirely realistic about how far the American public could be counted on to support imperial ventures: "As long as we occupy these countries [he was writing of Nicaragua] without great uproar and particularly without the loss of our own men, little attention is paid to our movements. . . . We may even kill a lot of natives of such countries without much comment . . . but, as soon as our losses begin to grow there is a big 'hubbub' . . . and the Corps comes in for unfavorable criticism."

Theodore Roosevelt thought Butler "the finest fighting man in the armed forces," and when TR's young cousin Franklin toured the island as Assistant Secretary of the Navy in 1915 he eagerly agreed, recommending him for a second Congressional Medal of Honor.

As commandant of Quantico after World War I, Butler liked restaging Civil War battles to keep his men in the headlines: at Gettysburg, in 1922, five thousand men replayed Pickett's Charge while President Warren Harding and other dignitaries enjoyed the spectacle—and a full case of illegal bourbon—from the shade of a sixteen-room temporary mansion Butler had ordered built for them of wood and canvas.

But peacetime duty bored him: it was "more stupid than a Quaker meeting," he said; he quarreled noisily with "swivel-chair admirals" and the over-educated products of the Academies who seemed to him to win more favorable treatment than scarred-up veterans like himself. In 1924, he took an extended leave to become director of public safety in Philadelphia, pledging to uphold prohibition and end street crime. He offered a promotion to the first officer who killed a robber, closed up 973 speakeasies in his first 48 hours on the job, and designed for himself a splendid military-style uniform with a blue cape lined with crimson. "Fighting crime," he said, "is just like war." Major crimes fell 40 percent during his two-year tenure; robberies at gunpoint fell *70* percent. Once, according to the *New York Times,* he spotted a notorious gunman on the street: "Stop!" he shouted. "They tell me you're a bad actor. Well, see this?" he pointed to a service stripe he wears. "I got this for killing your kind. Now get out of this town quick. Hear? Get out and don't come back, or I'll get you myself."

Eventually, the mayor and his aides got nervous about what they had unleashed upon their city, and when Butler tried to padlock the posh Ritz Carlton—after raiding a debutante party and excoriating the wealthy, tuxedoed young men his men found there for "feeding young girls wine and punch. . . . Jazzing them up a bit, they call it. . . ." —Butler was forced to resign. Finally, Philadelphians hadn't wanted their police militarized.

He returned to the Marines, but in 1931, passed over for commandant, and angry at having taken part in what he had now come to see as a series of cynical overseas adventures, he left the Corps for good. "I spent 33 years and 4 months in active service . . . ," he would write. "And during that period I spent most of my time being a high-class muscle man for Big Business, for Wall Street and for the bankers. In short, I was a racketeer for capitalism. . . . Like all members of the military profession I never had an original thought until I left the service."

Once out of uniform, Butler more than made up for lost time, proving as implacable in urging peace as he had been in waging war. He was a life-long warrior; it was just that his targets had changed. Now, he attacked the brass in magazines, wrote a best-selling book, *War Is a Racket*, the last words of which were "TO HELL WITH WAR!", and stumped the country—twelve hundred speeches in seven hundred towns and cities by his own count, before he was halfway through—inveighing against crime, big business, and the bosses. Lowell Thomas, his official biographer, called him "a stick of human dynamite . . . [a] Major General who would as leave spit in your eye as look at you." When he spoke over the radio, he got excited and could not stop himself from swearing like a Marine.

His fellow officers no longer knew what to make of him, but he was a great favorite of the Bonus Marchers: "You hear folks call you fellows tramps," he told them, "but they didn't call you that in '17 and '18. . . . You have as much of a right to lobby here as the United States Steel Corporation."

In 1934, he alleged, a gaggle of Wall Street financiers had come to him with a plot to lead a Fascist march on Washington and put himself in power as Generalissimo—if Butler refused the honor, they planned to turn to the Army Chief of Staff, Douglas MacArthur, or so Butler charged. (A congressional investigation confirmed most, if not all, of Butler's bizarre story.)

But if fascism appalled him, Huey Long-style Populism evidently did not: in his posthumously published *My First Days in the White House*, the Kingfish promised to name Butler his Secretary of War. When Long was assassinated, Butler said privately, "I lost most of my interest in the present political picture."

But Butler remained most fervid about anti-interventionism, drawing big crowds at first, and allying himself without embarrassment with isolationists as different from one another as Earl Browder and Hamilton Fish. Roger Baldwin thought him "the most colorfully outspoken opponent of war, armies, fascism and reaction I'd ever met."

As war spread across Europe and Asia, Butler's following fell away, his shrill old-soldier's warnings sounded increasingly hollow and irrelevant. He collapsed while campaigning against his one-time admirer, FDR, and died at fifty-nine on June 21, 1940—one day before the French were forced to surrender to Hitler at Compiègne.

In the end, the sheer complexity of things caught up with him, just as it apparently has with Colonel North.

American Heritage November 1987

THE GENERAL AND THE PRESIDENT: FDR AND GEORGE C. MARSHALL

A DAY OR TWO AFTER CHRISTMAS IN 1942, ELEANOR ROOSEVELT invited a young sailor, the son of an old friend and about to ship out, to join the President and a few guests for dinner at the White House. FDR presided at the head of the table around which sat the army chief of staff, George Marshall, and his wife; the President's closest civilian adviser, Harry Hopkins, and his wife; the Crown Prince and Princess of Norway; and Mrs. Roosevelt herself, with another personal guest—a pretty young woman the ex-sailor now remembers as "Miss Dental Assistant," in Washington to pick up her award, whom the First Lady had invited to stay at the White House so she wouldn't have to spend her first night away from home in a hotel.

The company was a little intimidating for an eighteen-year-old, but the conversation was not. While the main course was served, the one-time sailor recalls, Mrs. Roosevelt and the General talked about Coca-Cola. It seemed that Southern soldiers stationed in the North had written to Marshall complaining that their Cokes did not taste quite the same as they had back home. Mrs. Roosevelt had personally looked into it, and was happy to report that the president of the company had guaranteed to her that Coca-Cola syrup was the same wherever it was served: homesickness—or the water used by local bottlers—accounted for any apparent discrepancy.

Then the President interrupted to report to Marshall on his recent visit to the Ford plant at Willow Run, Michigan, now turning out aircraft instead of automobiles. Charles Lindbergh, whose strident prewar anti-interventionism FDR found it impossible to forgive, was working there as a civilian volunteer, testing the latest warplanes. He had been right inside when Roosevelt arrived, in fact, but had kept out of sight. "What do you think of *that*, George?" FDR asked, leaning forward expectantly.

Marshall, entirely amiable until then, stopped the President cold:

So far as he was concerned, he said, Charles Lindbergh was now loyally serving his country and for that reason, it was simply wrong to speculate further about him, even with his commander-in-chief.

The President's big smile froze. He returned to his dinner, and the weighty silence was broken only when Mrs. Roosevelt gently dismissed Miss Dental Assistant so that she could make it to her award ceremony on time, carefully explaining how to get back into the White House for the night once it was over.

The President's normal gaiety eventually returned, and he and the General turned to less controversial topics.

That dinner is not described in Thomas Parrish's fine book, *Roosevelt and Marshall: Partners in Politics and War*, about the unlikely but hugely effective partnership between FDR and the career soldier he picked to help him run the greatest war in history. But it points up two of the most important of Marshall's many admirable qualities: his consuming interest in the well-being of his men and his willingness to say what needed saying, even in the presence of superiors famously sensitive to criticism.

Aloof and self-contained, Marshall refused to write his memoirs, not wishing to reopen old wounds, he said, and believing it wrong, in any case, to profit from serving one's country. And he has been a hard man for others to write about. "I cannot afford the luxury of sentiment," he liked to say; "mine must be cold logic. Sentiment is for others." Even his stepchildren felt most comfortable calling him "Colonel," his rank when he married their mother.

Like George Washington and Robert E. Lee, the soldiers Marshall himself most admired, he seems to have been almost uniformly virtuous, and, as every biographer knows, virtue palls, especially when described at length. Forrest C. Pogue's magisterial, five-volume biography, *George C. Marshall*, is indispensable but removed, a full-dress portrait. Eric Larabee included an elegant sketch of Marshall in his study of Roosevelt's wartime leadership, *Commander-in-Chief*, and Mark A. Stoler more recently published a brisk one-volume biography, *George C. Marshall: Soldier-Statesman of the American Century*, which is especially good at relating its subject's extraordinary fifty-year career to the national rise to global power he helped make possible.

Thomas Parrish shrewdly chose to get at the mystery of Marshall obliquely, by contrasting him with the no less elusive President with whom he managed to work so well. The result is a vivid double portrait that no one interested in the way we fought and won the war should miss.

Candor served Marshall well long before he met FDR. He was still a promising captain on the staff of the commander of the U.S. First Division in 1917, when General John J. "Blackjack" Pershing stopped in to watch maneuvers, then dressed down the staff for minor mistakes that actually grew out of confusion at his own headquarters. Marshall's fellow officers took it in silence. Captain Marshall could not. Seizing the startled commander's arm to make him listen, his words tumbling upon one another, he stated the facts exactly as he saw them. At the end of his tirade, Pershing stammered: "You must appreciate the troubles we have."

"*We* have them every day," Marshall insisted, "and we have to solve every one of them by night."

His comrades were certain he'd ruined his career, but Pershing attached Marshall to his staff as Chief of Operations, a post in which he earned the nickname "Wizard" for somehow managing to move into position on the Meuse-Argonne front 3,980 guns, 4,000 tons of ammunition, 34 evacuation hospitals, and 93,032 horses without arousing the enemy's suspicion. When American troops marched up the Champs-Elysées in triumph, Colonel George Marshall rode just behind his commander, at the head of the procession.

"General Pershing as a leader always dominated every gathering . . . ," Marshall later told an interviewer, in words that might also have served to describe his own style of leadership. "He was a tremendous driver, if necessary; a very kindly likable man on off-duty status, but very stern on a duty basis." Among Pershing's gifts, Marshall added, was an ability to see himself as others saw him; "he could listen to severe criticisms, just as though it was about a man in another country." It was one of Marshall's greatest strengths that he could do that, too.

Other soldiers found the peacetime army stultifying, and Marshall himself was often impatient with the glacial pace of promotions, the niggardly budgets and obsolete armaments with which he and his attenuated commands had to make do, but he made the most of every assignment, nonetheless. As assistant commandant in charge of instruction at the Infantry School at Fort Benning, he played down theory in favor of practicality, teaching young officers to move and maneuver with imperfect maps and faulty intelligence as they really would in war, to think fast—and for themselves. "I insist we must get down to the essentials . . . and expunge the bunk," Marshall said. "We must develop a technique and methods so simple and so brief that the citizen officer of good common sense can readily grasp the idea."

And he began to keep what he called "my little black book," in which he jotted the names of those young citizen officers who showed the kind of good common sense he was looking for: Omar Bradley, J. Lawton Collins, Matthew Ridgway, Walter Bedell Smith, Joseph Stilwell. (Someone once asked Marshall if he'd also listed in his book the names of officers who showed *no* promise. No, he said, "there wouldn't have been room.")

In Marshall, FDR would find a kindred pragmatic spirit, impatient with orthodoxy, willing to try things. When Roosevelt put the army in charge of the Civilian Conservation Corps in 1933, some regular officers were annoyed at being asked to "baby-sit" civilians. Marshall found it "the most instructive service I have ever had and the most interesting," and actively enjoyed seeing ill-nourished, undisciplined city boys transformed into healthy, self-confident workers. It was the best possible training for a man who would one day be asked to build a mighty army out of the same raw material. "I'll be out to see you soon," he warned the officers in charge of the camps under his command, "and if I find you doing something, I will help you, but if I find you doing nothing, only God will help you."

Marshall was not an especially modest man, but he was congenitally averse to self-promotion, and, despite lobbying by General Pershing and others, did not make it to the War Department in Washington until 1938, as chief of the War Plans Division. There, his candor paid off for him again. Attending his very first White House meeting on November 14, 1938, just six weeks after Munich, he listened with growing impatience as FDR spun out ambitious plans for aircraft production that seemed to him entirely to overlook the care and training of the men needed to fly and service the new planes. Everyone in the room nodded pleasantly, nonetheless. Everyone but Marshall.

"So he turned to me . . . ," the General recalled, "and said, 'Don't you think so, George?' "

Marshall did not like being called "George" by a man he barely knew— it was a "misrepresentation of our intimacy," he thought—and his irritation showed: "Mr. President, I am sorry, but I don't agree with that at all."

Roosevelt shot him a "very startled look," and the conference came to an abrupt end. As he left the White House, Marshall remembered, his associates "all bade me goodbye and said my tour in Washington was over." It wasn't. In fact, Marshall's stubborn veracity—and his refusal to push himself for the job—helped persuade Roosevelt to name Marshall his new chief of staff. "Maybe he thought I would tell him the truth so far as I personally was concerned," the General said much later, "—which I certainly tried to do in all of our later conversations." And although FDR's lordly style led him to call almost everyone—

including visiting royalty—by their first names, he rarely called Marshall anything but "General," at least in public.

He was sworn in on September 1, 1939, the day the European war began. The outlines of the story Parrish tells will be familiar to anyone who has read anything about the war years: the desperate struggle to prepare the country for a war it did not wish to face; the shock of Pearl Harbor; the great wartime conferences—Argentia, Casablanca, Quebec, Cairo-Teheran, Yalta; the delicate working out of a common Allied strategy and the creation of the joint command structure that made victory possible. But Parrish is so adept at selecting telling details, and has ferreted out so much fresh material (much of it from living witnesses only rarely heard from till he took the trouble to look them up), that the reader is never tempted to skip a paragraph. There are entertaining asides about everything from Charles de Gaulle's verdict on FDR's Groton French ("not very good"), to the machine-gun speed with which Marshall dictated (160 words per minute and rarely a correction) and his chronic difficulty with remembering the names even of those closest to him: he called his loyal secretary, Mona Nason, Miss "Mason" about half the time, thought his closest aide's name was McCartney when it was McCarthy, and relied on experienced associates to know just who he meant when he ordered them to "Get me that fellow I want to see."

It would have been hard to conjure up a more apparently mismatched pair than FDR and George Marshall.

Marshall was a clean-desk man. No good decision, he liked to say, was ever made after four in the afternoon, and he rendered his own decisions in a way calculated to intimidate all but his most self-confident aides: "When duty brought an officer to his presence," Parrish writes, "the man was supposed to walk into the office, not saluting, and quietly sit down in the chair opposite the general facing him. Marshall would not look up until he had finished reading the paper in front of him; the officer would sit silently until the chief had completed his task. Marshall would then look at his caller and wait to hear a brief explanation of the purpose of the visit." In the course of listening to such a presentation, most men would have indicated their reaction by a nod or change of expression. Not Marshall: his ice-blue gaze never wavered, though impatience sometimes burned through if anyone went on much longer than ten minutes. When his visitor had finished, Marshall would ask a question or two, indicate his approval or disapproval, and return to his papers until the next man took his seat. Inarticulate or insecure officers got nowhere with Marshall. (It was said—and believed within the War Department—that one officer, receiving a summons to the General's office, suffered a heart attack.) But "yes" men got nowhere, either.

Franklin Roosevelt's desk was anything but clean, was famously littered, in fact, with books, mementoes, pictures, figurines, and knick-knacks that constituted a mirror image of his cluttered, restless, omnivorous mind. The convoluted process by which he made his decisions, which followed no easily discernible pattern, his refusal to have a written record of even the most important substantive discussions, and his standard administrative practice of playing off strong men against one another all strained Marshall's patience, but he quickly adapted to Roosevelt's way of doing things. "By making all the lines radiate directly from himself," Parrish writes, "Roosevelt could sit at the center of the administrative web and feel tugs slight enough to go unnoticed by a more orthodox executive."

Marshall, too, learned to be sensitive to every tug on that web, while remaining careful always not to allow himself to get too close to the sinuous, seductive man who wove it. Imprisoned in his wheelchair, Franklin Roosevelt overwhelmed his visitors with talk. He was not so much a conversationalist as a monologist, holding forth on anything and everything, especially when he did not wish to say—or hear—anything substantive. (One frequent luncheon guest always ate before he arrived so that when the President interrupted himself to fork in a bit of food, he could get in a thought or two of his own.)

Marshall refused to play the courtier. He visited the White House only on serious business (his presence at the White House dinner the young sailor attended was a rare event), and he gently but firmly turned down all invitations to visit FDR at his ancestral home at Hyde Park, fearful that under the relentlessly beguiling power of Roosevelt's spell even he might agree to things he would later regret.

Few men ever understood Roosevelt better than Marshall. The President should never be pressed "to see this or that or understand this or that," he warned the commandant of the Infantry School on the eve of a presidential visit: " . . . whatever is furnished to him in the way of data [should] be on one sheet of paper . . . he is quickly bored by papers, by lengthy discussions, and by anything but a few pungent sentences of description. You have to intrigue his interest, and then it knows no limit."

There was no limit to Roosevelt's love of secrecy, either, and even Marshall—whom FDR may have trusted more implicitly than any other man but Harry Hopkins—sometimes had to scramble to keep up with his chief's delight in clandestine decision making. When he was unable to find out from the President just what he and Churchill were telling one another in their private correspondence, he quietly arranged for his friend Sir John Dill, the chief British military representative in Washington, to show him copies of Roosevelt's messages, sent to him all the way from London. "I had to be very careful that nobody knew this," Marshall recalled, "—no one in the War Department and certainly not the [British] chiefs of staff," for fear he and Dill would lose their jobs. (When Dill died at his post in 1944, Marshall saw to it that he was buried in Arlington National Cemetery, the first foreign national ever to be laid to rest there, and he later helped raise funds for the equestrian statue that now marks his grave.)

There were stormy moments between the President and his favorite general, most memorably in May of 1940, when Marshall's need for more men and materiel clashed with Roosevelt's inclination to avoid asking for too great an increase in his defense budget in an election year in which he was already being accused of warmongering, and in 1942, when Marshall's stubborn advocacy of an early assault on occupied France rather than North Africa led him and his naval counterpart, Admiral Ernest J. King, to send FDR a hasty, uncharacteristically petulant memorandum arguing that if France were not to be the first Allied target, American forces should turn to the Pacific instead and "strike decisively against Japan." Roosevelt's handwritten response was withering:

> My first impression is that it is exactly what Germany hoped the United States would do after Pearl Harbor. Secondly, it does not in fact provide use of American troops in fighting except in a lot of islands whose occupation will not affect the world situation this year or next. Third: it does not help Russia or the Near East. Therefore it is disapproved as of the present. Roosevelt C in C.

But the storms always blew over. FDR, who did not easily tolerate opposition from subordinates, remained faithful to Marshall—and the General remained faithful to him. "I'm not always able to approve [Marshall's] recommendations," Roosevelt once told Sam Rayburn; "history may prove me wrong. But when I disapprove his recommendations, I don't have to look over my shoulder to see which way he's going, whether he's going back to the War Department. I *know* he's going back to the War Department to give me the most loyal support as chief of staff that any President could wish."

There is a nice irony in the fact that this professional soldier, who refused even to vote for fear of being thought partisan—his father had been a Democrat, he liked to say; his mother was a Republican; and he was an Episcopalian—may have made his greatest single contribution to the defeat of the Axis as a lobbyist on Capitol Hill. He dealt with politicians with the same bluff candor that characterized his dealings with his fellow soldiers and it was precisely that fact that made him such a credible advocate for the army. Men who distrusted FDR's every word and deed found themselves believing George Marshall when he said the same things the President was saying. Rayburn thought him the most influential witness he had ever heard on Capitol Hill: "It is because," he said, "when he takes the witness stand, we forget whether we are Republicans or Democrats. We just remember that we are in the presence of a man who is telling the truth. . . ." Passage of the draft extension in 1940 that ensured his newly created army would remain intact—won by a single, all-important vote—can be said to have been more his victory than the President's.

When the time came at last to invade France in 1944, and the decision was made that an American would act as Supreme Commander, Marshall devoutly hoped to be that man. Command of the greatest invasion in history would be the most fitting possible capstone to his career.

At first, Roosevelt agreed. "You and I," he told Dwight Eisenhower on his way to the Cairo Conference, "know the name of the Chief of Staff in the Civil War, but few outside the professional services do." Marshall was no Henry Halleck; Roosevelt wished to give him a chance to claim his rightful place alongside U.S. Grant as a battlefield commander. The British and Russians agreed. But field command was technically a demotion, and when rumors of the change reached opposition newspapers, they charged that by supplanting him as chief of staff, Roosevelt was somehow trying to transfer overall command to the perfidious British, perhaps plotting to establish a global New Deal.

"Marshall had been put in a strange position," Parrish writes. "The great national faith and trust in his wisdom and integrity stood in the way of the move both he and Roosevelt hoped to make." In the end, FDR decided that the domestic political cost of sending Marshall overseas would be too great; besides, no other officer was likely to serve him so well with Congress. There remained the most tactful way of telling him; Roosevelt hated directly disappointing anyone. "After a great deal of beating around the bush," Marshall recalled, FDR finally asked him what *he* wanted to do, gambling that the General would never be able to bring himself to ask for the honor. He knew his man: "I just repeated in as convincing language as I could," Marshall remembered, "that I wanted him to feel free to act in whatever way he felt was to the best interests of the country, and to his satisfaction, and not in any way to consider my feelings."

"I feel I could not sleep at night with you out of the country," Roosevelt said, and Eisenhower was named to lead the Allied forces to victory. Marshall never complained and late in 1944, FDR saw to it that Marshall was named General of the Army, the service's most exalted rank.

By then, Roosevelt was himself failing—perhaps the most moving part of Parrish's book deals with the President's precipitous decline, which he attributes, not to the heart disease that finally caused his death, but to the cumulative effect of twenty-three gallant, uncomplaining years spent battling the ravages of infantile paralysis, the condition which has in recent years come to be called "postpolio syndrome."

In April of 1945, Marshall did finally make the journey to the President's Hyde Park home, but it was at Mrs. Roosevelt's invitation, not her husband's: she would trust no one else to make the arrangements for FDR's funeral journey from Warm Springs.

MHQ Summer 1990

THE SOLDIER WHO COULDN'T STOP:
JOHN PAUL VANN

IN THE AUTUMN OF 1970, NEIL SHEEHAN, THEN THE PENTAGON correspondent for the *New York Times,* agreed to review a new book for the Sunday paper. It was *Conversations with Americans,* transcripts of grisly interviews with thirty-two servicemen who claimed either to have taken part in or witnessed or heard about war crimes committed by Americans in Vietnam.

Sheehan might have been expected to be a receptive reader. He was anything but an apologist for the military: his doggedly skeptical reporting had angered both the American and South Vietnamese high commands during stints in Vietnam for United Press International and the *Times*—within a few months he would further incense officialdom by obtaining the Pentagon Papers for his newspaper—and he had himself reported on American atrocities with candor and concern. But Sheehan's skepticism was both inbred and unbiased and the book's editor was Mark Lane, the New York lawyer who, in making a good thing out of the John Kennedy assassination, had become, in one critic's words, "his own credibility gap." Sheehan began to check into Lane's interviewees: one, who claimed to have been taught in survival school that "we could rape the girls all we wanted," turned out to be a state-side stockroom clerk who had never attended such a school; another, who said he was the son of a murderous ex-Nazi then serving in Vietnam, was tracked to a mental ward and found to be wanted for murder himself. When Sheehan confronted Lane with this and other evidence that he had got things wrong, the attorney maintained that verifying facts and assessing the reliability of his witnesses was "not relevant," and an anonymous spokesman for Lane's publisher, while admitting that no independent effort had been made to check the manuscript, thought its worthy purpose had been reason enough to publish—after all, he said, "the motives were anti-war motives."

"Can the opponents of the war accuse those in power of cloaking the war's prosecution in deceit," Sheehan asked in his review, "and then practice deceit themselves?"

That difficult question is raised again in his extraordinary book, *A Bright Shining Lie: John Paul Vann and America in Vietnam.* No one can accuse Sheehan of failing to do his homework; it took him sixteen years to write this book, in the course of which he interviewed 385 persons and made two three-month trips to Vietnam. The richly detailed result is both a sobering history of the entire American effort in Southeast Asia, and a compelling portrait of a legendary soldier, Lieutenant Colonel John Paul Vann, who was once revered as a moral hero by Sheehan, David Halberstam, and the other eager young journalists who made their reputations in Vietnam, but whose character turns out, thanks to the author's tireless and objective research, to have been, like the war he always thought he knew how to win, something quite different from what it seemed. Even those who do not share Sheehan's uniformly rueful view of the war will respect the anguish and unblinking honesty out of which *A Bright Shining Lie* was written.

"Soldiers respect a leader who is competent," Sheehan writes. "They admire a leader who is competent and bold. When he is an accomplished student of war, leads boldly, and also savors gambling his own life, he acquires a mystique." No American who served in Vietnam acquired more mystique than Vann, a small, wiry Virginian, with the creased, sunburned neck of a Confederate veteran and an almost religious faith in the ability of American arms and fighting skill to perform any task. He entered the army at eighteen, commanded Rangers in Korea, and volunteered to serve as an adviser in Vietnam in 1962, so early in the American effort there that the skirmishes shown on the television screens in our living rooms were still being fought in black and white.

Vann was at once fond of the Vietnamese troops he helped to lead and patronizing toward them. "The first thing you'll learn," Vann told Halberstam not long after the reporter arrived, "is that these people may be the world's greatest lovers, but they're not the world's greatest fighters. But they're good people, and they can win a war if someone shows them how."

Vann did his damndest: slogging through rice paddies with enlisted men in the vain hope that their officers would be emboldened to follow suit, driving alone through the jungle to demonstrate that the enemy did not necessarily own the night, employing shameless flattery to build the confidence of his Vietnamese counterpart, Colonel Huynh Van Cao, who owed his exalted station to the favor of President Ngo Din Diem and wished to do nothing—like incur casualties—that might jeopardize it. Cao decorated his map room to resemble Napoleon's, brandished a polished swagger stick, and published an autobiographical novel modestly titled *He Grows Under Fire*, but he was made physically ill by the sound of artillery.

Vann did not find the diplomacy his job demanded easy: Once, warned that he must not push so hard that his allies would lose "face," he answered, "I'm not here to save their face. I'm here to save their ass." That kind of blunt candor made him a favorite of Sheehan, Halberstam, and their embattled colleagues, whose own integrity and patriotism were now routinely being questioned because they insisted upon reporting the war as they saw it rather than as the brass wished it to be. A celebrated exchange between the American ambassador, Frederick Nolting, Jr., and François Sully of *Newsweek*, a seventeen-year resident of Vietnam, soon to be expelled for daring to criticize Madame Nhu's pet corps of paramilitary girls, nicely summarized the ongoing conflict between the bureaucracy and the bringers of bad news:

"Why, Monsieur Sully, do you always see the hole in the doughnut?"

"Because, Monsieur l'Ambassadeur, there is a hole in the doughnut."

Vann helped Sheehan and his colleagues keep that void clearly in view. His problem, like theirs, was always with Saigon, its languor, its intrigue and blatant nepotism, its callous mistreatment of the people it was supposed to be protecting, above all, its corruption—whose pervasiveness as described here defies belief. One province chief made a tidy profit charging displaced peasants for the barbed wire with which he surrounded the Strategic Hamlets into which he had herded them against their will; another broke holes in an American-built dike, allowing sea water to destroy the rice crop just so that he could charge fishermen a fee to set up their nets and catch the fish that were swept inland with the rising tide. During one battle, the South Vietnamese pilots of medical evacuation helicopters let the wounded bleed to death on the airstrip while they did a brisk business selling space aboard to deserters; a commander sold artillery barrages to besieged outposts— "no bribe, no artillery when the Communists attacked."

With friends like these, it is not surprising that Vann came to admire the tenacity of the enemy. "There is a revolution going in this country," he once wrote,

> . . . and the principles, goals, and desires of the *other* side are much closer to what Americans believe in than those of [the Saigon government]. I realize that ultimately when the Chinese brand of Commu-

nism takes over, these "revolutionaries" are going to be sadly disappointed—but then it will be too late—for them, and too late for us
to win them. I am convinced that even though the National Liberation Front is Communist-dominated, the great majority of the people
supporting it are doing so because it is their only hope to change and
improve their living conditions and opportunities. If I were a lad of
eighteen faced with the same choice—whether to support the [Saigon
government] or the NLF [National Liberation Front]. . . . I would
surely choose the NLF.

Like other American advisers, Vann hoped for the day when the
shadowy enemy would stand their ground and fight so that his men
could demonstrate to the world—and to themselves—the skills he had
taught them and the determination of which he knew they were capable if properly led. On January 2, 1963, he got his wish at a place called
Ap Bac, just forty miles southwest of Saigon—but the battle that
followed, brilliantly described in Sheehan's book, demonstrated only
the incompetence of the ARVN leaders, all hand-picked for syco-
phancy, not courage, by President Diem. The armored commander
refused to rescue the crews of felled helicopters for three hours; the
officer commanding two infantry units refused to fight at all, despite
Vann's profane urging from a spotter plane; and the showy General
Cao deliberately dropped airborne reinforcements in the wrong place
to engage the retreating enemy and so late that his paratroops and their
anxious comrades on the ground began shooting at one another in the
fading light.

By day's end, a band of 350 guerrillas had demonstrated that they
could meet and master a modern, magnificently equipped army that
outnumbered them by a factor of four. They had withstood napalm,
shells, bombs, machine-gun fire; downed five helicopters; inflicted 180
casualties—and got away clean.

"I consider it a victory," the American commander, General Paul
Harkins, bravely told the press. Vann had had enough pretense: It had
been a miserable performance, and if the conditions that had caused it
were not changed, the American cause was doomed. "This is a political
war," he insisted, and it was being lost. When he failed privately to
persuade Harkins to confront Diem and force him to alter the policies
he considered self-defeating, he took his case directly to the press. "I
may be a commissioned officer in the United States Army who's sworn
to safeguard classified information," he said as he took Halberstam
aside, "but I'm also an American citizen with a duty to my country.
Now listen carefully . . . "

The *Times* story that resulted was a sensation, and Sheehan, Hal-berstam, and the other reporters in whom Vann had confided felt in part responsible when he decided shortly thereafter to leave Vietnam, retire from the army at thirty-eight after twenty years of active service, and try to make his case in Washington. (He got nowhere there, either; General Maxwell Taylor personally intervened to keep him from briefing the Joint Chiefs of Staff.) Vann, Halberstam wrote, had clearly been "on his way to becoming a full colonel with a very good chance of . . . promotion to general," but had instead "done . . . what no other American official has done in defense of his conviction about our role in Vietnam: he thought that the lies and failures were serious enough for him to retire from the service he loved." Halberstam published an admiring profile of him in *Esquire* and made him the hero of his 1965 best-seller, *The Making of a Quagmire*, memorably portraying him as an honest man whom the system had punished for his honesty.

In fact, Sheehan later discovered as he looked into his life, Vann was deeply, perhaps pathologically, dishonest. He had, for example, actu-ally given up nothing by going home. His army career had reached a dead end before he ever got to Vietnam: he had been accused of the statutory rape of a fifteen-year-old baby-sitter—had escaped court-martial for it, in fact, only because he had beaten a polygraph test by rehearsing remaining calm under questioning, and because his fiercely loyal wife had been willing to lie on his behalf—and he had been unsuccessful in his effort to steal and destroy the records of the investi-gation. At least some of his reputation for heroism was phony, too; in recounting his exploits in Korea, he routinely commandeered the deeds of a brave friend. Even his marriage was a lie—he was an obses-sive womanizer.

Astonished and intrigued, Sheehan probed further, seeking the early sources of Vann's contradictory personality, and suggests that they lie in the two sad, central facts of his boyhood: he was illegitimate, the son of an alcoholic prostitute so viciously scornful of him that for many years she refused out of simple spite to permit him to adopt the last name of the only father he ever knew; and he had been repeatedly molested by the pastor and Scoutmaster who was the first man ever to take much interest in him.

The army gave Vann the legitimacy he craved. War—and philan-dering—provided the excitement and the danger he apparently needed to face down in order to feel that he was fully a man. It seems clear that he could not live long without either, and in March of 1965 he returned to Vietnam, where he eventually installed two mistresses simultaneously and found even them insufficient for his compulsive needs.

The war had expanded since his first tour: Operation Rolling Thunder was already pounding the North, the first U.S. combat troops had landed, hundreds of thousands more were on the way, and the televised battles in American living rooms were now being fought in full color. An aide to General William Westmoreland promised to "stomp them to death."

Vann was technically a civilian, a shirt-sleeved worker for AID, but he did his best to blur that distinction, driving his truck along jungle paths controlled by the enemy, his sole protection his skill behind the wheel and a handful of grenades on the seat beside him. "Drove thru the ambush," he noted in his journal after running one gauntlet, "—must have been embarrassing to VC—that many men failing to get one vehicle and driver. Close!"

He was soon made chief of the civilian pacification program for the eleven provinces surrounding Saigon, where he again irritated the army by noisily opposing the indiscriminate bombing and shelling that eventually drove one quarter of the South Vietnamese population off its land and into refugee camps and urban slums, calling again for a new kind of Saigon regime "responsive to the dynamics of the social revolution," and warning that Westmoreland's policy of attrition was sure to fail.

The Tet Offensive of 1968 seemed to bear him out, convincing many that the war was finally unwinnable. Lyndon Johnson halted the bombing of the North and announced he would not seek reelection. Hanoi agreed to open peace talks.

But "John Vann could not accept the death of the war," Sheehan writes, and now professed to see in Tet a fresh opportunity to continue the conflict he wished never to abandon. The Viet Cong had paid a fearful price for their great psychological and political victory—tens of thousands of guerrillas had been killed, many of them seasoned veterans—and it would take time for them to rebuild, Vann argued, time during which they would have to rely on North Vietnamese regulars ill-equipped for guerrilla war and "nearly as alien to the South as are our U.S. forces." American troop strength could be reduced to "pacify" public opinion at home, while the ARVN was built at last into the kind of fighting force which, if backed by U.S. airpower, could hold the North Vietnamese at bay. He was suddenly popular in circles where he once had been anathema: Richard Nixon received him at the White House; Henry Kissinger told him Vietnamization was "your policy"; Joseph Alsop declared him "infinitely patriotic. . . ." He began to dream of one day serving as Secretary of the Army.

"Vann had lost his compass . . . ," Sheehan writes. "The John Vann his old friends had known had disappeared into the war. Each year, South Vietnam had become a more perfect place for him. The war satisfied him so completely that he could no longer look at it as something separate from himself. He had finally bent the truth about the war as he had bent other and lesser truths in the past."

He had always opposed cross-border incursions as diversionary: "If we go across the border," he had told a reporter in 1967, "there will always be one more sanctuary just beyond the one we clean out." Now, he enthusiastically endorsed the invasion of Cambodia because it would buy Saigon precious time and keep the war going. He had always bitterly opposed corruption, too, but in 1970 he urged that a famously mercenary relative of President Nguyen Van Thieu be given a regimental command on the grounds that "He'll steal less with a regiment."

In 1971, he was rewarded with appointment as senior adviser for the II Corps region comprising the Central Highlands and the adjacent provinces on the central coast, a post always previously held by a major general and one which allowed him officially to command U.S. soldiers in the field, and, unofficially (thanks to his pliant South Vietnamese counterpart), to command ARVN troops as well. He planned to turn the tables on his old enemy; instead of sending troops to seek him out, as Westmoreland had done, he would fortify the provincial capital of Kontum and wait for the attack he was sure would come. "The sons of bitches will have to fight or die," he said.

It is a tribute to the skill and sensitivity with which Sheehan has built his book that despite all the reader now knows of the web of lies Vann has spun and the pain he has caused to those who believed in him, it is impossible not to care about his fate during these final days.

As 35,000 NVA troops poured out of the Demilitarized Zone and the battle for the highlands began at the end of March 1972, Vann raced from outpost to outpost to shore up morale, personally leading the Cobra gunships that hurled the enemy back from one critically important fire-support base, then flying six times through machine-gun fire to resupply it.

But Vann could not be everywhere. On the coast, the ARVN broke and ran, and at Tan Canh, a regimental base vital to the defense of Kontum where he counted on aggressive counterattacking by the South Vietnamese, he did not get it. The enemy overran Tan Canh, the ARVN fleeing so fast the local tribesmen called them "the rabbit soldiers," and Vann barely escaped with his life, four desperate ARVN troops clinging to the undercarriage of his helicopter.

Kontum was all that now stood between Vann and disaster. "If [we] don't hold it," he said, "I no longer have any credibility or career." He took over every detail of its defense, as if by sheer will he could save the city, and seemed suffused with what Sheehan calls a "rage and exaltation" remarkable even for him, ordering in strike after B-52 strike upon the North Vietnamese, then swooping low over the roiled hillsides to fire his M-16 into the bomb craters. "Anytime the wind is blowing from the north where the B-52 strikes are turning the terrain into a moonscape," he gloated to a visitor, "you can tell from the battlefield stench that strikes are effective. Outside Kontum, wherever you dropped bombs, you scattered bodies."

In the end, Kontum did hold. Vann's deputy later said that without him it would not have; the ARVN troops would never have stayed to see the battle through. Such talk pleased Vann, but he failed to see that by seizing control whenever a crisis occurred, he had only demonstrated again that the Saigon regime was powerless to defend itself, that without the Americans the South Vietnamese still could not survive. Hanoi itself failed to grasp how true this was: even with U.S. combat troops at last withdrawn, the North Vietnamese thought their final offensive would take two full years to defeat the South. In the end, it took less than one for Saigon to fall and the last American evacuation helicopter to lumber into the air from the roof of the U.S. Embassy.

John Vann did not live to witness that final American humiliation. He was killed instantly when his helicopter crashed on a forested mountainside not far from Kontum on the night of June 9, 1972. The exultant enemy claimed to have dealt the American cause "a stunning blow" by shooting him out of the sky. In fact, the North Vietnamese had not shot him down; Vann's inexperienced American pilot had slammed into the forest canopy while trying to fly through blinding weather without instruments. But South Vietnamese troops, sent to bring him out of the jungle, did strip him of his watch, wallet, and class ring before placing his broken body on a stretcher for the first leg of the long journey home to Arlington.

MHQ Autumn 1988

DELANOS AND
ROOSEVELTS

★

"A FAIR, HONORABLE AND LEGITIMATE TRADE": THE DELANOS IN THE OPIUM WAR

EDWARD DELANO ARRIVED AT MACAO OFF THE SOUTH CHINA coast aboard the American vessel *Oneida* on December 7, 1840. His initial impression of the tiny Portuguese colony was reassuring. A crescent of handsome whitewashed houses with a dozen church spires scattered among them, clinging to a green hillside, Macao often reminded seasoned travelers of Naples.

Massachusetts boys like Ned thought of Nahant.

It had been a long, uneasy journey of 160 days. Ned was just twenty-two and prone to seasickness. He had never before been more than one hundred miles from the family home at Fairhaven, and he had not seen his older brother, Warren Delano II, since he had sailed for China as a supercargo seven years before. Now Warren was the head of Russell & Company, the biggest American firm in the China trade, and had sent for Ned to join him as a clerk.

Their reunion was restrained at first. "W. came in . . . with his dressing gown on," Ned reported. "I should not have known him under circumstances different from which I was now placed—he appeared to me worn out—a yellow cadaverous visage [he was recovering from an attack of jaundice] added to a slow gait and body [a] little inclined forward—we embraced—scarcely a word was said—only that he was heartily glad to see me— . . . he said that I had arrived . . . at a time when he could do much for me and hoped that I should not have to stop here [in China] as long as he had. . . . "

Warren is "a perfect number One," an admiring Ned wrote home. "Of course he feels his authority—yet he does not abuse it—a *young man* of 31 at the head of R. & C[ompany]— . . . he can carve a duck, eat curry, be interesting in conversation, be sarcastic in his remarks, tell a good story, and do many other things 'too numerous to mention.' "

Macao was only the off-season residence of the China traders; most business was conducted at Canton, in the single riverfront block of thirteen factories, or "hongs," to which the Chinese tried to keep all foreigners confined. A few days later, the brothers set out together on the eighty-five-mile voyage to Canton. It was a pleasant three-day trip aboard a dispatch boat propelled by crimson sails and eight oarsmen.

Away from the other traders, Warren abandoned his public reserve, and he and his younger brother engaged in what Ned called "a delightful frolic . . . biting and pulling ears, pinching flesh, etc. . . . ," then lay back on carved benches and talked of old times as they glided among brilliant green islands, past weathered pagodas, orange groves, and fields of rice. "We amused ourselves," Ned remembered, "with shooting birds, snipes and magpies, the boatmen swimming on shore after them."

Only one thing intruded upon this idyll. From time to time shrill voices reached them across the water, shouting *"Fan Kuei! Fan Kuei!"* ("Foreign Devil! Foreign Devil!") When Ned scanned the shore to see who was calling to them, some of the villagers grinned and made an odd hacking gesture at the side of their necks.

Warren explained that the villagers were warning them that before long all the foreigners' heads would be cut off.

Ned had arrived at a tense but profitable time for the American traders. A curious, on-again, off-again war had been under way between Britain and the Chinese emperor since June, and the neutral Americans were its beneficiaries.

Tea was the staple of the China trade, and December marked the height of the Canton season; as Ned was shown to his room on the second floor of the Russell factory, the smell of the tea chests newly stored in the godown below was almost overpowering, and he would spend much of his first weeks in China weighing and tasting teas, "a dirty business . . . the tea getting into the nostrils, soiling the hands, etc."

But opium ran a close, shadowy second.

Though China and opium remain linked in the popular mind, the drug was not native to that land; the first opium poppy seeds are thought to have arrived from Egypt in the saddlebags of Arab traders toward the end of the seventh century, and for centuries it was used only in small quantities as a medicine and restorative. Dutch traders at Formosa are said to have been the first to smoke opium—mixed with tobacco and betel nut to fend off the effects of malaria—in the eighteenth century. Chinese merchants along the South China coast imitated them, gradually eliminating from their pipes everything but the drug and thereby inducing a state of euphoria unknown to those who simply swallowed it. Soon, this indulgence became addiction and spread from the wealthy to the poor.

The growing or importation of the drug had been officially barred by the Manchu emperors at Peking since 1729, an inconvenient fact which, until shortly before Ned arrived in China, Chinese officials and Western traders alike had found it easy enough to ignore in the interest of profits so vast that by 1830, the opium trade at Canton was said to be the most valuable trade in any single commodity, anywhere on earth.

The British dominated it as they did every aspect of the China trade, but their American competitors were fast gaining on them. The very first American in the China trade, Samuel Shaw, who brought the *Empress of China* to Canton in 1784, had foreseen the big profits those who followed him would make handling opium, which, he said, "could be smuggled with the utmost security." It had taken a little time for Americans to make good his prediction, not because they had higher moral standards than their British rivals but because they had a less dependable source of supply.

When the Honourable British East India Company established its grip on India in the eighteenth century, it inherited a system of state control over opium that had been an important source of revenue for the Moghul emperors. Warren Hastings, India's first Governor General, had understood both the drug's dangers and its attractions: "Opium is not a necessary of life," he said, "but a pernicious article of luxury which ought not to be permitted *except for purposes of commerce.*" At his direction, the Company planted vast fields of pink-and-white opium poppies on the Ganges plain, then monopolized the sale of the drug they yielded. (Hastings's encouragement paid off; opium exports to China eventually accounted for one seventh of British India's revenues.)

The Americans, on the other hand, had to make do at first with the drug produced in Turkey. Hard economic facts helped boost American participation in the drug trade. The United States had precious little silver with which to pay for tea, silk, and porcelain; the Chinese were uninterested in the "strange or ingenious objects" in which American manufacturers were beginning to take such pride; and the sandalwood and seal and otter skins which the Chinese had once accepted as payment were fast running out.

Opium proved as good for the dollar as it was for the British pound.

By 1839, every American house at Canton handled the drug, with the lonely exception of D. W. C. Olyphant & Company, opposed to the trade on moral grounds and ridiculed by their rivals as "Zion's Corner."

Russell & Company, which Warren now headed, was the biggest U.S. dealer in opium, and the third largest firm in the trade, British or American.

The drug business bred hypocrisy on both sides. In response to a new imperial edict, for example, the British East India Company had solemnly vowed to abandon the drug traffic in 1800, then expanded its poppy fields and sold the opium produced from them at auction to freelance "country ships" owned by British and Indian traders. The drug supply never even slowed.

The emperor deplored the trade. It drained precious silver from his empire, for one thing; not only coins but heavy bars of raw bullion called *sycee* flowed steadily out of China to the West. And opium vitiated his people; there were said to be more than 2 million Chinese addicts by 1835, and the number grew each day; even members of the imperial household were infected with the deadly craving for the "foreign mud." This seemed to him ungrateful behavior from outsiders to whom he had granted the right to trade, a concession about which the Manchus had never been enthusiastic in the first place.

Chinese officials were frankly contemptuous of the West, and the eagerness of Western nations to do business with them only underlined their scorn. To the emperor, all the other peoples of the world were vassals, a conviction which no amount of evidence seemed able to surmount. When Lord McCartney, an official British emissary, arrived at the gates of Peking with enough gifts to fill ninety wagons in 1793, for example, hoping to demonstrate that a commercial treaty with London would be to the emperor's advantage, the Chinese ruler thanked George III for this gratifying evidence of his "respectful spirit of submission," but he saw no need to encourage commerce since "there is nothing we lack. . . . "

To minimize the damage done to his empire by the barbarians, the emperor restricted the traders to the Canton factories, licensed just thirteen merchants to handle all dealings with foreigners, and held these hong merchants personally responsible should anything go wrong. Foreign traders were not to venture inside the city walls; foreign women were barred even from the factories; foreign ships were forbidden to approach closer than Whampoa, twelve miles downriver.

But Canton was a long way from the Manchu emperor's northern capital at Peking, and events in this southern city had long resisted imperial control. Officials dispatched there soon found themselves overburdened, underpaid, and subject to heavy taxes, for which they leaned heavily on the hong merchants. Some took bribes and in exchange promised to be less than rigorous in enforcing the opium laws. When an opium ship anchored offshore, for example, war junks were likely to be held back until all the precious chests were safely landed and the vessel was under way again, then dispatched to fire a noisy salvo into the sea so that their commander could boast to Peking that he had bravely driven off the barbarians.

If the Chinese authorities ever really became serious about halting the trade, Warren once wrote home, "Foreigners *cannot* by any possibility sell or smuggle the drug into the country."

Most drug transactions were handled briskly at Canton. Incoming opium vessels halted briefly under the lee of Lintin Island in Canton Bay, before proceeding upriver to the official anchorage at Whampoa. Chinese buyers paid for their orders on shore and with hard cash and were given a chit as proof of purchase. Then, aboard the red-painted buyer's boats rowed by as many as sixty men that the Chinese called "fast crabs" or "scrambling dragons," they raced one another to be first at the side of the latest vessel. Ned soon learned to recognize opium ships from afar by the smaller boats that invariably swarmed around them even before they dropped anchor.

On deck, a representative of the firm filled the buyer's order, weighing out the fist-sized cakes of the drug from the 133½-pound chests and receiving a five-dollar commission for every chest he handled. Robert Bennet Forbes, Warren's friend and predecessor as head of the firm, boasted that he made $30,000 for himself this way in just two years. Warren was always more circumspect about his earnings, but the firm's opium profits soared while he was in charge, and his own commissions may have, too.

The traders could not plausibly claim to be ignorant of the human toll the drug took. In 1844, William C. Hunter, a former Russell partner, showed a visitor two flourishing dens within a few hundred yards of the factories themselves, each filled with men in various stages of stupefaction. During a visit to Singapore that same year, Ned Delano himself visited several licensed dens: "Found smokers in all of them. One man was prostrate under its effects—pale, cadaverous, death-like . . . for when I took his pipe from his hand he offered no resistance, though his eyes tried to follow me."

The Americans argued that they only *carried* the drug; what the Chinese did with it once it was out of their hands was not their concern. It was the British who *manufactured* opium, and it was the corruption that pervaded China itself that made its distribution there possible. "The high officers of the Government have not only *connived* at the trade," Warren wrote home, "but the Governor and other officers of the province have bought the drug and have taken it from the stationed ships . . . in their own Government boats."

The sharp, self-serving distinctions the traders made among the Chinese may have helped ease their consciences—which were otherwise well enough developed. (A number of opium traders held strong opinions about such moral issues as slavery, for instance, including Warren, and Ned, who carefully pasted abolitionist doggerel into his scrapbook:

> A boasted flag of Stripes and Stars
> Once fluttered oe'r the waves
> Hangs dripping down in deep disgrace
> Wet with the tears of slaves.)

The Americans treated the hong merchants upon whom they relied for their licit profits with considerable courtesy and respect, for the most part. Warren and his partners had great admiration for Wu Ping-chien, Houqua II, for example, the grave, cultured old merchant who traded heavily with Russell & Company and was considered one of the world's richest men. (He was worth $26 million in 1833, the year Warren first knew him, according to another Russel partner, William C. Hunter.) Even in Warren's old age, Houqua's portrait hung in his library, and he often quoted to his own children something this closest Chinese aquaintance had once said to him: "Mr. Delano, I strive to serve my Heavenly Father on earth as I would have my sons serve me."

But cut off from Canton by both law and custom, the traders had little opportunity to know ordinary Chinese other than as servants, shopkeepers, laborers, or members of angry street mobs. Traditional Chinese xenophobia had a good deal to do with that. But so did the American zeal to get rich and get out fast. "From this country it is impossible for me to write any thing descriptive that can be interesting," John R. Lattimer, a Canton trader who left China about the time Warren arrived, once wrote home, "being debarred the privilege of going into the Country and even into the city, with no other society but our own countrymen. Our business constantly occupies our attention. From the hour of our arrival our constant study is to be away as soon as possible."

Only one Russell partner, William Hunter, ever even bothered to learn Chinese; the rest made do with the curious amalgam called "pidgin" (business) English. And the pages of Ned Delano's diary are filled with evidence of his ignorance of the people and customs of the city that started just a few yards behind his bedroom. Perhaps the opium traders' inability to see most Chinese as other than menials or curiosities helped them keep faceless the hundreds of thousands of Chinese who craved the drug they sold.

In any case, huge profits were being made, and the Delanos and their fellow Americans saw no reason not to compete hard for a share of them. The protests of missionaries and others that the drug trade was intrinsically wicked they found provoking. "I do not pretend to justify the prosecution of the opium trade in a moral and philanthropic point of view," Warren wrote home, "but as a merchant I insist that it has been a fair, honorable and legitimate trade; and to say the worst of it, liable to no further or weightier objections than is the importation of wines, Brandies & spirits into the U. States, England &c."

Robert Bennet Forbes agreed. "As to the effect on the people, there can be no doubt that it was demoralizing to a certain extent; not more so, probably, than the use of ardent spirits," he wrote later; "indeed, it has been asserted with truth that the 20 or 30 thousand chests—say, 12 to 15 million lbs of opium, distributed among 350 millions of people, had a much less deleterious effect . . . than the vile liquor made of rice, called 'samshue.' "

Besides, he added, all the best people did it: " . . . I considered it right to follow the example of England, the East India Company . . . and the merchants to whom I had always been accustomed to look up as exponents of all that was honorable in trade—the Perkins's, the Peabodys, the Russells, the Lows."

The drug trade was risky for the Chinese, who called it "the black tiger" because it had ruined so many: official crackdowns sometimes cut into profits; captured smugglers were occasionally strangled; pirates cruised the coastline; prices shifted wildly, depending on how much of the drug had made it to shore.

But for the foreigners, who usually lingered just long enough to hand over the drug and reap their profit, and were always paid in advance, it was relatively safe and wonderfully lucrative. Many years later, William Hunter recalled the drug traffic with something like rapture: the trader's "sales were pleasantness and his remittances were peace. Transactions seemed to partake of the nature of the drug; they imparted a soothing frame of mind . . . and no bad debts!"

It had all threatened to end suddenly in March of 1839, nine months before Ned arrived, when the emperor appointed the incorruptible Lin Tse-hsu as Imperial Commissioner to Canton, with orders to enforce his long-standing edicts and end the trade forever. Lin surrounded the factories with troops, ordered the traders to turn over to him all their opium for destruction and, further, to promise to import no more. Those who resisted, he warned, would be decapitated. Warren and the other traders had spent several nervous weeks locked inside their hong before the British superintendent of trade, Captain Charles Eliot, gave in, surrendering 20,280 chests—*each* of them containing enough narcotic to render 8,000 of the most hardened, three-pipe-a-day addicts insensible for most of a month. Russell & Company turned over an additional 1,540. All of the drug was dissolved in water, diluted with salt and lime, then dumped into the sea after apologetic prayers were offered to the gods for its defilement.

The British then withdrew to their anchored ships—taking with them in a crate the life-sized portrait of George IV that hung in the mess hall of their hong—and waited for London to dispatch an expeditionary force to punish the Chinese and force the emperor to pay them for the drug his agents had destroyed.

The Americans did not go with them. When Elliot asked them to do so, and thereby help "bring these rascally Chinese to terms," Robert Forbes had responded with considerable heat. "I replied," he recalled many years later, "that *I had not come to China for health or pleasure, and that I should remain at my post as long as I could sell a yard of goods or buy a pound of tea. . . .*"

The British squadron had arrived in June of 1840, blockaded the approach to Canton, and begun a series of small, fierce actions up and down the coast designed to intimidate. The sporadic conflict which followed, and which came to be known as the First Opium War, would last almost three years.

American opinion about the war was divided—just as British opinion was. Some people, including many churchmen, argued that the opium traffic was simply evil. English overseas adventures were never popular, especially along the east coast. The former President and Secretary of State, John Quincy Adams, now chairman of the House Committee on Foreign Affairs, nonetheless rose to England's defense in a widely reported paper read before the Massachusetts Historical Society at Boston. Opium was no more the cause of the quarrel, he said, "than the overthrowing of the tea in the Boston Harbor was the cause of the North American Revolution."

The cause of the war is the *kowtow!*—the arrogant and insupportable pretensions of China, that she will not hold commercial intercourse with the rest of mankind, not upon terms of reciprocity, but upon the insulting and degrading forms of relations between lord and vassal.

Adams's views proved so unpopular that the editor of the *North American Review*, who had already accepted his paper for publication, thought it wise to return it to him.

Still, it was also true that the end result of a British victory—a China more open and receptive to outsiders—would benefit both those who wanted to make money and those who wanted to save souls there. God did sometimes work in truly mysterious ways, and as the conflict dragged on, even some missionaries began to see some virtue in a British triumph. "Although war is bringing its train of horrors upon this heretofore peaceful land," wrote S. Well Williams, a missionary from upstate New York stationed at Canton, "and the still sorer scourge of opium is slaying its thousands, we will encourage ourselves in the name of the Lord. The cause of the war is exceedingly objectionable, [but] so has been many of those in ages past which at the end have brought blessings upon the scene of their devastation." Christ might follow commerce into the heart of China.

The Delanos' sympathies, too, were divided. They had little affection for the English: Captain Warren Delano I, the brothers' mariner father, had been captured and mistreated by the British during the War of 1812. Warren and Ned both sympathized with the Chinese determination to defend their homeland even against modern weaponry, and they were outraged to hear that British sailors were raping and plundering along the coast. "I truly wish that John Bull would meet with one hearty repulse," Ned wrote, "for why should he enter their peaceful habitations and commit the horridest brutalities upon the women?", and when news came of a British defeat in another colonial war being fought in far-off Afghanistan, he was privately pleased: "I very nearly hope that the true owners of the soil, the natives of India, may succeed and drive from their country, the ever-usurping and proud-hearted Britons—that they may never get a foothold in China is a wish connected with that."

At the same time, the Delanos and their friends had often chafed at the same Chinese hauteur that so angered the British. "Great Britain owes it to herself and to the civilized world (in the West)," Warren wrote early in the conflict, "to knock a little reason into this besotted people and teach them to treat strangers with a common decency." And they prayed that if the British were to strike they should strike hard, for a less than telling victory might rouse the Cantonese to take revenge on the factories, and the Americans knew they could not count on the mob making fine distinctions among the traders they found there. Even "the mandarins cannot tell the difference between us," Warren noted; all foreigners remained *Fan Kuei*.

Meanwhile, with the British traders away, the field was left to the Americans, and by the time Ned began his duties, Russell & Company was cleaning up. Robert Forbes had sailed for home, leaving Warren in charge of the firm; as the most senior trader in Canton, he was also the American vice consul. Under his shrewd direction, British tea was being carried out through the Chinese counterblockade to waiting British ships—all at stiff rates, about which the British traders could do nothing but complain. "While we hold the horns," one Briton wrote, "they milk the cow."

"The English are awfully envious of the success of their rivals," Ned noted, "& throw at them every abuse you think of—quietly the Americans pursue a straightforward course, without condescending to notice them. . . ."

That straightforward course also earned Warren profits from the Chinese. A 900-ton British ship, the *Cambridge,* had been trapped inside the Chinese perimeter. Warren bought her cheap, renamed her the *Chesapeake,* then resold her at a comfortable profit to Commissioner Lin who, in turn, had her towed above Whampoa and lined her decks with cannon and barrels of powder; brilliantly colored streamers reading "Courage" fluttered from her masts, meant to scare off any foreigners that sought to sail past her.

Despite the rumors of riots in the city and assault from the sea that from time to time forced the Russell men to pack their belongings and flee to Macao, the life they led at Canton was comfortable—the company chef was superb; there was still plenty of Calcutta ale on hand; each man continued to have his own servant to lay out his white linen suit, see to the mending of his mosquito netting, and stand behind his chair at meals that, one American guest wrote, "could not have been more completely like home if . . . transported by lightning line."

But it was also often a lonely and dispiriting existence. Neither Ned nor Warren ever saw Canton as anything more than a place to make money. Ned pronounced it "a vile hole" even before he got to China; Warren thought life there "about as monotonous as at sea on a long passage." Letters from home arrived months after they were written, if at all. During Ned Delano's seven years at Canton, four of his five sisters died; it became difficult for him to open new letters for fear of more tragic news. Portraits were sent back and forth just so that family members could remember how one another looked. Six months after their sister Susan died of "the fiend consumption," the brothers eagerly opened a parcel containing a memorial portrait of her: "Did not look farther than the head—my dear sister Susan was unlike the picture," Ned wrote, "I am much disappointed." Warren sent home at least two portraits of himself, painted by the celebrated Cantonese artist Lamqua, though he was not overly impressed with either likeness: " . . . in my humble opinion," he wrote, "neither of them look any more like me than they do—like—like—like Martin Van Buren."

There was little to do but work. Office duties filled the daylight hours. In the evenings, Ned sometimes played bowls at a distressingly bumpy lane attached to the factory; more often he joined the other traders in the square out front for a stroll or a game of what one visitor called "the prim and healthful sport of leap-frog," a favorite spectacle of the Cantonese who gathered there at dusk each day to see what the barbarians were doing.

On especially warm evenings, the Russell men sometimes ventured out onto the river, being careful to stay out from under bridges and far enough from shore to remain beyond the range of the stones and garbage that were often hurled at them from hiding.

Locked up together in the hongs for months at a time, the traders got on one another's nerves. Ned was especially sensitive to slights, real or fancied; an overly familiar joke about his girth or youthful appearance, or an unexplained shift in his place at table, could sour him for days.

Private smuggling sometimes added a little excitement. Ned evidently conducted a brisk independent business in silks; he got up early one morning, for example, and "Saw 67 cases of silk smuggled into the Lena's launch. $10,000 at risk. Gained by operation $500. E. King [a Russell partner] discovered the move but I persevered and succeeded."

Hong life was unrelievedly masculine. Traders were at least theoretically barred from the brightly painted floating bordellos called Flower Boats that were tied up here and there along the crowded riverfront. One evening Ned noted that he had "played the gallant to a young lady in a boat. . . . Modesty would not force a kiss from me and I left her with only a squeeze of the hand. Chinese laws being against foreigners entering the boats de plaisir, I did not venture my person in the lady's chamber." Other persons were ventured, however, and some of the sturdy women who rowed the traders up and down the river also proved pliable.

Several of the Delanos' friends kept Chinese mistresses at Macao. William Hunter's bore him at least two children. He proved so fond of her that after setting out for America and his first vacation in eighteen years, he turned back halfway, apparently unable to be apart from her any longer. Ned was disgusted: "The man must be insane. . . . A man who has been from home since 1825 . . . and amassing more than $200,000, return[ing] to China and his miserable Tanka mistress."

On January 7, 1841, the British demolished Chuenpi and the Big Taikok, two fortresses guarding the mouth of the river. Ned and several other Russell men had themselves rowed out to Chuenpi six days later to see the damage firsthand. Three British steamships had first perforated its walls and silenced its guns; then, landing parties of infantrymen and sailors trapped some seven hundred defenders and slaughtered all but a handful as they tried to flee into the sea.

Poking through the ruins, Ned wrote: "I saw the burned body of a Chinaman. Some [British] sailor had put a bamboo in his mouth surmounted by a Chinese scroll. In another room [a] large stain of blood . . . then a mandarin's boot and remnants of hats . . . , guns, bows. . . ." A British marine showed him five still-unburied bodies and cheerfully cut a souvenir for him from the coat of one of them, a wooden tag painted with the dead man's name and unit in Chinese characters. The rest of the bodies had been hastily buried in a mass grave just outside the walls, over which the British had put up a bamboo topped with a coolie's straw hat and a hand-lettered sign: "This is the Rode to Gloury."

Ned was appalled—"What horrid butchery!", he noted—but he was not undone: "Ate a hearty dinner," he added before going to bed that evening.

Tension was high, and the Delanos themselves inadvertently added to it. A few days after Ned's visit to the ruined fort, he and Warren were once again on the river, an arsenal of arms on deck as protection against pirates and for shooting at waterbirds. The boatmen acted as loaders, and as one returned Warren's shotgun to the deck, it went off. Two men were hit: one died within minutes; the other was only scratched on the scalp. Their angry companions refused to row further until the rest of the Delanos' guns were fired into the water. The bloody corpse was wrapped in a blanket and carried below. The incident "saddened our hearts," Ned noted, "and therefore our dinner was not eaten with that good relish with which it ordinarily is."

Word of the shooting had somehow preceded them to Canton and, while they were still several miles from the factories, the dead man's family rowed out to meet them:

The wife or widow set up an ugly howling and wailing. Our boat was stopped until the matter should be settled. 2 of our servants

[went] to Canton for money. We offered [the grieving family] in charity one hundred and fifty dollars. The family and relatives after quarreling upwards of an hour about it, came to the conclusion that the brother of the deceased would in consideration of a . . . present of $200, marry the widow and receive said sum in consideration. This was granted, and after humbugging two or three hours more the body of the deceased was conveyed away with the whole concern. . . . The family have probably more money now than they ever have had or ever will have again. The deceased was employed as a common boatman, which class actually get from 1.50 to $2 p[er] month! of course . . . the death of this man is a lucky thing for them. . . .

Later, when an agitated trader whispered that he had heard some foreigners had killed two boatmen, Ned assured him "it is all nonsense."

The war seemed to be coming closer. On February 2, the British paddle steamer *Nemesis* landed a lone Congreve rocket among the barrels of powder lining the decks of the refitted *Chesapeake*, the ship Warren had sold to the Chinese. Looking out the factory window a dozen miles away, Ned saw the explosion, "a sudden and brilliant light" on the horizon: "This spectacle made my heart and I reckon the hearts of those with me, *go pit a pat* quite seriously."

That evening there were nine for dinner, eight Americans and a Spanish silk merchant unable to arrange passage home. It was a less convivial evening than usual for, as Ned noted, all the guests nervously believed that they represented "the entire foreign community of the city and most likely of the whole Empire."

A month later, when a British assault on Canton seemed only a matter of hours away and thousands of Chinese were fleeing into the countryside, the frantic prefect of Canton asked Warren to intercede with the British. Warren said he would see what he could do, but only as a strict neutral interested in protecting his firm's property. The British commander received him politely enough, but would guarantee nothing.

On the way back to the city, Warren's fast boat, flying a white flag of truce, was ambushed from shore. He described what happened next to Ned, waiting anxiously at Whampoa:

When near Canton . . . the cowardly Chinese let go a shot at my boat, which passed some 30 feet over our heads, two men jumped overboard, two or three threw themselves on the bottom of the boat and roared like squalling babies, while the remainder in the greatest error and confusion imaginable, screeched and screamed to the soliders, to desist firing. . . . The Lingo (translator) then went on shore, and after an hour or more of delay, half a dozen petty soldier Mandarins came on board, and took me in triumph to the city of Canton. Yes, I was marched into the City, the distance of three-quarters of a mile, a prisoner, to the wondrous astonishment, admiration and gratification of a gaping multitude. The gallant soldiers informing those we passed of the terrible conflict which had taken place. . . . I was brought before his Excellency, the Commissioner Yang [General Yang Fang, assistant commander at Canton], a decrepit-looking man of the age of *74 years,* with bleared eyes, and deaf as a haddock, who asked me some foolish questions, examined my clothing, hat, shoes and cane, and expressed his surprise that my head was not shaved. He took my hands, examining them carefully, and *smelling them,* asked me to unbutton my shirt-bosom, and show my hide, which I did, and he then pronounced me a good man, an excellent man, one of the best men he had ever known, and seizing a lousy, ragged, dirty soldier, who stood within three inches of His Excellency, said I was "all the same as he."

Warren was released after urging his captors to seek some sort of compromise with the city's besiegers. They did, agreeing to pay the British within seven days a ransom of $6 million, more than twice the annual British revenue from tea.

The British traders finally returned to Canton in March 1841, under the protection of naval guns that fired over the factories into the city itself. Most of the Americans, including Ned, took cover when the first shot was fired, but Warren stayed on the roof watching the shells arc over his head to crash into the tangled streets.

The Delanos had mixed emotions at seeing a semblance of normal trade return: the threat of war seemed to have lessened, but business was no longer exclusively in their hands. Looking over the books for 1839 and 1840, Ned could not help sighing over the "Magnificent profits, the like of which I think cannot again accrue."

The war moved on northward along the coast and up the Yangtze as far as Nanking, the British fleet blasting its way through the war junks to stop at one fortified village after another just long enough to plunder it before moving on to the next prize. (British soldiers and sailors and Indian sepoys alike competed for treasure, and the Hindustani word for plunder—*loot*—entered the language after this expedition.) The

Chinese regiments could do little to stop them; their special whistling arrows and the sword-waving warriors who turned brave somersaults as they advanced were no match for British firepower.

Ned was disgusted that the British victory had been so effortless. Had the Chinese had "any of the Tartar spirit," he wrote, "not an Englishman would escape from his present *interior* position to tell the tale of bloodshed, and of punishment to the invader of the soil of a peaceable people . . . I have no pity for them—the idea of 10,000 men submittancing 10,000,000!!"

The Treaty of Nanking that officially ended the war in 1842 extorted from the emperor $21 million in indemnities and forced him to open five new ports to commerce and to cede Hong Kong to the British. There was no mention of opium—both sides pretending to know nothing about it—and so the trade continued. The American Treaty of Wang Hiya, negotiated by Caleb Cushing two years later, expressly declared the drug "contraband," but Yankee traders, including the Delanos, continued to ship and sell it with more ease and enthusiasm than ever.

(The Second and bloodier Opium War of 1858 ended again in British victory; the Treaty of Tientsin opened still more trading ports and fixed a tariff rate for opium, thereby finally giving the trade at least quasi-legitimacy. The opium problem grew steadily worse. Since the drug could now be imported without harassment, the emperor decreed that his subjects might grow it themselves; by 1880, fully one third of the arable land in the mountainous province of Yunnan was blanketed with poppies, and at the turn of the century there were thought to be 15 million Chinese addicts. In 1906, the British and Chinese jointly agreed to phase out the traffic in Indian opium over ten years, but it continued to flourish inside China until 1949, when the Communists began to stamp it out.)

In the autumn of 1842, Warren sailed for home for the first time in almost a decade, leaving Ned to look after his interests; he returned just over a year later with his sister, Dora, and a new wife, Catherine Lyman of Northampton, Massachusetts, and their lady's maid, aboard Robert Bennet Forbes's new *Paul Jones*. The ship was sleek and swift—the passage took just 106 days—and fitted out with the very first icehouse in the China trade. "We had ice from the [*Paul Jones*]," Ned noted in wonder. "Sent out for mint and for the first time in China . . . mint juleps were concocted and drunk." There were crisp New England pippin apples, too, "and I need not say that I have eaten

[them] with much gusto," and the next day there was still enough ice left to make "ICE CREAMS, things before unheard of in China."

Life seemed to be improving for the Delano brothers. Warren and his little family—a child named Susan was born in 1844—bought a big abandoned bungalow overlooking the busy harbor at Macao, called variously Arrowdale (because the Delanos enjoyed archery in the garden) and Rat's Retreat (because of the original occupants, which had to be evicted before the family moved in).

Ned, soon to be a full-fledged partner in the firm, lived with them whenever he was at Macao. In 1844, he traveled to India to oversee the inspection and buying of opium, throwing himself into amicable but sometimes frantic competition at Bombay and Calcutta with the representatives of other companies. (He was greatly pleased when the clipper *Antelope*, which he had managed to load with 1,400 opium chests, delivered that cargo to Warren at Whampoa before proceeding on to Macao with just 250 chests for his chief rivals, the British firm of Lancelot Dent & Company.)

While Ned was away, however, Warren's infant daughter died, a second was born but seemed alarmingly frail, and Arrowdale was gutted by fire. By the time he got back to China, his older brother had decided it was time to go home. "Before dark," Ned wrote a few days after his return to Macao, "I accompanied Warren to the Deadhouse . . . to see the case containing the remains of his sweet little Susie. Warren was a good [deal] affected—and coming home he discoursed freely to me about his fears for Katie's mind—its safety. Since Susie's death, K. has been queer. . . . The voyage home—the change of scene, mode of life, etc. etc. I think must restore K. to her usual sanity." Warren and his family returned to America in the summer of 1846, accompanied by a Chinese wet-nurse and manservant.

Catherine Delano did recover her equilibrium, and eventually bore nine more children; one of them, named Sara, would become the mother of President Franklin Delano Roosevelt. Within a few months of his return, Warren was "heels & head in business," according to Ned. "Mixing in all kinds"—railroads, coal mines, shipbuilding; "I fear he is branching out too much."

Ned found Canton insufferable without his brother's benevolen protection. More senior partners were overseeing tea, opium, and imports, leaving him with only the firm's correspondence to handle, a clerkish task he now thought beneath him. He detested the new head of the company, Paul S. Forbes—"a miserable, sneaking fellow"—and the feeling seems to have been reciprocated; though the two men worked in the same small office every day and dined together nearly every night, they often did not speak. Ned felt left out of things, had difficulty sleeping for "thinking, fretting, brooding," resented what he considered "a great deal of undertone conversation, whispering," and came to believe that "the *looks* of *people* betray the most horrible intentions toward me."

Finally—and probably to everyone's relief—Ned managed to work out satisfactory terms under which he could withdraw from the firm and sail for home, carrying with him almost $80,000 in profits. He began his journey on July 31, 1847. "Leave Canton," he wrote that night, "and wish I could say, never to be bothered more with the place. . . ."

He never really was. Ned did not marry and lived much of the time at Algonac, Warren's stately home at Newburgh, New York, dabbling in several businesses without much energy or success and growing hugely fat. He died suddenly of a heart attack aboard his yacht in the summer of 1881.

Warren Delano did have to bother about China again, for Ned's fears about his overextending himself proved accurate. He had made himself a millionaire by the age of fifty, but the Panic of 1857 ruined him, and in 1860 he was forced to go back to China, to Hong Kong this time, where he spent five more years recouping his losses in the two trades that had initially made him so rich so rapidly—tea and opium.

In 1879, more than thirty years after Warren left Canton, his old friend Robert Forbes asked him to write up his memories of life there in the old days. Both men had since earned distinguished reputations and several fortunes in fields unrelated to the China trade, but Forbes had grown nostalgic for it. He hoped that Warren and all the surviving Russell men would contribute memories, he said; there were nearly one hundred of them; the results would be used to compile a colorful company history.

Warren sent him a terse summary of his career in China in which he did not mention his participation in the drug trade. Some of Forbes's other former partners were still less obliging, wanting no part of any history that might prove too intrusive. Even Forbes finally thought better of his scheme: "The only thing I fear," he confessed to Warren, "is that in giving a sketch of the causes and effects of the opium traffic . . . I may say too much." He finally chose to say nothing.

Warren may have been relieved. He devoted his old age to keeping track of his investments, running his big estate, contributing to Republican candidates and to other causes he considered worthy, among them Booker T. Washington's work among Southern blacks.

The old opium days were allowed to fade from memory.

Some years after Warren Delano's death in 1898, an elderly Unitarian clergyman who had benefited from his generosity wrote a tribute to him. "This man seemed to have intuitions of right, justice and equity in small matters, as in great," he said. "Dishonesty, pretense, chicanery, come how they might and in whom they would, felt themselves rebuked in his presence. . . . His moral intensity and practical earnestness never relaxed their hold on what he felt to be good: the rest he left to God."

For a long time, American historians also seem to have been content to let the Yankee traders' pursuit of opium profits largely be forgotten.

Even Admiral Samuel Eliot Morison devoted just three uncharacteristically defensive pages to it in his monumental *Maritime History of Massachusetts 1783–1860* (1921). He found comfort in the fact that while "For English firms [opium smuggling] was vital, for Boston firms it was incidental," though it is not easy to see why. Morison was perhaps on firmer ground when he went on, "at the risk of appearing to black the kettle," to argue that "there is a difference between smuggling opium under the official wink [as the Americans did] and driving in opium with cannon and bayonet when officials are making a sincere if tardy effort at moral reform."

More objective study of the American opium trade and its impact on buyers and sellers alike had to await a more recent generation of scholars with access to Chinese as well as American sources, writers such as Jacques M. Downs, John King Fairbank, Peter Ward Fay, and Charles C. Stelle.

No one knows what FDR knew of his grandfather's involvement in the drug business. When the columnist Westbrook Pegler accused the President and his wife of living off the fortune left by "an old buccaneer" who had wrested it from "a slave traffic as horrible and degrading as prostitution," the White House maintained a discreet silence.

But Eleanor Roosevelt had been stung by Pegler's charge, and when she visited Hong Kong in 1953, she made a point of asking a veteran British merchant about the opium era. After talking with him, she reluctantly concluded, "I suppose it is true that the Delanos and the Forbeses, like everybody else, had to include a limited amount of opium in their cargoes to do any trading at all."

I wrote this piece for the August 1986 issue of *American Heritage* in collaboration with Warren Delano's great-great-grandson, Frederic Delano Grant, Jr., an authority on the China trade and his own distinguished family. I first told the tale in *Before the Trumpet*, but this version includes material unearthed since.

"GET ACTION!": THEODORE ROOSEVELT

I'M NO ORATOR," THEODORE ROOSEVELT ONCE SAID, "AND IN writing I'm afraid I'm not gifted at all. . . . If I have anything at all resembling genius it is the gift for leadership." That gift helped propel him to the presidency at just forty-two, making him the youngest man ever to occupy that office, to the anger and astonishment of a good many older politicians who thought themselves far better equipped than he for power. It is easy to see how they were led to underestimate him.

There was nothing physically prepossessing about Theodore Roosevelt. He stood no taller than 5 feet 9 and was built like a barrel. His blue eyes squinted out nearsightedly through a pince-nez, and his brown mustache framed teeth so large and white they sometimes frightened friends as well as enemies. The British writer H. G. Wells once recalled "the friendly peering snarl of his face, like a man with the sun in his eyes." His voice was high-pitched, even squeaky, his delivery rapid and explosive. "I always think of man biting ten-penny nails when I think of Roosevelt making a speech," an old admirer wrote.

Nor was it any special suppleness of thought that accounted for his rise. His mind did rove widely: there was very little that did not interest Roosevelt, and there was still less about which he did not have a vigorous opinion. And he was a prodigious writer: he managed to produce some 150,000 letters during his crowded life, and 38 books, far more than any other American politician, let alone any other President. His subjects included everything from naval history to the habits of grizzly bears, personal conduct to national preparedness. But he did not often pause to probe deeply; his views often seem simply muscular and self-evident on paper, somehow better suited to his own confident time than to our uncertain one. "My problems are moral problems," he once said, "and my teaching has been morality."

Yet when he shrilled such sentiments aloud, he drove audiences to delirium. The vivid force of his character and personality, his unabashed, contagious joy in taking charge made the difference. That power winks only faintly now through the jittery silent footage that provides all but the oldest among us our only glimpse of him. But those who experienced it firsthand never got over it, and struggled to find the words with which to describe the experience. A political foe called him "a steam-engine in trousers." A British visitor thought him comparable only to Niagara Falls among the natural wonders of the New World. One woman journalist who sat next to him at a concert found him unnerving even when he was momentarily at rest: "I felt his clothes might not contain him, he was so steamed up, so ready to go, to attack anything, anywhere." "His personality so crowds the room," another reporter remembered, "that the walls are worn thin and threaten to burst outward. You go to the White House, you shake hands with Roosevelt and hear him talk, and then go home and wring the personality out of your clothes."

"Roosevelt bit me," said the Kansas journalist William Allen White, "and I went mad." So did much of the United States. During his tenure in office, TR may have been the most admired President in history; he was undoubtedly the most colorful. When he won the election in his own right in 1904 (he had originally succeeded to the office at William McKinley's assassination in 1901), he did so by the largest popular majority in history up to that time. Four years later, had he not felt obliged to fulfill his own pledge not to succeed himself, he might have done still better. And when he did finally try for the White House again in 1912, as the leader of his own Progressive or "Bull Moose" Party, he swamped the incumbent Republican, William Howard Taft, and came within striking distance of the Democratic winner, Woodrow Wilson.

Roosevelt's ability to lead—and the rugged, restless constitution that went along with it—was not really a gift at all, but a hard-won achievement. To an extraordinary degree, Theodore Roosevelt was his own creation.

Everything about his earliest years convinced him, he once wrote, that life was one "long campaign where every victory merely leaves the ground free for another battle." His first battle was fought simply to survive. He was born to wealth, but as every schoolboy once knew, he was also a small, spindly child with feeble eyesight, a sufferer from asthma so severe that he sometimes could not summon the strength to blow out his bedside candle. He wrote that often he had lain in bed, frightened that he might not be able to pull enough air into his lungs to make it through the night. He taught himself to face down such terrors. "There were all kinds of things of which I was afraid at first," he confessed in his autobiography, " . . . but by acting as if I were not afraid, I gradually ceased to be afraid."

Still, that struggle left him so weak that he had to rely on his younger brother, Elliott, to shield him from bullies. Unable to win through size and strength his rightful place in his loving but fiercely competitive family, "Teedie" learned the power of words and charm and book learning to call attention to himself. He read endlessly, battling his way through heavy, grown-up tomes in search of facts; and he talked incessantly, his thoughts sometimes tumbling so far ahead of his words that some early observers thought he suffered from an impediment. At Harvard, one professor would finally have to remind him, "See here, Roosevelt, let *me* talk. I'm running this course." But within his family it worked perfectly: his siblings idolized him all their lives. So would a good many of his countrymen.

Just as TR learned to will away fear and to make himself heard, so he willed himself to become strong. His father was a formidable man. "The best man I ever knew," Roosevelt once wrote, but also "the only man of whom I was ever really afraid," at once so strong and so upright, energetic and affectionate that members of his family sometimes called him "Greatheart" without a hint of irony. He took his son aside when the boy was eleven or twelve, and told him that a good mind alone would not ensure success—he must build himself a powerful body to match it. Theodore did so, spending thousands of hours chinning himself, lifting weights, and rattling a punching bag that was set up for him on the back piazza of the Roosevelts' Manhattan brownstone. Although he never became an outstanding athlete, he was a dogged and enthusiastic one, good enough to make the lightweight boxing finals in college.

TR never abandoned any of the battles begun in boyhood. He successfully dominated others all his life through torrents of words. His Secretary of State, John Hay, once calculated that during one two-hour White House dinner, the other guests had been permitted to talk for a combined total of four and half minutes; all the rest had been Roosevelt. He continued to test his ability to overcome fear, facing Spanish bullets and enraged water buffalo alike without flinching, and undertaking a perilous expedition into the South American interior after leaving the presidency. And he never stopped trying to build his body: in the White House he went several rounds each week with one of a number of artillery officers recruited for the purpose and instructed not to pull punches. When a blow from one of his opponents accidentally destroyed the sight in the President's left eye, TR later wrote, "I thought it better to acknowledge that I had become an elderly man and would have to stop boxing. I then took up jiu-jitsu."

Tragedy and disappointment were to be ignored, so far as that was possible. His first wife, Alice Lee, died in childbirth; his autobiography does not even mention her name. Nor does it more than touch upon TR's single loss at the polls, in the race for mayor of New York in 1886.

"The most fundamental characteristic of Theodore Roosevelt was his aggression," his fine modern biographer, Edmund Morris, has written, "conquest being, to him, synonymous with growth." But he did not so much conquer fear or weakness or self-doubt as learn to hold them at bay through willpower and unending activity. "Get action," he once exhorted a young friend seeking guidance, "do things, be sane. Don't fritter away your time; create, act, take a place wherever you are and be somebody; get action!"

There was an excess of energy in everything he did. At his inaugural reception in 1905, he eagerly clasped 8,150 hands, still a record for any man anywhere; he routinely smashed mosquitoes with blows that would have stunned lions. Even his rocking was hyperactive, his chair edging its way across the piazza as he devoured a book. He did not organize his time, exactly, it was more that he filled every moment of it. When he went to Africa on safari in 1909, he took with him one hundred books so as not to waste a minute between stalks; each volume was especially bound in pigskin so that the blood from his kills could easily be wiped off. His own admiring but weary family liked to recite a poem about him which included the lines: "At five o'clock he takes the air, / He does not take it *all*, of course . . . " Roosevelt himself once stated the reason underlying his ceaseless activity: "Black care rarely sits behind a rider whose pace is fast enough."

Few could match his pace. "I rose like a rocket," he once said: elected to the New York legislature at twenty-three; candidate for mayor of New York at twenty-eight; U.S. Civil Service Commissioner under two presidents; president of the police commission of New York; Assistant Secretary of the Navy; organizer and leader of the Rough Riders in the Spanish-American War and a national hero at forty; then, in three still busier years, governor, Vice President, President.

For all his energy and initiative, he could not have risen so far so fast on his own. The press was his enthusiastic partner. His career coincided with the growth of a new kind of newspaper aimed at the growing big-city readership interested in the doings of the rich and famous and filled with photographs and reforming zeal. He could be counted on to provide glorious, gaudy copy. "Roosevelt has the knack of doing things," one publisher wrote, "and doing them noisily, clamorously; while he is in the neighborhood the public can no more look the other way than the small boy can turn his head away from a circus parade followed by a steam calliope." Within weeks of his arrival at Albany as a freshman legislator, he was known throughout New York as "the cyclone assemblyman" for his noisy frontal assault on corruption and old-line politicians. Frontline dispatches from Cuba spread the news of his courage under fire to a country avid for heroes. It is not surprising that as TR entered the Buffalo, New York, parlor in which he took the presidential oath of office after McKinley's death, he asked, "Where are all the newspapermen?" and held up the ceremony until some two dozen of them elbowed their way inside.

No President before him had ever allowed such easy access to the White House. Through the newspapers, ordinary Americans came to know him and his big boisterous family almost as if they lived down the street, or, more aptly, in the big house on the other side of town. They learned the names of all six of his children; read aloud to one another his hunting adventures; delighted in the moral fervor with which he championed everything from the Panama Canal and the preservation of the wilderness to simplified spelling. "Roosevelt's fighting was so much a part of the life of the period, and was so tied up with the newspapers . . . as to constitute almost the whole of the passing show," the journalist Mark Sullivan once remembered.

TR had considerable personal dignity: for all his geniality, no one who knew him well ever slapped his back or called him "Teddy." His pleasure in people, every kind of person, was huge and unfeigned. But, unlike most politicians, he insisted on remaining himself. Others had to take him as he was or not at all. When, fresh from Harvard, he resolved to shove his way into what he called "the governing class," he knew, as Edmund Morris has written, that it was "socially beneath his own," and on his early visits to Morton Hall, the smoky Republican club over a Manhattan saloon where he broke into politics, he wore evening clothes. "I insisted on taking part in all the discussions," he later told a reporter about his earliest contacts with shirt-sleeved politicians. "Some sneered at my black coat and . . . tall hat. But I made them understand that I should come dressed as I chose. . . . Then, after the discussions, I used to play poker and smoke with them."

Roosevelt was not given to introspection. He would always rather lead than theorize about leadership. But he despised those who sought to succeed out of simple greed. "If there is one tendency of the day which more than any other is unhealthy and undesirable," he wrote in 1900, "it is the tendency to deify mere 'smartness,' unaccompanied by a sense of moral accountability. . . . The successful man, whether in business or in politics, who has risen by conscienceless swindling of his neighbors, by deceit and chicanery, by unscrupulous cunning, stands toward society as a dangerous wild beast. The mean and cringing admiration which such a career commands among those who think crookedly or not at all makes this kind of success perhaps the most dangerous of all the influences that threaten our national life." Nor did he think fame or riches the best measure of success. "If a man lives a decent life and does his work fairly and squarely so that those dependent upon him and attached to him are better for his having lived, then he is a success."

By that relatively modest definition, TR was certainly successful. No more attentive, loving husband or father ever occupied the White House. But professionally, he was never satisfied as anyone's subordinate: even the name he chose for the big comfortable house he built as a young man at Oyster Bay, New York, suggests the scope of his ambition—Sagamore (Chieftain's) Hill. No President ever enjoyed his job more. He never agonized over how lonely it was at the top: he loved it there, loved to feel his hand "guiding great machinery," he said, though he sometimes complained that even a President's power was not enough to accomplish all that he wanted to accomplish. "Oh," he once said to his admiring young cousin, Franklin Roosevelt, "if I only could be President and Congress, too, for just 10 minutes." He was never content merely to preside, as a good many of his predecessors had been. The office provided an unrivaled opportunity for the action without which he was never happy. "My view," he wrote after leaving the White House, "was that every executive officer in high position, was a steward of the people bound actively and affirmatively to do all he could for the people, and not content himself with the negative merit of keeping his talents undamaged in a napkin."

It sometimes seemed that he could never get enough of leading. On summer weekends he loved to take as many as fourteen children—his own six, plus a lively, shifting cast of small relations—on long, strenuous dashes through the woods and marshes around Sagamore Hill. The game was called "Point-to-point," and it had a single inviolable rule: Obstacles were to be overcome, not circumvented; one pushed through brambles, waded streams, crawled under fences or scrambled over them, and never, never went *around* anything. Sometimes older people took part. His sister, Corinne Roosevelt Robinson, recalled one race when TR came upon "an especially unpleasant-looking bathing house with a very steep roof." She prayed he would somehow contrive to lead the pack around it. Not a chance. "I can still see the sturdy body of the President of the United States," she wrote long after, "hurling himself at the obstruction and with singular agility chinning himself to the top and sliding down on the other side." Point-to-point was a good metaphor for Theodore Roosevelt's leadership style—or at least for the style he advocated. Adversaries were to be met head-on.

His own relentless buoyance was not always perfectly suited to the occasion: under fire in Cuba, he came upon one of his Rough Riders, propped against a wall and clearly dying of his wounds. TR stopped, clasped his hand, and said, "Well, old man, isn't this splendid?" But his old comrades-in-arms overlooked such lapses. Introducing him to a Texas audience during the 1900 campaign, one over-enthusiastic veteran shouted, "My fellow citizens, vote for my colonel! Vote for my colonel, and he will lead you, as he led us, like sheep to the slaughter!"

He could be savage in his denunciations of those who opposed him. He saw himself as battling away always for the right, and was able to convince others of that vision. But he treated those who worked with him with care and kindness, for the most part. He exaggerated only slightly when he wrote: "Most of the men who did the best work under me felt that ours was a partnership . . . that it mattered not what position any one of us held so long as in that position he gave the very best that was in him." Roosevelt was "the most advisable man I ever knew," recalled one member of his cabinet.

Mike Murphy, an Irish-born athletic trainer then famous for fielding great Yale teams, never forgot his visit to the President. Roosevelt, he said later, was the greatest trainer he had ever seen: "Give me 60 men and every one a champion, and let that man at Oyster Bay have 60 other men, and every one of 'em a dub, and his team would lick mine every time. . . . That man . . . would tell a miler that he could reel off a mile in four minutes. And not only would that man *think* he could run in four minutes, but by God, he'd do it!"

Theodore Roosevelt was just fifty when he left the White House, and only fifty-nine when he died on January 5, 1918. As the pallbearers carried his coffin through the snow-covered trees to a hilltop grave at Oyster Bay, and the family followed along behind it, a New York police captain said to his sister: "Do you remember the *fun* of him, Mrs. Robinson? It was not only that he was a great man, but, oh, there was such fun in being led by him."

Success! April 1985

THE LONG REIGN OF PRINCESS ALICE: ALICE ROOSEVELT LONGWORTH

UNION STATION IN WARTIME WASHINGTON. A YOUNG MAN IN a navy uniform escorts a short, stocky blond woman in her fifties along the crowded platform toward a waiting train. There is nothing especially striking about her, but she carries a big framed caricature of Franklin and Eleanor Roosevelt that attracts the attention of most of the people who pass along on either side of her: "I'm just a peasant," she says again and again to all these perfect strangers, her bright blue eyes rolling upwards. "I won't go *anywhere* without a picture of my king and queen!"

The woman was Alice Roosevelt Longworth, the eldest child of Theodore Roosevelt, and this incident was recalled for me recently by her long-ago escort, the son of a girlhood friend, who also vividly remembered his own relief when he finally got her settled on her train.

She is best remembered now for the maliciously witty things she said over the course of some seventy years in Washington: it was she who suggested that Calvin Coolidge had been "weaned on a pickle" (though she liked to credit her dentist with having said it first); she who compared Thomas Dewey to "the little man on the wedding cake" and said about Douglas MacArthur's fastidiously arranged pate, "Never trust a man who combs his hair from his left arm-pit"; and she really did have a sofa pillow embroidered with the legend "If you can't say something good about someone, sit right here by me."

She was hard to pin to paper. At least two early biographers failed to get far beneath her spiky surface. Mrs. Longworth failed, too: her autobiography, *Crowded Hours,* is uniformly and atypically bland. Until now, the most graphic portrait has been Michael Teague's *Mrs. L.,* compiled from taped interviews that captured something of the relentless irreverence that held the fascinated attention of everyone from Kaiser Wilhelm II to Richard Nixon, Robert Taft to Robert Kennedy.

An inveterate gossip, Mrs. Longworth might have enjoyed Carol Felsenthal's book, *Alice Roosevelt Longworth,* had it been about someone else: it is far more candid than its predecessors, and written with far less wary reverence. But she was always careful to keep her own private life off-limits to strangers, and on the evidence of this latest study, hers was a wise decision. For all the glitter of its cast and the good gag lines repeated along the way, the tale it tells is mostly sad.

When her mother, Alice Lee Roosevelt, died within hours of giving birth to her in 1884, her father fled west to forget, leaving her in the care of his remarkable sister, Anna. Alice's first "hazy recollection" of the mysterious man her aunt insisted was her father came when, not yet three, she watched him return from a fox-hunt during which he had characteristically shattered an arm and cut his face trying to leap a five-foot stone wall. When he dismounted and came toward the little girl, one arm dangling useless at his side, grinning through the blood pouring down his face, she tried to run away. "I started screaming at this apparition," she remembered, "and he started shaking me to shut me up which only made me scream more. So, he shook more. It was a theme which was to be repeated with variations, in later years."

TR never spoke of his first wife after her death, failed ever to mention her even to her own daughter, apparently because he believed that his decision to marry again in 1886 was a sign of his inconstancy: remarriage was a sin and Alice a reminder of his having committed it. "My father obviously didn't want the symbol of his infidelity around," she once recalled, writing of herself. ". . . It was all so dreadfully Victorian and mixed up."

Edith Kermit Roosevelt, however, insisted she be permitted to raise Alice as her daughter. It was a gesture made out of conscientiousness rather than affection, a fact made increasingly evident to Alice as her stepmother gave birth to five adored children of her own. She would always seem an outsider in her father's house. "Father doesn't care for me, that is to say one eighth as much as he does for the other children," she once confided to her diary, and for this she blamed herself: "It is perfectly true that he doesn't, and, Lord, why *should* he?"

There was another waif in the Roosevelt family: Cousin Eleanor, the orphaned daughter of Elliott, TR's alcoholic brother, raised by maternal relatives whose feelings for her were no more genuinely fond, no less grimly dutiful, than Edith Roosevelt's for her stepdaughter. She would develop into a shy, self-conscious woman, chronically unsure, despite the great fame that came to her, whether she truly belonged anywhere or could be loved by anyone, convinced she could carve a place for herself only through service to others. Alice was scornful of her cousin's sometimes excessive piety: "I can still see those large blue eyes fixed on one," she told Michael Teague, "worrying about one, and wanting you to know that in her you had a friend. She always wanted to discuss things like whether Contentment was better than Happiness, and whether they conflicted with one another. Things like that, which I didn't give a damn about."

Alice learned early not to give a damn. Her insecurities were nearly as great as Eleanor's, but she dealt with them entirely differently: if others failed to pay enough heed to her, she would be heedless in return. "I pray for a fortune," she wrote. "I care for nothing except to amuse myself in a charmingly expensive way."

She was an excitable tomboy as a child, clamoring for short hair and trousers to match her brothers', and as the striking "Princess Alice" of the White House, she reveled in the publicity she generated by carrying a live snake in her purse, smoking in public, eating asparagus with her gloves on, waving at the crowd from the inaugural stand. (Her father hissed at her to stop this last, and when she asked him why, replied, ". . . this is *my* inauguration!") A family friend called her "a young wild animal . . . put into good clothes."

To everyone's relief, she married Nicholas Longworth in 1906. As she left the White House on her wedding day, her stepmother pulled her close: "I want you to know that I'm glad to see you go," said Edith Roosevelt. "You've never been anything but trouble." The marriage was a disaster. Longworth was a charming, wealthy Republican congressman from Ohio who played both poker and the violin with consummate skill, but he was also a part-time drunk—"He'd rather be tight than President," Alice said—and an almost full-time philanderer: the last of a long line of his mistresses made a point of attending his funeral in 1931, veiled in black and stalking up the aisle in full view of his widow to lay a bunch of violets on his coffin. Alice herself shed no tears, went home and burned most of her husband's papers—and his Stradivarius.

She took up with at least two other men, both of them flamboyant and leonine—the labor leader John L. Lewis, and Republican Senator William E. Borah of Idaho, who, according to Felsenthal, was the real father of her only child, a daughter named Paulina, born to her at the age of forty-one in 1925, while she was still married to Longworth.

Spurned as an infant, Alice now ignored her own infant daughter, and when the girl grew old enough to speak, ensured that she did not do so often by interrupting or belittling her whenever she made the attempt: in the home of Alice Roosevelt Longworth there was room for only one child. Paulina developed a stutter, lapsed into long silences, rarely bathed. In 1944, she married Alexander McCormick Sturm, an alcoholic eccentric whose grandiose ambitions for himself did not include sustained work of any kind. The same family friend who escorted Mrs. Longworth through Union Station during the war also remembers a spooky evening with Paulina and her fat, pallid husband, during which they consumed a bottle of Scotch while playing at being an eighteenth-century German noble and his consort, complete with phantom tenants and servants whom they addressed by name. According to Felsenthal, Alex drank himself to death and Paulina attempted suicide several times before finally succeeding at it in 1957, leaving her body to be discovered by her own ten-year-old daughter, Joanna.

Mrs. Longworth was devastated. "She kept saying, 'I wonder, I wonder, is it all my fault?' " a friend remembered. "Could it be my fault?" Perhaps in part as expiation, she took on at the age of seventy-three the raising of her granddaughter, forging the closest thing to a genuine, reciprocal friendship she seems ever to have been able to manage. But she dealt with the memory of her dead daughter precisely as her father had dealt with that of her mother: no one was to mention Paulina's name; no pictures of her hung in her picture-filled house.

Alice's craving for financial comfort eventually tapered off, but her carefully cultivated frivolousness remained obstinately intact. Frightened of public speaking, perhaps frightened, too, of venturing much beyond the Washington salons in which she knew she shone, she shied away from an active role in politics, working behind the scenes against the League of Nations and aid to the Allies before World War II, but discouraging those who wanted her to run for Congress, or for Vice President under Herbert Hoover to help offset the appeal of her cousin Franklin.

FDR's four presidential victories were to her usurpations. "There we were," she explained later, "descendants of a popular president, and what happens? A fifth cousin comes along and gets into the White House. Can you think of anything more distressing." Her contempt for the *nouveaux* Roosevelts was unmerciful: "My poor cousin," she liked to say, "he suffered from polio so he was put in a brace; and now he wants to put the entire U.S. into a brace. . . ." She saw even Pearl Harbor in purely personal terms: "Well friends," she told her luncheon guests on December 7, 1941. "Franklin asked for it, now he's got it."

She was largely uninterested in the substance of political debate: it was the spectacle she enjoyed; she attended all the McCarthy hearings, for example, alternately cheering on the senator from Wisconsin and his victims; ". . . she didn't care who got banged in the head," a friend said, "as long as it was an exciting show."

Alice outlived almost all of her contemporaries, presiding over dinners at which generation after generation of feuding politicians found themselves seated next to one another so that she could enjoy their discomfiture, keeping her regal chin high even after a double mastectomy left her, she said, "the only topless octogenarian in Washington."

Moments before she died at ninety-six in 1980, she stuck out her tongue at a family friend.

American Heritage May 1988

"THE PEACE OF IT IS DIVINE":
ELEANOR ROOSEVELT

THERE IS NOTHING ESPECIALLY IMPOSING ABOUT VAL-KILL, Eleanor Roosevelt's retreat at Hyde Park. Visitors approach it along a bumpy lane that threads its way between woods and ragged fields, circles around a pond, crosses a noisy plank bridge, and ends in a grove of spindly pines. There are two main buildings on the property: a small, handsome fieldstone cottage, flanked by beds of flowers, which Franklin Roosevelt had built for his wife and two of her friends in 1925; and behind it, half-hidden at first among more substantial trees, an ungainly two-story gray stucco structure that still resembles the furniture factory it once was. That is where Mrs. Roosevelt lived for much of the last quarter century of her life; characteristically, when her partnership with her friends dissolved, it was she, not they, who moved into the converted factory.

Still, it is an evocative place, the only National Historic Site dedicated to the memory of a First Lady, and a monument both to a remarkable but troubled marriage and to its owner's determination to have a life and a home of her own.

The story of Eleanor Roosevelt's struggle for independence is much better known now than it was during her lifetime: she was far more than her crippled husband's "eyes and ears," and during their dozen years together in the White House she often acted as FDR's conscience as well, and sometimes as his goad, reminding him of the needs of people otherwise without access to him, while pursuing a host of political and social interests of her own. She set the standard against which every President's wife since has been measured, and after her husband died she became if anything more active, campaigning tirelessly for human rights and international cooperation—and for political candidates whom she believed would best carry forward the traditions of the New Deal. The title "First Lady of the World," which was inevitably conferred upon her during the final busy years of her life, may have been a little cloying, but it was also accurate; no woman was more universally admired.

Yet no matter where she went or what she was doing, she yearned to come back to this modest house and the woods and fields that surround it. "My heart is in the cottage," she once told a friend, and a glance back at her parched beginnings suggests why. Her father was Theodore Roosevelt's alcoholic younger brother, Elliott, whose noisy disintegration preoccupied her beautiful but distracted mother. Even before she was orphaned at nine, she had been rootless, parceled out to relatives in a succession of exiles and abandonments which helped persuade her that she was somehow odd, unattractive, unable to count on anyone's love for long. At two and a half she asked her aunt, "Where is baby's home now?" and received no satisfying answer; there was none to give. At eighteen, she told another aunt, "I have no real home," and burst into tears.

Her marriage in 1905 to her buoyant fifth cousin Franklin seemed at first to promise just the sort of stability and support for which she longed, but, although the Roosevelts had six children over the next eleven years (five of whom lived), she never found in her husband a wholehearted emotional partner. He was unable even to provide her with a home of her own. Their first house in New York City had been rented and furnished for them by his fond but iron-willed mother, Sara Delano Roosevelt. In 1907, Sara had their second home built as a Christmas gift, then moved into its twin next door, connected with theirs by doors that were never locked. Summers were spent on Campobello Island, New Brunswick, in a cottage which stood just down the beach from hers. Even Springwood, the big comfortable old house at Hyde Park, in which FDR had been born and raised, and with which the public always associated him, was actually his for only the four years between his mother's death in 1941 and his own. It was still less his wife's: when the Roosevelts adjourned to its book-lined living room after dinner, FDR sat in one of the two massive carved chairs that flanked the fireplace, his mother in the other. "I sat anywhere," Eleanor recalled.

By the 1920s, the Roosevelts' relationship was more merger than marriage, an affectionate and hugely effective partnership based on a shared past and mutual interests but without passion or intimacy. Mrs. Roosevelt's discovery of her husband's romance with her social secretary during World War I, and her refusal ever to forgive him for it, had seen to that. And she had begun to carve out for herself in political and social work a career allied to his but independent of it as well.

Among the women she came to know and like were two who had

lived and worked together for some years, Nancy Cook and Marion Dickerman. Miss Dickerman was tall and somewhat mournful-looking, an educator and social worker who had run for the New York legislature in 1919. Nancy Cook had been her campaign manager: she was short, sturdy, vigorous, and able to "do almost anything" with her hands, Mrs. Roosevelt wrote—jewelry, gardening, cabinetmaking.

Sometime in the summer of 1924, Franklin and Eleanor Roosevelt, Cook and Dickerman spread a picnic on the grassy bank of the Val-Kill, a cold clear stream about two miles east of Springwood, on land FDR had bought for himself. It was a lovely place and a beautiful day, and Mrs. Roosevelt lamented that this would be one of the last picnics of the year; her mother-in-law was soon to close the big house for the winter. FDR then suggested that the three women build a cottage on the spot; Cook and Dickerman could live there year-round if they liked, and his wife could join them whenever she wanted. He would give them a life interest in the land and supervise construction.

It was a generous gesture, but it also gave him an interesting project to oversee at a time when he had little else to occupy him other than his struggle to come back from infantile paralysis. "My Missus and some of her female political friends want to build a shack on a stream in the back woods," he wrote a contractor friend in the affectionately patronizing tone he sometimes used to discuss his wife's activities. The stream could be dammed to form a pond, and its water diverted to fill a pool in which he might exercise away from the claustrophobic solicitude of his mother. He signed on an architect, Henry Toombs, and told his wife, "If you three girls will just go away and leave us alone, Henry and I will build the cottage." They did, and on New Year's Day, 1926, it was officially inaugurated with a dinner party to which the whole Roosevelt family was invited; everyone, including Sara Delano Roosevelt, sat on kegs of nails.

"The peace of it is divine," Mrs. Roosevelt told her husband the first summer she spent there. She and her two friends all slept for a time in the same big dormitory-like bedroom upstairs, in a proximity that some visitors found startling; even their towels were embroidered with their intertwined initials. Life in the stone cottage in those early years had something of the air of Allenswood, the boarding school in England where Eleanor Roosevelt had spent three adolescent years, "the happiest years of my life."

Yet this was only the first of a series of extraordinarily fervent friendships Mrs. Roosevelt would form over the decades. The recipients of her devotion would eventually include not only Cook and Dickerman but the newspaperwoman Lorena Hickock, a genial strapping state trooper named Earl Miller—who was first her husband's and then her own bodyguard when FDR was governor of New York—Joseph Lash and his wife Trude, and in her later years her physician David Gurewitsch and his wife Edna. All would frequently visit Val-Kill and some would live there off and on. These men and women had little in common other than that there were ways in which Mrs. Roosevelt had felt she could help them. Unable to attain the emotional support that she needed from her husband, she found satisfaction in gathering around her those whom she believed needed her.

In 1926, the three women built a furniture factory behind their cottage, intending to operate a successful business while helping local farmers and their sons stay on the land and earn a living during the lean winter months. Nancy Cook ran it, basing the designs for her bedsteads and trestle tables and bookcases on Colonial models. Mrs. Roosevelt provided most of the financing and saw to the marketing, making the rounds of New York department stores herself, sample book in hand.

She still stayed overnight at Springwood whenever her husband or her children were there. But sometimes the strain became too great, and one summer evening, Marion Dickerman remembered, a distraught Mrs. Roosevelt appeared unexpectedly at the cottage. For three days, she refused to take calls from Springwood. Finally, Cook called FDR and told him to come over and talk to his wife. "But will she talk to *me?*" he asked. Cook thought she would, and so he drove over in his hand-controlled Ford. Mrs. Roosevelt reluctantly joined him in the front seat of his open car and they sat talking in low tones for nearly two hours before FDR started up the engine and took his wife home with him to his mother's house.

The furniture business foundered, and in the spring of 1936 the factory was closed. Mrs. Roosevelt's friendship with her partners had begun to falter, too, for reasons never made entirely clear by anyone involved, and the following year she moved into the remodeled factory building. This was truly her own home and she eagerly saw to every detail of its furnishing. Her life at Val-Kill seemed almost consciously to mock the formality of her mother-in-law's establishment. The walls were knotty pine, the rugs laid down straight from the department store. "There wasn't a lamp shade that wasn't askew," a frequent visitor remembers, "and nobody cared if the cups and plates matched." There were framed pictures everywhere—103 in her sitting room alone—mostly photographs of friends and family.

"Tommy"—Malvina Thompson—her dedicated secretary, who devoted her life to working for Mrs. Roosevelt, lived in an apartment of her own in one wing of the first floor. Mrs. Roosevelt lived in another wing with a bedroom upstairs, but she spent all but the coldest nights on an adjoining sleeping porch where she could enjoy what she called the "peace of nature . . . healing and life-giving." She especially liked being snowed in on winter days, undisturbed except by the occasional creaking of a branch or the distant crackling of the ice in the brook; and every summer morning she watched from her bed as the sunrise was reflected in the still surface of her pond, its shore blanketed with purple loosestrife and punctuated by birch trees, their mirrored white trunks seeming to "reach down toward the bottom."

Time for contemplation was rare, however, for Val-Kill soon became the social center for the Roosevelts whenever informality seemed in order. A large stone fireplace on the lawn permitted big cheerful picnics at which Mrs. Roosevelt happily presided, spooning out potato salad and grilling hot dogs for her husband's friends and for her own. (A smaller grill was placed next to FDR's chair on the lawn so that he could prepare his own steaks as blood-rare as he liked.)

Nancy Cook was an enthusiastic maker of home movies and her thousands of feet of jittery film provide an intimate record of life at Val-Kill during the gubernatorial and presidential years. One by one, the supporting players in the Roosevelts' vivid drama flicker past the camera. Tiny, wizened Louis Howe, already dying of a host of ailments, feebly tries to blow out the candles on his birthday cake. Harry Hopkins, almost equally frail, capers barefoot within the President's outsize bathrobe. While someone else holds the camera, Nancy Cook and Marion Dickerman skip rope girlishly in shirtwaists and long dark skirts. Sara Delano Roosevelt sips tea beneath a parasol, queenly and apparently serene even on her daughter-in-law's hard-won territory. Big Earl Miller, his handsome face split by a grin, his hair parted precisely in the center, strolls arm-in-arm with Mrs. Roosevelt, and later rides laughing alongside her through the snow, three police dogs barking silently at their horses' heels.

There are fleeting glimpses of FDR, too: performing childish hand-tricks; playing water polo, his thin hair plastered flat, hurling the ball like a bullet; and seated on the edge of the pool in a dark bathing suit, teeth clenched around his cigarette holder, his enormous torso swollen to the point of caricature above his white, withered legs.

He died in 1945 at Warm Springs, Georgia. On the slow, sad trip north, Mrs. Roosevelt resolved to live out her widowhood at Val-Kill: ". . . it was mine," she wrote, "and I felt freer there than in the big house."

She planned a quiet life, working on behalf of her many causes but blessedly out of the Washington spotlight. "When I warn my friends that I am going to sit by a fire with a little lace cap on my head and a shawl about my shoulders and knit baby things for the newest generation," she wrote, "they look at me with some incredulity. The day will come, however, and when it does I think it will be rather pleasant." It never came. She could never stand to be idle, "could not bear to be alone," her last secretary, Maureen Corr, remembers.

"When you cease to make a contribution," she said at seventy-four, "you begin to die." She maintained a New York apartment so as to be near the United Nations and her other interests, and she actually accelerated the peripatetic travels she had begun as First Lady. Val-Kill was meant to be her retreat, a place to relax, but her notion of relaxation was different from anybody else's. She spent as much time there as she could, but surrounded whenever possible by friends and family. And after 1947, when Cook and Dickerman finally vacated the stone cottage and Mrs. Roosevelt's son John and his family moved in, there was always a full complement of grandchildren all summer as well, riding horses and boating on the pond. "Where Mrs. Roosevelt was, life flourished," Edna Gurewitsch remembers. "Dogs barked. The cook's grandchildren were being scolded. There was the smell of baking. Someone was diving into the pool. Something was *happening.*"

Her guests were encouraged to rest while they were with her. She herself never wasted a moment. "I never saw her when she wasn't doing something," a friend remembers. She rose early to cut flowers so that when her guests arrived they would find in their rooms vases filled with varieties she knew they especially liked. Nearby were books she thought they might enjoy, along with bowls of favorite fruit or candy. She planned the day with Marge Entrup, her able and patient cook during her final years, who grew accustomed to having her employer tell her that she was at last growing old and would have to cut back on her entertaining; meanwhile, "Only fourteen for breakfast tomorrow, Marge."

She wrote all her own checks, and balanced her checkbook, and she liked to shop, too, standing in the checkout line at the Grand Union or driving across the Hudson to a favorite farm stand in search of bargains. At least once a day she took a long walk in the woods with her dog, first her late husband's Fala and then with one or another of his boisterous Scottie successors, and in warm weather she plunged briefly into the pool, an activity she hated but thought "good for my character." And she found time to dictate her "My Day" column, write articles and books, brief herself for public appearances, and keep up with the mail that was delivered by the sackful.

Luncheon guests might include one or two of her sons, Princess Beatrix of Holland and her lady-in-waiting, Adlai Stevenson, two Mormon missionaries who had happened to knock on the door, an out-of-work actor, an astonished couple she had chanced to meet on a train. And there were far larger events, including the ceremonies honoring FDR on Memorial Day each year, to which scores and sometimes hundreds of old colleagues and new admirers came; and the picnic for the delinquent boys who lived at the Wiltwyck School at Esopus across the river, some 150 of whom descended on the grounds annually to eat hot dogs, roam the woods, and listen more or less attentively as Mrs. Roosevelt seated herself on a log and read to them from Rudyard Kipling's *Just-So Stories*.

Foreign statesmen came, too, bringing with them their ravenous entourages: India's Prime Minister Jawaharlal Nehru and his daughter, Indira Gandhi; Marshal Tito of Yugoslavia; Ethiopia's Emperor Haile Selassie, for whom lunch was delayed half an hour so that he might watch himself on television for the first time in a pretaped interview. No extra help was hired. Marge Entrup had to manage with just the six burners in her small kitchen. Her husband, Les, supervised the serving. Overnight guests pitched in, tossing the salad or setting the table. Mrs. Roosevelt herself dished up the food, chewing on her tongue in concentration, making sure that everyone had just what they wanted. And, after the dignitaries left, Marge would ask, "Well, Mrs. Roosevelt, how'd I do?" and receive a grateful kiss.

Nikita Khrushchev's visit in 1959 almost permanently altered the look of Val-Kill. The Secret Service warned before he came that its agents could not adequately protect him there unless a number of trees were cut down. Nonsense, Mrs. Roosevelt replied; the Secret Service had always protected her husband perfectly during *his* visits to the cottage. The trees stayed. As many of her opponents learned to their sorrow, Mrs. Roosevelt could be very tough and shrewd, and that side of her, too, sometimes showed at Val-Kill. When old friends gave her two piglets as a Christmas gift and the animals proved impossible to keep penned, she told her farmer to slaughter them right away; a pair of less adventurous pigs was bought, fattened up, and later enthusiastically shown off to the donors as the originals. One year, a visiting Wiltwyck boy stole her keys. She asked the whole school back later that day, ostensibly to help her search for them. When one boy "found" the keys, she thanked him for being so very helpful. After that, every time the school came, she quietly suggested to her guests that they lock their cars and pocket their valuables so as not place temptation in the boys' way. (She needn't have worried; the word had gone out among them by then that "you don't lift from Mrs. Roose-velt.")

Even on comparably uneventful days there was often a handful of new guests at dinner. Mrs. Roosevelt took a brief nap beforehand, sleeping on her good ear to block out the shouts of her grandchildren. Drinks were served exactly fifteen minutes before dinner—a single drink, usually blond Dubonnet on ice for Mrs. Roosevelt. "The food was delicious those last years," Edna Gurewitsch insists, no matter how famously mediocre it had been in the White House, and the talk was relaxed and wide-ranging. Even then, a certain brisk but gracious efficiency was often in evidence. Mrs. Roosevelt sometimes filled and passed the dessert bowls so rapidly that her hands seemed actually to blur, and there was rarely much after-dinner conversation.

At a few minutes before ten she would turn, smiling, to one dinner guest and suggest that since he or she happened to be going in the same direction as another, perhaps they might travel together. And when they left, they often found that flowers wrapped in damp paper to keep them fresh had been placed in their cars, alongside jars of cooked rhubarb from the kitchen garden. She then spent a few minutes more with her overnight guests before saying, "Well, children . . ." and rising from her chair, bid each visitor good night: "Blessings on you," "Thank you for a lovely day," "Sleep well."

She was left alone at last. While her guests settled in for the night, she stayed up until two or three in the morning answering letters from friends and total strangers, the only sounds the frogs in the pond and the scratching of her fountain pen.

Christmas was the highlight of the Val-Kill year. Mrs. Roosevelt kept meticulous lists of all the gifts she had sent to scores of persons over the years so that she might never repeat herself, and she began Christmas shopping "about January second," or so it seemed to Edna Gurewitsch. Items she had ordered by mail arrived almost daily during the spring and summer, and she brought others home from every-where she traveled. The staff had orders to wrap them whenever they had a few moments to spare. Everything was in readiness by early autumn, a big upstairs closet no longer able to contain all the red and green packages.

In the early hours of Christmas morning, Mrs. Roosevelt padded silently along the corridors of her cottage, leaving stockings stuffed with sweets and small but skillfully chosen presents outside each guest's room. There were more gifts at each visitor's place at the dinner table. Mrs. Roosevelt offered her traditional toast—the same one she gave on the Fourth of July and Thanksgiving—"To the United States of America. To the President. To those we love who are not with us today." Franklin Roosevelt, Jr., carved the turkey with as much of his father's old flourish as he could muster. John Roosevelt carved the ham.

After dinner everyone filed into the living room, where there was a tree, and the guests found their assigned chairs, each one heaped with still more gifts. Mrs. Roosevelt moved around the room as they were unwrapped, making sure that sweaters fit, toys pleased, books had not already been read. Her own gifts were left for last; one guest recalled that she liked best those things such as cheese and champagne which she could immediately share with others. She was firm about only one thing: paper and ribbon were to be saved and handed back to her to be used the following year.

Eleanor Roosevelt died in her New York apartment on November 7, 1962, at the age of seventy-eight. She had not wished to die at Val-Kill, she told friends, because to do so would have inconvenienced so many people who might wish to come and see her. She was buried at the big house, in her mother-in-law's rose garden beside her husband as he had wished. A few weeks later, however, packages from Mrs. Roosevelt arrived in the mail for many of the friends and family members who had traditionally spent Christmas with her at Val-Kill. The gifts had of course been wrapped and ready since the summer.

Smithsonian October 1984

FRANKLIN D. ROOSEVELT, BIRD-WATCHER

FRANKLIN ROOSEVELT'S OPEN BLUE FORD MOVED STEADILY across a muddy field near Springwood, his family home at Hyde Park, New York. The President was behind the wheel, skillfully negotiating the rough terrain with the special hand controls his paralysis required, and as he drove, he chatted amiably with his friend and adviser on forestry, Nelson C. Brown, sitting to his right.

Three big cars filled with Secret Service agents moved warily along the rough forest road that skirted the field, their occupants nervous that the man they were there to protect had left the road and driven onto boggy ground where their heavy, bulletproof vehicles could not follow. They knew that Roosevelt often chafed at their perpetual presence, but was especially resentful of it here, deep in the woods he'd known and loved since boyhood, and if his protectors got too far from him, they never knew when he would try to lose them altogether, laughing as he careened down one or another of the rough tracks with which he had honeycombed his forest.

The President halted his car at the edge of the field, and appeared to be staring intently into the trees. The Secret Service men stopped, too, hands on the handles of their revolvers, straining to see what the President clearly saw.

Then, Roosevelt beeped his horn. The agents leaped from their cars and pounded into the muddy field, pistols in hand, ready to eliminate whatever menace had made the Boss sound an alarm.

When they reached the car, FDR was roaring with laughter. There was nothing to worry about, he explained as they holstered their weapons and fought for breath.

He had been peering into a clearing in the woods beyond the field's edge, he said, when he noticed the head of a large bird just visible through the blowing grass.

"What's that bird?" he had asked his companion.

Brown said he wasn't sure, "but if you sound the horn very lightly we will soon find out."

Startled at the sound—and by the shouting of the anxious agents that followed it—a ring neck pheasant had drummed away into the woods, feathers blazing in the afternoon sun.

As the agents stumped back to their cars, the mud sucking at their polished shoes, FDR started up his Ford and moved off again, still grinning, his cigarette holder at an especially jaunty angle.

Roosevelt's interest in birds began in early boyhood. Few Presidents— few *Americans*—have led a more comfortable and sheltered existence than did Franklin Roosevelt during his first years. His father, James Roosevelt, was almost twice his mother's age, but a lively, vigorous presence in his son's life, inculcating in him his own serene Episcopalianism, his sturdy sense of a wealthy citizen's duty toward those less fortunate than he, his love for trees and the land. But Franklin's day-to-day activities were then left to the loving but determined care of his mother, Sara Delano Roosevelt. He was her only child, and she poured into his raising all of her formidable energy. Few boys have ever received more maternal devotion—or had to grow up under more intense scrutiny. His mother picked his books and toys, screened his infrequent playmates, oversaw his games, even stood at the side of the tub while he took his baths until he was at least eight.

About that time he began to show an interest in the rich variety of birds that flapped and fluttered in and out of the great trees in which he had been taught to take such pride. It is probably no coincidence that his new-found scientific interest gave him his first legitimate excuse to stray at least a little way from the house in which he was watched so ceaselessly.

Like most birders of his generation, he started as an oologist—a collector of eggs and nests. When she was a little girl, the daughter of the Episcopal rector at Hyde Park remembered, she attended a Springwood Easter party at which her small host had arrived late, emerging slowly from the woods and inching his way across the lawn, oblivious to his guests, a brilliant blue robin's egg cupped in his small hands.

His father insisted that only a single egg ever be taken from a nest and that no nest could be collected until the winter, but several drawers in Franklin's upstairs bedroom were quickly filled with fragile specimens, and he began to read everything about birds on which he could get his hands, demonstrating for the first time his extraordinary ability to read and remember prodigious amounts of material.

At eleven, he laboriously wrote an essay on "Birds of the Hudson

River Valley," filled with the special scorn only a young hobbyist can summon for those less knowledgeable than he:

> Many people do not know what a great variety of birds we have. They can always point out a robin but probably could not tell the difference between a Fox Sparrow and a Song Sparrow and will think that a nuthatch is a woodpecker. . . .

At the enthusiastic urging of his mother, Franklin began giving little lectures on birds to patient relatives, delivering one entitled "The Shore Birds of Maine" so impressively that his grandfather gave him a life membership in the American Museum of Natural History and took him there to meet its president, the paleontologist Henry Fairfield Osborn, and the great ornithologist Frank M. Chapman, who let him poke through the trays of bird skins.

Franklin spent the summer of 1893 abroad with his parents, and was desolated to find that a business appointment in London had forced them to cancel a long-planned visit to Osberton-in-Worksop, the Nottinghamshire seat of the Earl of Liverpool, Cecil Foljambe, one of England's most knowledgeable bird fanciers, whose collection of mounted birds was unmatched outside of museums.

"Mummie, can't I go without you?" Franklin begged.

"You mean you'd visit people you had never met?" she asked, genuinely surprised. Until that moment, she had thought her sheltered son well mannered but awfully shy with strangers.

"I'd go anywhere to see those birds," he answered, and his parents nervously allowed him to take the train alone, so that the elderly earl and his eleven-year-old visitor could spend the afternoon together talking about birds and gravely examining the brightly colored exhibits in their glass cases.

The Foljambe birds dazzled Franklin—he would later take his bride Eleanor to see them on his honeymoon—but there was another collection almost as spectacular much closer to home, just up the Albany Post Road, in fact, on the sprawling Hyde Park estate of Colonel Archibald Rogers of Standard Oil. Rogers's British butler, Arthur Bloomfield, was an entirely self-taught ornithologist whose collection of hundreds of stuffed and labeled specimens, amassed while traveling with his peripatetic employer from one stately home to another, had grown so large that the colonel eventually built him a little stone building just to house it all. Young Franklin liked to go there whenever Bloomfield had a few moments free from his duties in the main house.

In any case, as soon as Franklin got home from Europe in the autumn of 1893, he began lobbying his parents for a shotgun. Nests and eggs were no longer enough for him. He wanted to shoot and mount his own collection. His mother was appalled—her son was far too young, too delicate, for firearms, she said—but his father acquiesced, presenting him with a gun on his eleventh birthday, January 30, 1893. With it came another set of rules which, if not obeyed, meant confiscation: there was to be no shooting during the mating season; nesting birds were off-limits; only one member of each species was to be collected.

That shiny new gun meant many things to Franklin. It enabled him to create a collection of stuffed birds, first of all. But ornithology also licensed him to kill, to stalk Springwood's forests at dawn, alone and unwatched, to affect things directly on his own and out from under his mother's anxious love. Something of the feeling of liberation shooting gave him can be read in a schoolboy essay called "Guns and Squirrels": "Many Mamas think guns are very dangerous things & think they will go off without cartridges or without being cocked, but if properly handled they are not dangerous. . . . It is great fun shooting . . . and it is not very easy. . . ."

For Franklin, it seems never to have been very hard. In shooting, as in most things, his assumption always was that he would find a way to bring home any prize he sought. One of his mother's favorite stories about him had him strolling in from the river side of the house, requesting his shotgun. She asked him why he needed it.

"There's a winter wren up in one of those big trees down there," he said. "I want to get him."

His mother unlocked the cabinet in which the gun was kept. "Why do you think the wren is going to oblige you by staying there while you come in and get your gun?"

"Oh," said Franklin, shouldering his shotgun. "He'll wait."

He did, and the young hunter returned a few minutes later with another addition to his collection.

He became an "insatiable" hunter, his mother recalled, and in a small *Bird Diary* for 1896 began to keep a running tally of his kills and sightings:

January 31, 1896
    Shot 3 pine Grosbeaks and saw 18 others. Sent the birds to T. Rowland one to be stuffed & 2 to be skinned. . . .

    February 14, 1896
    Saw about 50 Pine Grosbeaks while driving on the avenue. I

noticed a blue-gray bird fly out of a pine tree and immediately a pine grosbeak fell to the ground. It was still warm, though dead. I suppose that the blue-gray bird was a Great Northern Shrike. . . .

February 18, 1896
New York. Went to Museum [of Natural History] & Mr. Frank M. Chapman put me up for Associate membership of the A. O. U. I am to send about 1 dozen grosbeaks to Museum for Local Collections. Mr. Chapman gave me a card of introduction to Mr. L. S. Foster, publisher of "Auk," etc. as I intend to buy back no's of the "Auk." Mr. [Arthur] Dumper [Franklin's tutor] reported some grosbeaks at Hyde Park.

February 19, 1896
(In snow—15 degrees)
Shot a Pine Finch. The bird was alone in a small pine tree, & he appeared very shy. Had great difficulty in shooting him. . . .

February 25, 1896
Shot 1 male Pine Grosbeak for Museum and saw 30 others. . . . Mr. Dumper saw a woodchuck & I smelt a skunk. . . .

March 7
Saw Red-Shouldered Hawk. . . .

April 15
Cowbirds at Newburgh. . . .

April 16
Cooper's Hawk near Staatsburgh. He flew up quite close to me and appeared to be tame.

April 18
Saw near Barrytown about 100 red-winged Blackbirds.

April 25
Shot a barred owl at 5 P.M. in Newbold's Gully [a declivity in the woods between his house and his neighbor's next door].

May 7
Shot a Scarlet Tanager. Also an Inigo Bunting.

May 8
Shot a red-headed woodpecker.

By the age of fourteen he had collected and identified more than three hundred different species native to Dutchess County. At fifteen, the American Museum gratefully acknowledged his gift of ten carefully prepared pine grosbeak skins.

In collecting, as in so many other things, Franklin received additional inspiration from the example of his celebrated cousin, Theodore. TR, too, had been a voracious collector of specimens as a boy and he had relished the noisome hobby of taxidermy as well, although it made the lives of his parents and siblings and servants miserable. In the end, Franklin found he could not stomach the stench—it made him "green," his mother remembered—and, after trying two or three times to stuff his own trophies, he asked to have his skins sent off to professional taxidermists in Poughkeepsie and New York instead. His ever-indulgent parents agreed. (His mother considered his birds too precious for anyone but herself to dust and, when Springwood was greatly enlarged in 1915, had a special glass-fronted case built for twenty-seven of his best specimens in the front hall where they remain today, a little the worse for wear, but each still labeled in Roosevelt's boyish hand. A harrier hawk hung from a wire nearby, and a prominent place was also found in the living room for her son's largest prize, a green-backed heron.)

The acclaim Franklin's ornithological knowledge and shooting skill elicited from his proud parents and pleased relatives evidently inspired him to compose an article for *The Foursome*, a typed magazine gotten up by three of his contemporaries who lived at Tuxedo Park. So far as I know, it has not seen print in its entirety since 1896.

THE SPRING SONG.
    by F. D. R.
Listen! The bugler has come. A few shrill notes and a trill, and we see our friend the Song Sparrow.

In quick succession the robins and the Bluebirds arrive. This is the advance guard.

A few days more, and Blackbirds appear. Hear their juicy note, which reminds you of strawberries and cream, but, venture too close, and they will be off, with a cheery "can't catch me." You see the Robin on your lawn, busily engaged in grubbing, but you would be surprised to hear that he eats about seventy worms every day. If those worms were laid end to end, their length would extend fourteen feet. The American Robin is an entirely different species from the English Robin Redbreast of Nursery tales. The latter is smaller, in form resembling our Bluebird.

The Bluebird, the color-bearer of the Spring Army is gladly welcomed as a harbinger of Spring, as, flitting about the orchard, his mellow note mingles with the Spring Chorus.

Walk now along the Creek and, with angry rattle, a Kingfisher will startle you from revery. There you will also see a lazy Heron, slowly flapping his way from pond to pond. With neck drawn in, and legs dangling, he will remind you of Japanese Screen pictures.

Suddenly, a loud "tapp, tapp," will ring out on the clear air, and you will see a fine red head stuck out inquisitively from behind a branch. A black-and-white body will follow as the Wood-pecker climbs into view.

But what is that soberly clad bird hopping about near the Spring? You will soon see, as, when he faces about, his spotted breast will come into view, and you will know that a Wood Thrush has arrived.

Now will come numbers of small birds, known as Warblers. Their song is feeble and they are very shy, only staying a few days.

A little brown bird is seen hopping about the patch; this is the chippy or Chipping Sparrow. Always cheery, he will be with you all summer, but an even smaller and browner bird will attract your attention. The House Wren, for it is he, will scold from the start, but we will put it down to a disagreeable wife.

The Peabody-bird, or White-throated Sparrow comes at this time, and he will stay with us until driven southward by the cold, when sitting on a fence-rail, he bids us

"Farewell."

How much of this essay was his own work, how much that of the nanny who presumably typed it up for him, and how much may have been cribbed from someone else's article, we will probably never know. (It has something of the weary tone of the overwrought outdoor writers whom his cousin Theodore dismissed as "Nature fakirs"; certainly nothing else Franklin wrote at the same age has anything like the clarity of this little essay.)

Franklin entered Groton School at fourteen that fall, perhaps the only new boy ever to boast of a complete set of bound volumes of the *Auk*. But bird-watching was not thought robust enough a sport for Groton. The enthusiasms of its resolutely manly headmaster, the Reverend Endicott Peabody, ran toward Football (which Franklin was too light to play well), Boxing (at which he was no better, having had his nose bloodied by a far smaller boy in his only known public match), and Baseball (which he also played poorly, finding at least a measure of compensatory success as manager of the team in his senior year). And so he began to keep his enthusiasm about birds mostly to himself, at least when among his schoolmates, although he did lecture about them at least once more: At his cousin Muriel Robbins's request, he spoke before her settlement house class of Irish immigrant boys from the mean streets of East Boston. The call of the Peabody Bird was a very long way from the daily concerns of his listeners, and the enthusiasm of this slender, over-eager young man for such things must have been at the very least a novelty.

He never lost his interest completely, however. Eleanor Roosevelt was often surprised in the early years of their marriage by the curiously selective keenness of his eyesight, chiding him gently when he blamed near-sightedness for his failure to recognize an acquaintance on the street. "That," she explained, "has always seemed strange to me. For as long as I have known him, Franklin could always point to a bird and tell me what it was."

During the summer of 1907, Franklin, two Harvard friends, and his younger brother-in-law Hall Roosevelt left Eleanor behind in the Roosevelt cottage at Campobello and sailed north to Oak Island off Nova Scotia, intent on digging up Captain Kidd's pirate treasure rumored to be buried there. They found no treasure, but on the way back, Franklin spotted a cormorant's nest at the top of a tall tree on a small rocky island. Hall, then sixteen, was sent ashore to bring it down. He clambered up the tree and returned with the nest and the four baby birds it held, so that Franklin could send them to the American Museum. The nest and its contents reeked so, Eleanor remembered, that when the expedition got back to Campobello, Hall "had to take off all his clothes and leave them on the beach and scrub himself before he could enter the house."

Although the hectic public career that began with Roosevelt's election to the State Senate in 1910 and only accelerated after his appointment as Assistant Secretary of the Navy in 1913 kept him apart from his family much of the time, he seemed anxious to pass on his hobby to at least the eldest of his children. Anna Roosevelt treasured all her life her memories of the times when he would swing her up onto the saddle in front of him and canter off into the Hyde Park woods, identifying each bird they scared up along the forest path.

As with a good many enthusiasts of his time, bird-watching and bird-shooting remained inseparable in Roosevelt's mind. He took a shotgun with him on a semi-official horseback inspection tour of Haiti in 1917, shot a dove and had himself photographed with it, then liked to explain to friends who saw the picture that he had really bagged a "Great Haitian Shrink Bird," a big exotic species, measuring four feet from wing tip to wing tip, which had dwindled after death because it had not been immersed in boiling water.

Almost his first thought after James M. Cox and he were spectacularly trounced for President and Vice President by Warren Harding and Calvin Coolidge in 1920 was to head south for a week of wildfowl-shooting in Louisiana. He was photographed there, too: in just one noisy morning in the flooded cane fields, he and seven friends accounted for some sixty ducks and geese.

Infantile paralysis struck Roosevelt down in the summer of 1921, leaving him unable ever again to take a step unaided, threatening to end forever his political hopes. He stayed out of politics for seven long years, struggling with only marginal success to recover the use of his wasted legs and forced to fall back on his more sedentary hobbies—collecting stamps, books, naval prints—to stave off the boredom and depression that might have crushed a less resilient and resolute man.

Hunting birds was now virtually impossible for him, of course—although he did once try shooting driven quail at Warm Springs, Georgia, banging away at the tiny targets hurtling over his head, the brakes on his wheelchair locked so that the recoil would not send him rolling backwards. And the twisting forest paths around Springwood he had prowled as a boy in search of birds were closed to him as well—at least until, in the late twenties, he began widening some of them to accommodate his hand-controlled automobile.

But, his son Elliott remembered, even as President, wherever he was and whenever he had the opportunity, he enjoyed identifying the birds that came within his range, keeping binoculars near at hand at Hyde Park and Warm Springs and sometimes halting the conversation to identify a distant song. Even when cruising aboard warships at sea, he liked to keep an eye out, and at least once—at St. Joseph's Island off Texas in 1937—he had himself carried onto the beach so that he could get a better look at the shore birds.

One day during the winter of 1942, his wife's distant cousin Margaret Suckley told him that she and two other members of the staff of his newly created Franklin D. Roosevelt Library at Hyde Park planned to take part in the annual census of Dutchess County birds in the spring. Would he like to come along?

To her surprise, "he said he would love it," James L. Whitehead, another bird enthusiast on the staff, remembered, "and so we made our plans."

Those plans were not universally popular with the President's entourage: "The Secret Service men not enthusiastic," his secretary William Hassett noted, "when they learned the President plans to leave home at 4 o'clock Sunday morning to go with friends . . . to hear the spring bird notes." But the President was almost pathetically eager to go—he had not been able to indulge his boyhood passion for more than twenty years—and just as soon as Whitehead and the others drew up in front of a still-darkened Springwood well before dawn on Sunday morning, May 10, "the door to the 'Big House' opened, and there sat the President in his wheelchair, all ready to go. He had evidently been ready before we got there, and this was only shortly after four o'clock. . . ."

Roosevelt was lifted into the car and seated in the back alongside Miss Suckley. Ludlow Griscom of Harvard, the author of *Birds of the New York City Region,* and one of the country's preeminent authorities on bird identification, sat up front with the Roosevelt chauffeur. Five sleepy Secret Service men rode in a second car behind them. "I'm sure they thought us all crazy—the president included," remembered Whitehead, whose own car brought up the rear.

It was a chilly, wet morning and it took almost an hour to reach the census site, Thompson's Pond near Pine Plains in the northern corner of the county, but halfway there, Roosevelt asked the driver to stop and fold down the roof so that he could hear the night sounds—whippoorwills, sparrows, a catbird.

The small convoy reached the pond just after five, Whitehead recalled, and "stopped on a little road built right through the center of the marsh—reeds and grasses growing thick on both sides." Everyone but FDR got out in the gray light and stood around his car to listen to the marsh birds greet the dawn. The Secret Service men, "all of them bored," stood in a sleepy cluster a little distance away.

The chorus was so "awe-inspiring," Whitehead noted, that even FDR spoke in half-whispers. At first Roosevelt seemed a little bewildered by the sheer variety of calls and songs—Whitehead was afraid that "the President knows little now of birds"—but with Ludlow Griscom's help, "lots of it came back to him," and the birders heard or saw Virginia rails and American bitterns, northern flickers and eastern meadowlarks, cedar waxwings and scarlet tanagers, and seventeen separate species of warbler. The President himself filled out the check list in his bold hand: "Total for day 108 species. Franklin D. Roosevelt."

A soft but steady rain began to fall around seven o'clock, and the cars pulled beneath the trees for shelter. Roosevelt sipped hot coffee and ate sandwiches, and told stories of his boyhood pursuit of birds, of the blue heron that used to come year after year to the marshy riverbank below the house and the robins he used to tease by tying a string to a branch.

About eight, the President said goodbye and headed back for Springwood. He had to see to his house guests, the Crown Prince and Princess of Norway, and could not be away too long from the special telephone that linked his country home with the White House.

Despite the early hour at which he'd risen and the time he'd spent in the damp cold, he seemed "fit as a fiddle and full of enthusiasm" when Bill Hassett saw him shortly after noon. "His face lighted up when he related how at the break of the day he heard the note of a marsh wren, then a red-winged blackbird, after that a bittern. All told, he recognized the notes of twenty-two different birds."

Roosevelt told Miss Suckley he'd like very much to go birding again some time, if it wouldn't be too much trouble. But then the war closed in around him and he never again could quite find the time.

Audubon January 1990

FDR'S "YANKEE PYRAMID"

I T IS FITTING THAT TWO OF THE FIRST SIGHTS THE VISITOR SEES upon entering the Franklin D. Roosevelt Library on the old family estate at Hyde Park, New York, are the massive Dutch family Bible on which FDR took the presidential oath of office four times—twice as many times as any other man—and his White House desk, its broad top forested with knickknacks, the high-backed chair behind it frayed by a dozen years of hard use by a President who could not rise from it unaided.

From that threadbare chair, Roosevelt struggled to resolve the two gravest crises Americans have faced since the Civil War—the Great Depression and World War II. In the process, for better or worse, he forever altered the relationship between the citizen and his government, the presidency and the people, America and the world.

The Roosevelt Library itself is a symbol of the profound transformation over which he presided: no President before Roosevelt ever built one; no President since has failed to do so. And the story of its creation half a century ago is, in microcosm, the story of Roosevelt's exuberant style of leadership, with all its ego and energy, boldness and cheerful duplicity.

A President's papers had always been considered his personal property. George Washington himself set that precedent, bundling up his files and taking them home with him in 1797 to Mount Vernon. There, he hoped to build a library for his "civil and private papers which are voluminous and may be interesting," but never quite got around to it. No other President ever did, either, and during the 142 intervening years, precious historical documents were sold, swapped, given away as souvenirs, cut up for autographs, scattered among repositories all across the country.

Bushrod Washington lamented that some of his stepfather's papers had been "excessively mutilated by Rats" while on loan to a biographer. Ulysses S. Grant mislaid a good many of his own letters: "The only place I ever found in my life to put a paper so as to find it again," he once confessed, "was either a side coat or the hands of a clerk more careful than myself." Most of Zachary Taylor's letters were burned when Union troops occupied his son's Louisiana home in 1862; two years later, Confederate soldiers seized Andrew Johnson's house in Granville, Tennessee, and gleefully destroyed the record of his early career. Chester A. Arthur saw to it that three garbage cans heaped with documents four feet high were set ablaze the day before he died. Warren Harding's widow sought to protect what remained of her husband's tattered reputation by ensuring that most of his personal papers would never be seen by historians.

There were rare exceptions to the slipshod rule: the papers of John and John Quincy Adams were carefully preserved alongside those of other members of their illustrious family at the Adams home in Quincy, Massachusetts, and after the death of Rutherford B. Hayes his admirers established a memorial library at his family estate in Fremont, Ohio, which became an important center for the study of Reconstruction. But for the most part, the records of the presidency before Roosevelt were ragged and disappointingly incomplete.

In 1903, the Library of Congress took it upon itself to remedy this, and by the late 1930s had managed to assemble the bulk of what survived of the papers of twenty-two chief executives.

This arrangement might have satisfied most of FDR's thirty predecessors, but it did not please him. No chief executive cheerfully ignored more presidential traditions than did Franklin Roosevelt, and none was more sure of his own special place in history. And so, in 1937, in the midst of the second presidential term which even FDR then thought would be his last, he decided upon an unprecedented solution to the problem of what to do with his papers. The scale of that problem was also unprecedented. Even before Roosevelt became the greatest war leader since Lincoln, volume alone made FDR's papers unique. Because of the special relationship his fellow citizens felt they enjoyed with the man who had allayed their fears and restored their faith during the Great Depression and who addressed them in their living rooms as "my friends," he received an unheard-of avalanche of mail: Herbert Hoover had received an average of four hundred letters a day, FDR said, while he routinely got more than four thousand. Meanwhile, the vast expansion of federal responsibility over which he presided was yielding an equally vast proliferation of official paperwork. (The Franklin D. Roosevelt Library would eventually contain

16 million pages of personal and official papers—more than 45 *tons* of documents, all of them generated in the pre-Xerox, pre-computer age.)

Then, too, FDR was incapable of throwing anything away. "As a result," he once said, "we have a mine for which future historians will curse as well as praise me." It sometimes seemed to his friends and family that Franklin Roosevelt collected *everything:* more than a million stamps in 150 matching albums; coins; medals; 1,200 naval prints and paintings and more than 200 fully rigged ship models (a collection begun long before he served as Assistant Secretary of the Navy during World War I); armies of miniature donkeys, elephants, Scotties, pigs; English political cartoons by George Cruikshank. There were some 15,000 books—2,500 about the U.S. Navy alone—miniature books, children's books, children's books in *French;* first editions; books about Dutchess County and the Hudson River. And there were stuffed birds and birding guides; Colonial documents and ships' logs and Christmas cards and walking sticks and thirty-seven leather-bound volumes filled with photographs of naval vessels, each carefully captioned in his own bold, slanting hand. Roosevelt himself once called his hoardings "a very conglomerate, hit-or-miss, all-over-the-place collection." No existing institution, not even the Library of Congress, had room for it all—and he could not bear to think of breaking it up.

But even if room for everything could somehow have been made somewhere, FDR did not want the record of his life buried amid those of others; "such a collection would be the tail on the dog," he told one admirer, "and . . . my idea is to have the whole thing in a place by itself." That place could be nowhere else but Springwood, the serene estate on which he had been born and brought up and to which he returned as often as he possibly could—as a young attorney, state senator, federal official, candidate for Vice President, while struggling against the ravages of infantile paralysis, as governor of New York, and some two hundred times as President.

To blunt the criticism of his enemies, who were certain to see in this novel scheme evidence of an unseemly desire to glorify himself, he first needed the support of what he called "the fraternity of historians." He began trying to win it in February 1938 with a letter to Samuel Eliot Morison, a fellow yachtsman and Harvard man already friendly to the administration. He had recently been harboring "a somewhat ambitious thought of creating a repository for manuscripts, correspondence, books, reports, etc., etc., relating to this period of our national history," the President wrote. Without such a repository, this material would be scattered everywhere: "For example, my own papers should, under the old method, be divided among the Navy Department, the Library of Congress, the New York State Historical Division in Albany, the New York City Historical Society, Harvard University and various members of my family."

Morison agreed: "In my opinion *all* your papers, even those of a personal nature and of college days, should be kept together in the order in which they are filed. It does not so much matter where they are kept, as long as the repository is fireproof and the guardians faithful—for I suppose you would wish to put a 50-year limit on their use by any save authorized biographers. But whatever you do, Mr. President, *don't* break up the collection, giving some to your children, others to Harvard, etc! although alma mater would profit, and dispersion offends all my professorial principles and professional prejudices!"

That was precisely what Roosevelt wanted to hear, and he got Morison to help him convene a luncheon for historians, journalists, and others who might be helpful to his project, personally drawing up the guest list with a practiced politician's eye toward balance that made sure to include "1 Texas man," and "1 Pacific Coast man" among the easterners. "The ostensible purpose of the luncheon," remembered Dr. Waldo Leland, the retired executive director of the American Council of Learned Societies, "was to attain [our] advice and approval . . . and this was reported to be entirely favorable and the approval unanimous. (But had it been otherwise I do not think it would have made any difference)."

Only moments after the luncheon ended, FDR held a rare Saturday-afternoon press conference and, with Professor Morison at his side, announced his plans. He had always intended to leave his boyhood home to the government, he said, "to be maintained for the benefit of the public by the Federal Government." Now he planned to donate in advance sixteen acres on which a new library and museum would be built. He stressed that it was not to be a personal memorial, but "for the first time in this country what might be called a source material collection relating to a specific period in our history." The building and the materials it would contain were to be overseen by the Archivist of the United States, but no public funds were to be used in building the gray fieldstone structure he had already sketched in the distinctive style he had persuaded himself was authentic "Hudson River Dutch." Rather, construction funds were to come from private individuals, plus the proceeds from the sale of anthologies of his speeches and whatever writings he might undertake once he left the White House. So far as possible, maintenance would be covered by the twenty-five cent admission visitors would pay to get in.

Anticipating the charge that Hyde Park was rather remote for most scholars, FDR said that it was merely two and a half hours from New York and just four and a half miles from "the city of Poughkeepsie, which has good hotel and other accommodations." At this last, the assembled reporters, all too familiar with Poughkeepsie's limited distractions, broke into laughter in which even the President joined. Later, FDR simply invented a statistic to further bolster his case: "far more people," he claimed, "pass over the New York-Albany Post Road [the narrow roadway that runs past the Springwood gate] in a given year than pass over every other road in the Nation. . . ."

His course now set publicly, the President moved fast. The Archivist of the United States, Dr. R. D. W. Connor, was deputed to ask Dr. Leland to head the executive committee.

"I'm a Republican," Leland protested.

"I know that," Connor said, "and that's all to the good."

But, Leland continued, he really didn't think much of the idea: "If the Library of Congress was good enough for [what remained of] the papers of Washington and Jefferson and Jackson," he remembered asking, "why wasn't it good enough for those of FDR?"

He finally agreed to serve, swayed in part by the argument that in a world threatened by war, it was safest not to concentrate the presidential archives in Washington.

Roosevelt kept up the pressure. The executive committee met with him just three days later, and archivists were appointed to survey some of his holdings. Asked on December 19 to draw up plans for incorporation, the Treasury and Justice Departments completed and delivered them within forty-eight hours. The fund drive was launched, consigned to the practiced hands of Frank Walker, former treasurer of the Democratic National Committee.

On April 28, 1939, FDR himself drove a government surveyor around the Hyde Park property through a steady spring drizzle, pausing here and there to show him where to hammer his stakes into the muddy soil.

Despite all the careful groundwork and the army of academics he had marshaled, his plans were not greeted with unanimous approval by the public. The columnist John T. Flynn compared FDR to a vainglorious pharaoh, intent upon immortalizing himself by building a "Yankee pyramid." A Chicago Republican was more blunt: "The decent citizens of this country are not at all interested in perpetuating your memory to future generations" he wrote the President, "—in fact, we are only anxious to forget the stench of your egotistical, incompetent, unscrupulous and unspeakably costly administration. . . . I suggest you *sell* Hyde Park and give the money to the 'forgotten men' you prate about so much (and then exploit) and let us get back to our Constitution."

The administration bill authorizing the government to accept Roosevelt's gift sailed through the Senate in April, but stalled in the House two months later, falling well short of the required two thirds. A Republican representative from Missouri charged that "only an egocentric megalomaniac would have the nerve to ask for such a measure," and when a Democrat announced that he would himself be happy to vote in favor of a comparable memorial to Herbert Hoover, Hamilton Fish, the Republican representative from Roosevelt's own Dutchess County, declared it inconceivable that any *Republican* "would even think of asking in his lifetime to have the Government maintain a personal library in his hometown." (Of course, every Republican—and every Democratic—successor to FDR has cheerfully asked precisely that, though not always in his hometown, and Herbert Hoover himself subsequently saw that his papers were trucked from Stanford University to a handsome new library at West Branch, Iowa, built along the lines Roosevelt had pioneered.)

There were further embarrassments. Bureaucrats in the Agriculture Department and Democratic officials in the District of Columbia, evidently overeager to please the Boss, exhorted their employees to contribute to the President's library fund, actions which the White House hastily disowned.

In the end, Speaker Sam Rayburn employed his legislative wizardry to maneuver the bill back onto the floor in such a way as to require only a clear majority—and then got it, 221 214, on July 18, 1938. The formal signing of the deed of gift, transferring title of the land for the library to the people of the United States, was set for six days later.

Franklin Roosevelt was this century's acknowledged master of Washington's levers of power, and the executive and legislative branches of the United States government had now responded to his touch with remarkable efficiency and dispatch. But there was a force closer to home that even FDR could not control: his eighty-four-year-old mother, Sara Delano Roosevelt.

She was at best ambivalent about her son's most recent enthusiasm. No one admired him more. She had assumed he would be a great man long before there was much reason to believe he would become one, and she sympathized with her son's desire to have a place where he could display his collections; it was she who had encouraged him to begin collecting when he was a small boy, and when the big house was renovated in 1915, she had worked with him to ensure that there was plenty of room to show off much of what he had already amassed. She found some comfort, too, in the fresh interest he was showing in Hyde Park; he had not revealed his thoughts about a third term even to her, yet perhaps his library scheme meant he really did plan to retire from the sordid world of politics in 1940, as she had always hoped he would.

But the building he now proposed to put up just a two-minute stroll from her door was to be enormous and, worse still, he was going to encourage the general public to visit it. Springwood belonged to her. It was her most precious inheritance from her late husband, James Roosevelt—his bold initials still marked the weathervane that turned above her rose garden—and for almost forty years she had done everything she could to keep it just as he had left it. When the President once gently suggested that the sizable dairy herd his father had established during the Civil War had become an unconscionable drain on her resources, she was unmoved: "So long as I am alive, Franklin, it is a matter of no consequence to me whether the cows make money or not."

She had only reluctantly accepted the changes to her estate demanded by the clamorous, peripatetic lives he and his wife had unaccountably chosen to lead: the crowds of well-wishers who trampled her lawns on election nights; the reporters and hangers-on who littered her flower beds with cigarettes; the ill-mannered strangers whom she had to pretend to be pleased to see at her dinner table. She had been deeply wounded when her daughter-in-law built a separate Hyde Park home of her own, and when her son later constructed for himself a hilltop cottage still further from the big house, she had made him promise never to spend a night in it so long as she lived—a pledge he faithfully kept.

At the very least, she felt she had been insufficiently consulted about her son's new plans for her old home, and she quietly boarded the liner for her annual summer voyage to France without ever having signed the deed or appointing anyone to do so on her behalf. This oversight was not discovered until ten o'clock on the morning of July 24, just two hours before the signing ceremony was scheduled to begin. It could not be put off: photographers and newsreel cameramen were already on their way to Hyde Park to record the historic moment and to see if they could pick up any hints about the President's plans for 1940.

And so, after hasty consultation with Justice Department lawyers, Roosevelt resolved to put on a sort of dumb-show. The cameras whirred as the President and his wife, seated in his open Ford beneath a spreading oak, solemnly but meaninglessly signed the deed of gift to property to which they as yet had no legal claim. Dr. Connor signed for the cameras, too, but on a blank sheet of paper, unable actually to accept the property on behalf of the government until the elder Mrs. Roosevelt had agreed to deed it over.

Meanwhile, a copy of the deed was rushed to Europe, along with a memorandum from the President, urging his mother to sign and "release your life interest in [the] field." There was no response until a White House telephone operator finally tracked her down at Chantilly, the château of the American ambassador, William Bullitt, and FDR himself gently coaxed her into putting pen to paper at last. "The joy I felt at hearing your voice!" she wrote him afterwards; his personal call and the telegrams that had preceded it offered welcome evidence, she said, that "you think of me."

She sat near him at the laying of the cornerstone on November 19, 1939, bundled against the chill wind blowing off the Hudson but smiling fondly as her son warmly recalled his earliest days at Spring wood.

Fifty years earlier, he remembered, "a small boy took especial delight in climbing an old tree, now unhappily gone, to pick and eat ripe Seckel pears. That was one hundred feet of west of where we stand. Just to the north he used to lie flat between the strawberry rows and eat sun-warmed strawberries. In the Spring of the year, in hip rubber boots, he sailed his first toy boats in the surface water formed by the melting snows. In the Summer, with his dogs, he dug into the woodchuck holes of this same field. The descendants of those same woodchucks still inhabit the field, and I hope they will continue to do so for all time."

The library was dedicated to "the spirit of peace—peace for the United States and, soon, we hope, peace for the world," Roosevelt said; but as building continued that autumn, much of that world was already at war, and by the time construction was officially completed on July 4 of the following year, France had surrendered and Hitler seemed poised to invade Britain. Two weeks later, FDR was renominated for a third term.

It took another year to ready the exhibits and arrange things to the President's liking—he had firm ideas about everything from thermostats and light fixtures to the precise shade of blue with which the backs of the museum cases should be painted to set off his ship models to best advantage.

The library was formally dedicated on June 30, 1941—the same day that Hitler invaded Russia. Two days later, the first visitor, Floyd

B. Avery of nearby White Plains, New York, paid his quarter and walked through the front door. He was "a life-long Republican," he told the press, but he had found the exhibits "very interesting," anyway.

The President's mother never fully reconciled herself to the library's massive presence, and when she realized her son planned to abandon his old cubbyhole of an office just off her porch for a spacious new study, she had a life-sized portrait of herself painted by the artist Douglas Chandor to hang near his new desk. She also found some of the exhibits distasteful, particularly the more bizarre gifts to the President displayed in an area officially labeled the Oddities Room but which the Roosevelts privately called "the chamber of horrors." She was not amused, for example, when the Gridiron Club gave the President the mammoth papier-mâché caricature that had served as the centerpiece of its annual dinner in 1940. It portrayed FDR as the Sphinx—an allusion to his long, exasperating silence about running for a third term—and its most prominent feature was its massive, jutting jaw. An innocent White House aide asked the President's mother if she didn't think it was a pretty good caricature.

It was *not*, she said; her jaw was identical to her son's. Did the aide think this grotesque object looked *anything* like her?

Sara Delano Roosevelt died at Springwood on September 7, 1941, in the bed in which she had given birth to her son. Not long afterwards, Grace Tully, the President's secretary, was arranging shelves in the new study when she came upon an unfamiliar carton and asked FDR about it. It was strange to him, too, he said, and they opened it together, finding coils of his baby hair, the lace dress in which he had been christened, bundles of his boyhood letters, each package carefully wrapped and marked in his mother's confident hand. Suddenly surrounded by these proofs of his mother's consuming love for him, Roosevelt's eyes filled with tears and he asked to be left alone for a while.

The world war that had finally come to America just three months after Sara Delano Roosevelt's death changed everything for Roosevelt, for his country—and for his library. The threat of it had already forced him to abandon his plans to retire to Springwood; now, its reality—and the gasoline rationing that accompanied it—ensured that the flood of visitors FDR had looked forward to remained a trickle.

It also imposed strict military security on the old estate. Helen Roosevelt Robinson, the Republican daughter of FDR's half brother, who had grown up right next door, already disliked the library—it was far too big, she thought, and "quite spoils the big field with the great oaks that I've known all my life. I'm afraid I don't like new things at Hyde Park." When she returned to her old home in the autumn of 1942, she found herself challenged at her own gate by "fixed bayonets . . . a horrid situation," had to endure the indignity of being fingerprinted, and late one evening, taking her dog out for his final walk before going to bed, found herself and her mortified pet blinded by a spotlight while an unseen guard shouted, "Who goes there?"

During his wartime trips home, Roosevelt managed to snatch as much time as he could in the library. His secretary William Hassett often found him there, "happy as a clam," signing and sorting books or dictating labels for the exhibits or personal anecdotes for the memoirs he still hoped to publish someday, and he loved to show the place off to important visitors: Winston Churchill, Manuel Quezon, Madame Chiang Kai-shek, Princess Martha of Norway, King George II of Greece, Queen Wilhemina of the Netherlands, ex-Empress Zita of Austro-Hungary, all walked alongside his wheelchair, stopping from time to time so that he could tell an old story or point out an especially fine piece of rigging.

Samuel Eliot Morison had been Roosevelt's strong ally during the campaign to get his library built, but at least once he unwittingly displeased his chief. Offering a few remarks at the dedication, the historian addressed Roosevelt directly: ". . . Mr. President," he said, "if you're going to keep a snug harbor for all your collections and your papers from the White House I shall have to warn you to give some of those 'Oddities' the 'deep six' or they will overflow and take up the space needed for documents. I know you are the Nation's Number One Collector but collecting can be overdone even by Number One." And he pleaded with Roosevelt's friends and neighbors in the audience who might be tempted to offer him their old horse-hair trunks and disused buggies, "Don't do it."

FDR laughed good-naturedly, but he emphatically did not agree. Old buggies, at least, were always fine with him—he hoped one day to build a separate building just to house them—and he continued relentlessly to accumulate miscellaneous objects, enthusiastically accepting for the library three fragments of petrified gingko wood; a silk hat worn by a fellow candidate during his first political campaign in 1910; a miniature stained-glass window fashioned from fragments of larger windows blown out of the House of Commons by Nazi bombs; a framed spray of flowers woven "entirely of hair from the heads of members of the Roosevelt family." In late 1943, he himself sent to the museum a rusty horseshoe he had spotted in the sand while picnicking with General Dwight Eisenhower after the Allied conference at Cairo.

Even Eleanor Roosevelt got into the spirit of things. Though she had been startled when FDR insisted in 1941 that letters she had written to her mother-in-law while on her honeymoon should not simply be thrown away, she was soon sending mementoes of her own to the library—including what little remained of the bottle with which she had christened a barge at Camden, Maine, on February 8, 1943. (In 1972, two new wings would be added to the library in part to house her papers and honor her extraordinary life.)

Nor did he seem ever to lose his eagerness to compile the most complete possible record of all the history he was helping to make, at least once with potentially disastrous results. One day a photograph album arrived from the White House, filled with memorabilia from the Cairo Conference. Included in it, to the horror of Dr. Edgar B. Nixon, acting director of the library, was the *Overlord* Agreement, giving both the location and the approximate date for the invasion of Europe. For months, the archivist worried that he would somehow let slip these most precious of all Allied secrets, and it was not until D-Day actually arrived that he began sleeping soundly again.

Roosevelt's most prized ship model, the USS *Constitution*, built in 1815 and laboriously rerigged by FDR himself, rested on the mantel of the Oval Room in the White House throughout his presidency. It was a point of pride in every office Roosevelt ever occupied, and once, Shipman recalled, when he innocently suggested that it would make a very fine centerpiece for the room that held his ship models, FDR "particularly rejected" the notion; it seemed clear that the library was not likely to inherit "Old Ironsides" before the President left office.

But nearly four years later, on April 7, 1945, the model unexpectedly turned up at Hyde Park, part of an unusually large shipment of objects, books, and papers that FDR had ordered sent to the library before setting out himself for a badly needed rest at Warm Springs, Georgia. The library staff was braced for still another shipment of books to be sent north from there after the President finished sorting them into the wooden crates he had unaccountably taken to calling "coffins," when he died at Warm Springs five days later. He was buried at Hyde Park on April 15, in the rose garden that stands about halfway between his mother's house and his own library.

When, in 1917, Theodore Roosevelt, the President with whom his distant cousin most often compared himself, just as subsequent presidents have measured themselves against FDR, sent locked boxes of papers from a bank safe at Oyster Bay to the Library of Congress, an archivist gently suggested that the ex-President send along the key. TR answered with customary vigor: "The Lord only knows where the key is. Break the case open and start to work on them!"

FDR had never been so ready to have strangers nose through his papers. His fierce drive to ensure his place in history kept him from discarding anything having to do with his career, public or private. But that impulse had been very nearly matched by his lifelong love of secrecy. And it had never been entirely clear during his lifetime precisely which of his papers he ultimately wished scholars to see. He could never be persuaded to sign a formal deed of gift for his papers, and he dictated a memorandum in 1943 setting up a "Committee of Three" of his most trusted aides to winnow through them should he not live to do so, deciding which should be released, which sealed for a time, and which withheld forever. He believed, for example, that his personal correspondence with the king of England should "never" be read by anyone else, and he once evidently planned to destroy all of the thousands of brief notes headed "The White House" and signed "F.D.R." with which he often made his wishes known. "Those chits are nobody's business," he told a Senate delegation, "so long as the final determination is made a matter of record. . . . But, in arriving at the final determination of any question of government, the machinery is not of interest to anybody, and it is not going to be." Of course, it is precisely the machinery of decision making that does interest biographers and historians—the final determination can be found in the files of any newspaper—and we can all be grateful that Roosevelt's compulsion to control access was not finally allowed to overcome his desire to leave behind as complete a historical record as he could.

The letters and telegrams and speeches and transcripts of 998 press conferences filed in row upon row of gray library boxes—250 manuscript collections at last count and still growing—constitute an unrivaled record of a period of unprecedented change, just as Roosevelt intended they should.

On the campaign trail in 1932, he pledged "bold persistent experimentation" to overcome the Depression: "It is common sense to take a method and try it. If it fails, admit it frankly and try another. But above all, try something." The formal record of all his trials and errors is here for anyone to see, but it is perhaps most memorably recorded in the letters from ordinary citizens. There are heartfelt messages from dust bowl farmers and jobless men, asking for help or giving thanks for help already given by one or another of the alphabet agencies whose mushroom growth signaled a new era in which, for the first time, the federal government was made to accept responsibility for the welfare of ordinary citizens. It was these letters that Roosevelt most prized.

But interspersed among them are other, angry letters excoriating him for attempting to enlarge the Supreme Court, for stretching the constitutional limits of his office, for simply daring to be "That Man in the White House."

The second great struggle waged by FDR—to persuade the American people to abandon their traditional isolationism and see that their fate and those of other peoples around the world were inextricably linked, that "our own well-being is dependent on the well-being of other nations far away"—is just as richly documented. Most celebrated perhaps are the almost two thousand letters and cables between FDR and Winston Churchill—"the Former Naval Person"—in which both men uncharacteristically rein in their considerable vanity in the interest of defeating the common enemy. But the most momentous of all the documents may be a single, short letter from Albert Einstein, written in August of 1939 and warning that the Germans had accomplished the fission of uranium and were likely soon to build "extremely powerful bombs of a new type," just one of which "might very well destroy" a whole city and its suburbs. "This requires action," Roosevelt wrote to his military aide, General Edwin "Pa" Watson, after reading it, and thereby launched the Atomic Age.

And everywhere there is firsthand evidence of the breezy confidence and extraordinary attention to detail that made it possible for FDR to preside for a dozen years over such cataclysmic change. Across the top of a memorandum from the head of the brand-new Civilian Conservation Corps estimating the cost of housing and feeding each recruit at $1.92 per day is his bold scrawl ordering that this "absurdly high" figure be "greatly reduced." When his old friend and neighbor, Secretary of the Treasury Henry Morgenthau, Jr., was tardy in paying his dues to the local Democratic Party, FDR took time to write him a reminder, ending with the words, "in other words, cough up!" And when members of his own staff dawdled over lunch, he took them to task, too: "From now on till the close of the session please don't take any afternoons off—and please don't be gone more than one hour for lunch. I've been put in [a] hole a number of times."

Still, while Roosevelt's papers are voluminous, they are also for the most part resolutely circumspect. For all his outward geniality, he kept his own counsel. "Never let your left hand know what your right is doing," he once advised Morgenthau.

"Which hand am I, Mr. President?"

"My right hand," FDR answered, "but I keep my left hand under the table."

The charm and guile and sheer force of personality that helped make Roosevelt irresistible when encountered face to face only rarely came to life on paper, and the relics he compiled are in many ways more revealing of his magnetic personality and magpie mind—restless, acquisitive, omnivorous, fascinated by everything. Even to a frequent visitor, the exhibits and public galleries that surround his battered desk are endlessly rewarding, hung with vivid proofs of a full life lived: The yellowed telegram on which his fifty-four-year-old father noted the arrival of "a bouncing boy" and the ribbon young Franklin wore while a Harvard freshman, marching through a steady Boston rain in honor of his Republican cousin Theodore; the diamond stick-pin he designed in the form of the Roosevelt crest worn by the ushers at his wedding to TR's favorite niece on Saint Patrick's Day in 1905 and the sheets from a legal pad on which he penciled meticulous instructions for his own funeral. There is even a case devoted entirely to collars and rubber balls and well-chewed toys that belonged to the playful Scottie Roosevelt immortalized in a masterful campaign speech as "my little dog, Fala."

But it is in the five big, behind-the-scenes storerooms filled with items for which there is simply no exhibition space that one feels closest to the complex and mercurial man responsible for assembling them all. A sweet-smelling cedar closet holds a selection of the elegant navy capes FDR loved to wear. A hat box contains the floppy cotton headgear with green sun visor he jammed on to his head while fishing. One drawer is filled with the preserved skins of birds he shot at twelve, each with its handwritten tag; another holds the contents of his desk drawer on the day he died, including several of his celebrated cigarette holders and the "Yello Bole" brand pipe cleaners he used to ream them out.

For me, however, the most immediately evocative objects are hidden away in a trunk on an upstairs shelf: five pairs of long, heavy, steel braces. The shoes to which they are attached look shockingly small and so shiny and smooth-soled they appear never to have been worn, but the leather straps that bound them to Roosevelt's shriveled legs are cracked and salt-stained and still seem to smell faintly of sweat, the most vivid possible evidence of the great effort infantile paralysis demanded of him simply to stand—and of the resolute courage whose existence only his most embittered detractors ever dared deny.

Roosevelt's motives for building his library were surely mixed, but to get to know it is to get to know its builder, which is, I suspect, what he had in mind all along. Few who have ever spent time here could disagree with what the poet Archibald MacLeish said at the laying of the cornerstone fifty years ago: "The records which will be collected here . . . are the records of . . . the man who refused, in the name of his generation, to continue to accept what was no longer acceptable—the man who demanded, for his generation, what his generation had the courage to expect. As such they have the unity which history remembers and even living man can see.

"They belong by themselves, here in this river country, on the land from which they came."

A slightly different version of this article appeared in the December 1989 issue of *Smithsonian*

INDEX

GEOFFREY C. WARD is the author of
*Before the Trumpet: Young Franklin
Roosevelt* and *A First-Class Temperament:
The Emergence of Franklin Roosevelt*, winner of the National Book Critics Circle
Award for biography, the Parkman Prize
of the Society of American Historians,
and the *Los Angeles Times* book prize for
biography. He is also the principal
writer for Ken Burns's PBS series
"The Civil War" and its bestselling
companion volume, *The Civil War: An
Illustrated History*.